Mary Fong

Two HEARTNUTS to CRACK!

Memoir One

(second edition)

Trilogy: A Magnificent Mess!

MARY FONG

with KARL

Two Heart Nuts to Crack!

Two Heart Nuts to Crack!

KDP ISBN:9798782740702

CONTENTS

Book Reviewers

"Mary Fong has written a moving memoir about growing up in Los Angeles as the daughter of Chinese immigrants. Her experience is at once unique and emblematic to the trials and tribulations facing immigrants of all faiths and ethnicities, and Fong captures the sometimes, troubling issues of transition and acculturation. Her story is a powerful one, earnest and true, rich with the passion of life, of the tender, unrequited love for a dear classmate, ultimately learning to overcome loss and embrace both the past and the future as one." James Brown, author of the memoirs, *The Los Angeles Diaries* and *This River*

"Mary Fong has written a wonderful and engaging memoir detailing her experiences of childhood, including witnessing her immigrant parents' struggle to survive in the restaurant business. As a result, I have much greater compassion for people in similar circumstances. Her descriptions of various emotions and experiences growing up are vivid and they stimulated reflections on my own path, letting me enjoy childhood once again." Walter Semkiw, M.D., author of *Origin of the Soul and the Purpose of Reincarnation,* and *Born Again*

DEDICATION

This memoir

dedicated to you,

the reader who is open

and ready to move forward

in your awakening that is part

of human evolution -- a process

of awareness in discovering

and being who you

truly are

in your

life's journey.

LOVE - LOVE - LOVE

Accessing Hyperlinks in This Memoir

Two Heart Nuts to Crack! of *A Magnificent Mess!* Trilogy (2nd edition) is in print for readers who prefer to read from a book. This first memoir of the trilogy allows the reader to access hyperlinks to informative videos and songs. How? Reading this book, you will encounter **[labels]** representing hyperlinks. Instructions are on the last page of this memoir for easy access to the hyperlink webpage.

Preface

Near the end of my ninth-grade year, a thought flashed in my mind that I would write a book for a wide audience someday. I had no inkling what the book topic would be. It was a quick, fleeting subliminal thought. During my graduate years studying Cultural and Intercultural Communications at the University of Washington in Seattle, I had read the novel *Joy Luck Club* by Amy Tan during my quarter break. I felt that I could write about my cultural and intercultural experiences from the lower socio-economic class point-of-view.

Midway through my teaching career, I felt I could include some of my spiritual experiences in my memoir. Since I was busy teaching and conducting research, I had no time to write my memoir. I decided to write my memoir near the end of my academic career to include more life experiences. I also delayed writing my memoir because I didn't have a theme that would string all my life experiences together. I didn't know what that push, that punch that will drive my life story from the beginning to now.

It is not until I passionately began studying, researching, creating, and teaching three spiritual communication courses: "Communicating Compassion and Love," "Personal Growth," and "Dying and Afterlife Communication," that more of my experiences like jigsaw puzzle pieces began fitting together. Following my passion helped me better understand who we are, our existence, life purposes, life's journey, and life after death. In learning about the spiritual field, I read books, researched the internet, listened to various internet programming related to these topics, attended conferences, seminars, and workshops. I love to learn and share the current research related to spirituality to educate and empower people to make choices for their well-being.

What finally gave me the punch to move forward to write my memoir was crossing paths unexpectedly with a former high school classmate, Karl. We agreed to record nontraditional inter-views regarding our past experiences and thoughts to assist me in this memoir. He's been a significant person in my life who gave his honest, insightful, and meaningful point-of-view on the events related to our past interactions. His responses were insightful that helped solve the mystery of our past interactions. More pieces of the jigsaw puzzle were snapping together continuously as I engaged in conversation with Karl that created a process of increasing momentum of awakening or awareness for me.

Sharing my journey with the reader gives me great joy, not only taking you on an adventure but in hopes of assisting you in expanding your awareness and self-discovery. This trilogy is for the reader who asks questions about who I am, my existence, or the game of life?

This memoir shares my actual cultural, intercultural, and spiritual experiences in my first 27 years of my life. This first memoir covers the early years of two people's lives that are mysteriously intertwined. Second, Karl and I have carefully selected and integrated 90+ songs from the nostalgic era of the 1960s through 2019 that perfectly matches the events and enhances the flavor of the storytelling.

I recommend to the reader if they wish to listen and enjoy the songs and the informative hyperlinks in an uninterrupted and advertisement-free manner, then sign-up for Premium YouTube. I understand there is usually a one-month free trial promotion. Understand that if a song, educational video or website is removed from YouTube, Rumble, Bitchute or another internet platform, it is beyond my control. However, you can easily search the song, video, website or concept on the internet.

The second memoir covers the next 20 years of our lives. Karl shares his experiences and some answers to the mysteries of life. I share my cultural, intercultural, and spiritual insights. The third memoir continues with the events in the recent twelve years of our lives while integrating some of the current spiritual literature and research I share with my students.

This trilogy's primary thrust is to educate and introduce some current research in a storytelling style that is significant and meaningful. All to enlighten and shift people's consciousness of discovering who they truly are and their life journey. All to help people's growth and awareness of their life journey will add insights to a happier and more meaningful one as they reflect, understand, learn, and create their lives.

In this memoir, I changed most of the names, a few locations, and a few characteristics to maintain people's anonymity and respect their privacy and identity. To respect the confidentiality of Karl's siblings, we decided not to include his interactions with them. Therefore, in part, Karl's childhood chapters are relatively brief. Otherwise, this memoir is accurate to the best of my recollection and based on the interview transcripts with Karl. The transcripts were edited for grammar, past to present tense, choice of another synonym, and sentence structure. Essentially, Karl's intent and meaning remain the same.

Two Heart Nuts to Crack! would never be possible without the primary collaborators in my life. First, I'm grateful for my Mom and Dad for their love and courage in immigrating and raising their family. Both of my brothers, thanks for their love and being a part of my life experiences. Karl, thank you for your friendship, love, and supportive collaboration in the importance of this trilogy to open people's awareness about the journey of life.

I have much gratitude for Emanuelle McIntosh for her friendship, generosity, assistance, and embarking on this memoir journey with me. Incredible thanks to my spirit counsel for their guidance throughout my life. Much thanks to Erik Medhus for his spiritual guidance and his Mom, Elisa Medhus, MD, for being brave, curious, and generous in the collaborative creation of *Channeling Erik* on YouTube. Both Erik and Elisa are big game changers in expanding the awareness of people.

After a three-month search, I'm grateful for Ann-Sophie Côte for executing my concept of the graphic design of the attractive book cover. Much gratitude to my students who registered for college credit to transcribe the recorded interview sessions: Nick Bess, Karina Gonzalez, and Daniel Banks, who did a careful and accurate job.

Much thanks to the creators of the educational videos that expand our understanding. I love all inspired musical artists for sharing their genius creativity, heart, and soul in their songs creating a slice of life that touches people's feelings of the ups and downs of life together as one. Also, appreciation for the YouTube video creators providing visual effects to the songs. **A BIG THANK YOU** to all the collaborative creators who have made this memoir rock!

Namästé,
Mary with Karl

Chapter 1: Introduction

If you had three big questions about life, what would they be? What are you most curious about in life? What do you find that is so mysterious? I have many questions, but for starters, here are my three biggest ones.

The first is, what is the meaning of life? Why do we live this life and feel we "ta-da" popped out into this world? The bottom line is: What is the name of the game of life?

My second big question is, why are so many variations and extremes in people's life circumstances? Why are some extremely wealthy where others are poor, and why are some healthy and others are not? Why do some have a good journey, and others suffer so much?

Lastly, my third big question is, what happens after we die? Are we dead, dead, never to have any existence, and we evaporate into thin air, or do we somehow continue to live? How does it work? Okay, I cheated a bit in stacking the questions. However, I say it still counts as three big questions. I'm just elaborating so that you clearly understand what I'm asking.

For the longest time, I've been in search of answers to my big life questions, like who am I, why am I here, what is the purpose of life, why do things happen the way they do, what is the game of life, what happens when we die, and so on.

My friend, Karl, will also be contributing glimpses of his own experiences as he has been a significant person in my life in which our paths have crossed at specific points through the years. I conducted recorded nontraditional interviews with him, in which I used the interview transcriptions to express Karl's point of view in this memoir. Importantly, Karl's intentions and meanings in his passages remain authentic.

I feel comfortable being "outside of the box," which has resulted in discovering, growing, learning, expanding, evolving, and increasing my awareness. I love being curious, progressive, and finding what is genuine. To search and discover answers to my big questions, I repeatedly jump outside the box to find pieces of the jigsaw puzzle of life.

How often do you think "outside of the box?" How comfortable do you feel and think whenever you are outside your box? As my life story unfolds, many events are relatable, while other happenings that you haven't experienced will lure you outside of your box. This memoir will challenge how you think about life events, your underlying belief system and life in general. It's taken me many decades to search for the answers to my big questions. So, welcome to my life adventures. Let me take you down memory lane.

Take a deep breath with me, exhale, and relax. Allow your memory to wander to when you were a toddler. Go back, further back, and relax your mind. Be patient. Float back to your earliest thoughts and images. What do these memories and experiences whisper or shout out to you?

As a two-year-old Chinese American girl, my earliest memory is living in a two-bedroom rental house on Gaviota Street in Long Beach, California, in 1961 with my Chinese immigrant parents from Mainland China and my two older brothers.

My Daddy immigrated from Guangdong province of Mainland China about 1949, prior to the communist regime of Mao Tse-tung in China. My Mommy and oldest brother, Leland, migrated to Macau after my Daddy comes to America. **[Ch. 1:1]**

Early years in America, my Daddy was diagnosed with tuberculosis and quarantined in the State Hospital for quite some time for treatment. My Daddy made little jewelry trinkets and sold them for a living. **[Ch. 1:2]**

Judge DeVries in Long Beach becomes acquainted with my Daddy when he is in America. Seven years later, Judge DeVries sponsors my Mommy and seven-year-old Leland to come to America. Leland is my oldest brother, ten years older than me. Jason is my other brother, almost two years older. Both of us were born in Northern California. I am too young to remember when the family moves to Long Beach. I'm perhaps around one year old.
[Ch. 1:3] [Ch. 1:4]

My parents work long hours in the Chinese restaurant business. Jason and I stay with a family of babysitters. Every time we're picked up, I'm always crying and looking disturbed. My parents don't know why. They assume that toddlers typically cry.

I don't remember at all what happened at this age. However, my Mommy tells me later when I'm older. As kids, we don't take a bath every day. Usually, it is once a week. My Mommy's angry surprise, she discovers burnt cigarette butt burns all over my back.

My parents are upset at the babysitters' abuse and never return. Soon after, to avoid irresponsible and abusive babysitters, my parents buy a small trailer and park it in an open gravel space behind their restaurant, *House of Fong*, where Jason and I sometimes stay. The trailer has two upper and lower beds and a middle table with two long cushion seats on both sides.

Chapter 2: Mary's Earliest Memories

Traveling from the restaurant, I'm sitting in the front seat between my Mommy and Daddy as he drives his 1950s pink Thunderbird. Sitting with an ugly face, feeling an unsettling discomfort grumbling in my tummy like something is about to come up. I feel weak, terrible, and nauseous. What's going on? I feel an uncontrollable sensation percolating in my tummy to my chest and throat. Repeatedly turning my head from left to right, searching where to put whatever is coming up. I couldn't speak.

Bursting out of my mouth like lava shooting out from a volcano, I reactively lean forward, turned my head to my right, spurting vomit all over my Mommy's lap! With a startled look, my Mommy stares down at this unexpected smelly puddle of vomit that gushed onto her dress. I'm squinting, moaning, and feeling so woozy and helpless, peering up at my Mommy, who looks disgusted. Her tight lips with wrinkled eyebrows stare at the puddle of stinky vomit. She doesn't scold me. My Mommy remains silent, holding her dress in place to avoid my vomit from spilling.

Glancing at us, my Daddy reassuringly says, *"Oh, ngwo dei jau faan heui a,"* meaning, "We will be home soon." Luckily, we're only three blocks away from home on Gaviota Street.

On another occasion, standing on the driveway, my parents see our neighbor, a senior woman zipping up the shared driveway in her golf cart mobile, where I'm standing. "Hey!" my parents yell. Feeling grabbed and pulled away fast like an eagle swooping down, carrying its prey away.

The senior woman abruptly stops her speeding mobile in her parking spot, gasping. I look at her. She's holding her chest with one hand, breathing heavily, straightening her spectacles and patting her grey hair with her other.

"Oh, I didn't see her, and by the time I did, I couldn't stop in time," she says breathlessly. Holding both sides of her face while shaking her head, she gratefully says, "Oh, my goodness. Thank God for moving her."

Why is she panicking? I stare at her with my round brown eyes seeing a relieved, stressed face and upper body slouching over her steering wheel. Although I feel everyone is in a panic, I'm unaware of what could have happened to me. Some would say I've experienced a brush with death. Fazed, I'm not at all.

I'm a tad over two years old, and my Mommy discovers a rip in front of my simple dress that I've been wearing for several days. Somehow my mischievous little hands and fingers pick at the small hole that coaxes and baits me to keep tearing at it little by little, day after day. My mischievous little hands have a mind of their own. Or perhaps I'm tired of wearing the same dress for days.

Tonight, my Mommy and Daddy show me a pretty yellow party dress. My Mommy likes to buy a larger than my normal size so I can grow into it. She holds it against my body as I'm peering down at it, almost touching the floor. I like the yellow dress with its ruffles, ribbons, and puffy princess look.

Early morning, I'm wide awake, eager to start the day. My brothers are still fast asleep in the same bedroom we share. I push my blankets aside, jump out of bed enthusiastically, pitter-patter across the room, and fly open the closet door. Standing on my tippy toes, stretching high with my fingertips, flicking on the closet light with a quick quarter-turn stopped my bare feet. Inhaling a quiet gasp, leaning with both hands withdrawing backwards, staring at an unexpected dark intruder.

Hanging mid-air, a hairy dark spider crawls about on its large weaved silky web that drapes from wall to wall in the narrow closet where it finds a home overnight. Peering through the spider's creepy veil hangs my yellow pretty princess party dress glimmering so still, so elegantly, and so preciously. I want so much to bring my pretty yellow princess party dress down to look at and try on, but that creepy spider web blocks my hope.

Dragging a chair over to stand on, I still cannot bypass that spooky, sticky, silky spiderweb hanging like fancy laced Victorian curtains while an intimidating black, hairy, eight-legged guard with fangs stares down at me.

For several days, I open the closet door to glimpse at my pretty yellow princess party dress that continues to be held captive behind an intricate, delicate, well-designed, sticky, silky web. The hairy, eight-legged guard with fangs camps out 24-7 with one eye open and one eye closed. Many eye-to-eye staring matches between us, each calling our bluffs, but nothing changes. I haven't told my Mommy as I do not know how to express this precarious situation.

Soon after, my attention lures away, inhaling the inviting aroma of freshly brewed roasted brown coffee beans. My parents pleasurably sip cup after cup at the breakfast table while enjoying bite-after-bite their tasty coffee cakes over their morning chat.

After their morning coffee ritual, they place their cups and saucers on the white stove. Hearing their footsteps exiting the kitchen back door that locks shut, I drag a chair next to the stove, climb up, sitting on top. Delightfully sipping the remaining sweet dark brown drops of coffee left in their cups.

My parents work long hours at their *House of Fong* restaurant from early afternoon to 11 pm. Their restaurant opens for business at 4 p.m. My Daddy is the cook, and my Mommy is the waitress. Sometimes, my Mommy cooks if it gets busy. My parents have their day off on Mondays. **[Ch. 2:1], [Ch. 2:2]**

House of Fong's dining area has two side walls of booths with high wood partitions for privacy. Three long banquet tables with white tablecloths and red cushion chairs reside in the center. Beautiful Chinese picturesque lanterns hang from the ceiling. **[Ch. 2:3]**

Three part-time junior college Caucasian waitresses serve at my parent's restaurant on different days. The waitresses are Donna, Sherry, newly married to Ken, and Kathy, married to Ming, a Chinese man. The waitresses wear black ankle pants with black low heel shoes and a glossy, silky red Chinese-style high collar top lined with black trim and Chinese-style black button ties. **[Ch. 2:4]**

I spend most of my curious time at home and at the *House of Fong*. Jason and I sometimes stay and sleep in the small trailer during the day and early evenings before dinner. My parents rarely have time during the week to interact with us because they work very hard and late long hours. Leland looks after Jason and me. Usually, Leland is busy doing his homework and school projects. Jason and I typically hang out together. We are latchkey children and are pretty much on our own. Monday is the only day our family eats dinner together.

I'm at home with my Mommy this morning, working in the kitchen. I'm terribly bored. Jason is at school. I'm walking around to find something to do. I get this bright idea to enclose myself in the corner of the kids' bedroom by bringing the bedroom door and the bathroom door together. With eyes shut, standing in the corner enclosed by the two doors, I pretend to cry in the dark, "Whhhaaaa, whhaaaaa, sniff, sniff, whhaaa, whhaaaaa..." for several seconds.

A simultaneous creaking of two doors opens with a crack of light lasering between my eyes, gagging my next breath of Whhhaaa before release. I freeze with my guilty brown eyes, mouth wide open, and my opera tone, whhhaaa instantly muted as if someone pressed a TV remote control button. My Mommy's eyes stare at me. Slowly closing my mouth, she says nothing and walks away, back into the kitchen before I rudely interrupted her with my naughty prank. **[Ch. 2:4A]**

Usually, during the day, Jason and I play together or watch TV if Jason is not in school. We always creatively think of something to do. Sometimes, we sit on separate sides of the rocking chair's padded armrest, rocking back and forth, pretending to play cowboys and Indians. We playfully yelp, *"yai-yai-yai-yai-yai,"* and alternate a string of vibrating vocal sounds like "wo-wo-wo-wo-wo," while patting our mouths with our hands, imitating what we see in western movies on TV. **[Ch. 2:5]**

Somehow, we find a blanket with a hole in the middle. Jason thinks of an idea and lays the blanket across two rows of chairs after lining them up together.

"Mary, climb up there and stick your hand in the hole," Jason instructs me as he sits under the blanket where it drapes across the chairs. I climb onto the chair and stick my arm in the blanket hole. With both hands, he grasps my arm that dangles in the blanket hole and suddenly yanks hard. I tumble down. He smiles and giggles as he gets up.

I'm moaning, feeling intense pain. Jason stops smiling and giggling. I slowly get up, squinting with an ugly face. My shoulder feels twisted like a pretzel; my arm feels pulled out of my shoulder socket. Moaning in intense pain, I walk to my bed.

"Are you all right, Mary?" Jason asks as he follows behind.

"My arm, my arm hurts," I say with my eyes closed while resting to remain calm and mentally relax the tension in my body.

Minutes later, our Daddy arrives home, bringing some food he cooked at the restaurant. I hear him say in Cantonese,

"Maly, hai bindouh a? meaning, "Where is Mary?"

"She's in the bedroom," Jason says as he points toward the bedroom.

My Daddy sees me lying down on my bed in anguish. He takes me to the restaurant, where my Mommy immediately rubs raw ginger and warm oil on my shoulder. I'm quiet, watching my Mommy do her therapy. With a ginger root in one hand, while holding a small vegetable knife with the other, she repeatedly chops the slice side of the ginger root to allow the juices to flow to the surface.

Flicking on the cigarette lighter, she heats the ginger. After dipping the ginger root's chopped side into the warm vegetable oil, she rubs it firmly into my shoulder area. The heat of the ginger penetrates my skin to help circulate the blood around my shoulder. She repeats her therapy for the whole week. The pain and discomfort eventually go away. My shoulder feels better after a week.

At home, one morning, my Mommy says in Cantonese to stick out my tongue as she briefly demonstrates sticking her tongue out. She examines the condition of my tongue. Are my taste buds protruding? What color is my tongue? Is it pale, pink, reddish, or flaming red? Does my tongue have any cracks? Is my tongue clean, or is there too much white coating? Does my tongue have teeth marks on the side? Is my tongue wide or narrow? Is my tongue wet or dry? Are my lips chapped? For 10 seconds, my eyes look back and forth from the ceiling, peering down, nearly crossed-eyed, at my Mommy as she analyzes my tongue hanging out of my mouth like a doggie.

She points her index finger at my tongue and says, *"Néih yáuh yiht hay,"* meaning, "You have too much heat in your body." I roll my tongue back into my mouth and peer at her. I'm learning that tongue reading originates from Chinese medicine and a routine Chinese doctors practice in the initial examinations of their patients. Chinese families also use this tongue diagnosis at home. **[Ch. 2:6]**

My Mommy concocts a Chinese herbal soup to drink to help lessen the heat in my body. Too much heat in the body creates an inflammatory condition, which health practitioners report is unfavorable if it goes on too long--ailments and diseases begin manifesting. Particular Chinese herbs have a cooling effect that helps balance the body system for better health. The *yin* and *yang* energy forces are complementary opposites that interact with one another. This condition constantly changes and transforms our bodies and the environment. **[Ch. 2:7]**

By early afternoon, my Mommy dresses me to go out with her. I have no idea where we are going. My Daddy drops us off in front of a tall, large apartment building. I'm sensing that my Mommy is displeased about something and where we are going. We arrive at the apartment of one of the blond-hair waitresses, Kathy, married to a Chinese man named Ming.

Kathy happily greets and introduces us to her husband. Kathy thinks I'm a cute doll and wants her husband to meet me. Eventually, figuring out that I am the focus of attention even though no one tells me. We all sit on the couch and the loveseat in their small apartment. My Mommy speaks a little bit of English. It feels awkward because there isn't much conversation.

Several plates of food fill the coffee table. Kathy and Ming chat with niceties while my Mommy smiles and sits there nodding, agreeing, or speaking in her broken English. I sit quietly, observing everyone. I feel like my Mommy's side-kick or tag along.

After all the chit-chat of niceties and the conversation going nowhere, Kathy enthusiastically smiles while referring to food dishes with her open flat palm. "You are welcome to any of the food," she says while lifting a plate of food toward us.

My eyes get big, my tummy growls, and I'm ready to devour any food. My hands move ever so slightly. Abruptly, my Mommy blocks my hands from the offered food while leaning away, saying, "No, no, no."

Kathy looks awkwardly surprised by my Mommy's rejection of her food offering. She nervously puts the dish down and awkwardly gestures at the food, saying, "You can have any of the food here."

"No, no, no," my Mommy says with a slight smile while holding my hands on my lap. I'm wondering, how can we refuse all of this free delicious food? I haven't had a thing to eat this morning.

It's appropriate and polite to reject any food initially offered guests in Chinese culture. Even a second rejection response to food is still appropriate, and the host keeps offering until the guest modestly accepts the offer. The rejection of food shows that we are not hungry pigs, even though I am a hungry piglet. We stay only a short while, and I never get a bite of any food! What a waste! *Mammamia!* **[Ch.2:8]** Or better yet, in Chinese, *Aiiyaah!* **[Ch. 2:9]**

My parents are busy at the *House of Fong* preparing to open their restaurant doors at 4 p.m. My Daddy wearing his long white apron holds my hand and walks me outside the restaurant to the street corner. I'm probably at least three years old. He kneels beside me and directs my attention to the signal lights across the street. He points to the signal light and says, *"Néih tái gin gó hung sik dang ma?"* meaning, "Do you see that red light?"

"Yeah," I nod.

"Hung dang, mo hàahng," meaning, "Red light, don't walk." "*Tái gó wong sik dang*," meaning, "look at the yellow light." *"Wong sik dang, mo han,"* meaning yellow light don't walk.

"Okay," I nod while looking at the signal lights across the street.

Luhksik dang, Néih han dak," meaning, “green light, you can walk.”

My Daddy reviews the meaning of the signal light colors as the lights change. *Néih ming baht ma?"* meaning, "Do you understand?" he asks.

I nod and say, "yeah."

"Néih sikh wei, faan ngukkéi ma?" meaning, "Do you know how to return home?" he asks. *"Na, hàahng yat go gaai hou, jeun jeuo sau,"* meaning, walk one block, turn left, as he motions his left hand to help in his directions.

"Néih ji dou ma?" meaning, "Do you know?" he asks.

"Yeah," as I nod.

He further directs me, *"Jeun jeuo,* néih *hàahng liang guo gaai hou, néih tái gin ngwo dei ngukkéi. Néih geidak ma?"* meaning, "Turn left, you walk two blocks, you'll see our house. Do you remember?"

I nod and say, "yeah."

"Dang go a luhksik dang, ho hàahng a," "meaning, wait for the green light, then walk," he explains. Within moments, the signal light turns green.

"Luhksik dang, hàahng a," meaning, "green light, walk," he instructs.

My Daddy releases me from his hands, and I walk across the street. I step up to the sidewalk, turning to look at my Daddy. He stands up, nods, and smiles at me. He points at the signal light, kitty-corner from him, to direct my attention to reading the signal light. The light turns green.

"Hàahng a!" meaning, "walk," he shouts as he gestures his hand forward.

I step down from the curb and walk across the street. Looking back at my Daddy, smiling. He motions forward to keep me walking down the block. I keep turning now and then to look back at him. He still stands and watches me. Before I make a left turn at the end of the block, I stop and turn to my Daddy, waving goodbye. He waves back, smiling. I continue to walk straight ahead. Soon I arrive home on Gaviota Street--my first lesson of independence. **[Ch. 2:10]**

A few months later, my Daddy comes home and announces that we are moving. He says to gather our things together because we are going to leave someday soon.

Chapter 3: 2026 E. 4th Street, Long Beach, California

On a rainy morning, I'm walking with my Mommy under our umbrella, following closely behind her as we climb a tall flight of wooden stairs at this pink apartment. Standing at the top of the stairs on the second floor, my Mommy complains in Cantonese, glancing at me as she wrestles with her ring of keys. My Mommy's negative energy reverberates in me. She seems stressed. She finds the key that opens the door. We go inside.

I soon realized that my parents purchased this four-unit one-bedroom pink apartment with a living room, a bathroom, and a kitchen. My family will live upstairs in both units, where the laundry room joins them, allowing open access. Downstairs my parents rent the two units separately to current tenants.

In front of my parents' pink apartment is a cafe with a gravel parking lot sandwiched between them. Directly across the street is the theatre's front entrance and a department store. On the corner of East 4th Street and Cherry Street is a 76-gas station. Three long blocks away, both my brothers attend Luther Burbank Elementary School.

Soon after my family moves into the pink apartment, I'm with my Daddy, who shakes hands with Mr. Cornfield, the owner of the café. Mr. Cornfield's arms and hands look pale, shriveled, and freckled with protruding blue veins that branch from his knuckles to his forearms.

Watching them introduce and engage in their chat, I continue staring at Mr. Cornfield, wearing a long white apron with his chef's white hat. He looks terrifying. Never in my entire life have I seen anyone who looks so old!

He's wearing thick coke bottle bifocals that enlarge the size of his eyes, similar to those alien invader bug eyes. His face wears deep wrinkles with hanging loose white, pale skin. His neck looks baggy and deeply wrinkled like a rooster wattle.

Mr. Cornfield smiles, patting me on the head when my Daddy introduces me. Gripping my Daddy's hand tighter with my small hand while holding his pants with my other, standing close to him, staring up at Mr. Cornfield with no expression. Mr. Cornfield and my Daddy have welcoming smiles and nods throughout their pleasant neighborly chat.

No more than a couple of months later, overhearing a neighbor saying urgently to my Daddy, "Mr. Cornfield died this morning." I'm shocked. Fearful after hearing the urgent and intense commotion of Mr. Cornfield's death. My image of Mr. Cornfield burns deep in the recess of my mind from the very first time seeing him.

Soon after, my parents go to their restaurant to prepare to open. My brothers and I stay at home. I still feel the chilling resonance of the alarming commotion that occurred only a couple of hours earlier. I wander to my parent's room and climb up on my Mommy's padded bench in front of her vanity table.

Kneeling on the padded bench, looking in the mirror at myself for several moments, and revisiting my disturbing feeling of urgency and commotion just hours earlier about Mr. Cornfield's death. Hearing only silence, feeling so alone. My tears begin flowing, looking at myself in the mirror. Incredibly scared to get old like him and die. My heart pounds in my chest, feeling chills all over my body while brushing my hands several times over my goosebump arms to soothe them.

Clasping my small hands tightly together while resting my tilted forehead and nose on them while praying so fervently, "Dear God, please, I don't want to get old. I don't want to die. Please keep me young forever and ever. I don't want to die. I don't want to get old. Please, God, keep me young forever and ever." In my prayer, I think of the highest number imaginable in a future year that I could live to be—never praying so hard in my entire life. It's my first prayer. I keep praying over and over again, pleading to God. Finally, saying, "Thank you, God."

Lifting my head, seeing the tracks of my tears on my face, tears dripping off my chin, moistening my t-shirt. Wiping my face and taking several deep breaths, I feel relief after my prayer. Looking into my eyes and face reflecting in the mirror, remaining motionless.

Moments later, I'm reliving a flashback of my family driving home on Gaviota Street. Black smoke and orange-red flames burst ferociously out of a home. Firefighters in their yellow helmets and heavy jackets grip a large hose, blasting water shooting high in the sky, cascading powerfully down like Niagara Falls, drenching the top of the flaming deteriorating roof. The heavy black smoke penetrates our cupped nose and mouth, making breathing difficult.

Everyone in the car rubbernecks as my Daddy slowly drives past the intense, chaotic scene. Peering between the gaps in the crowd, seeing a few people lying on their backs on the front lawn with oxygen masks. Witnessing my first serious, urgent, and frightening event.

Jason comes to wake me up from my nap. He taps on my shoulder and says, "Mary, wake up. It's time to wake up."

Swipe! Abruptly swinging and scratching like a fierce tiger, Jason's face is scratched while I'm in a deep sleep. Jason feels my stinging swipe, jumping back, holding his face. His hands lift quickly to block any other fierce swings. I vaguely recollect this. My Mommy later points out the bleeding scratch mark on Jason's face.

Whenever Leland tells Jason to wake me up, he's hesitant and a bit fearful of getting scratched across his face again. Next time, Jason strategically stands at the foot of my bed.

He gently calls me, "Mary, are you awake? It's time to get up." Still sleeping, he pats me on my foot. "Mary, wake up. It's time to get up. It's time to go and eat." I eventually wake up.

Ever since I can remember, I have had vivid dreams, more like nightmares. Sporadically, having nightmares of someone chasing me, trying to hurt me.

One time in the middle of the night, I wake up from sleep. Peering at the plastic-lit Santa Claus face on the wall between our twin beds. Feeling uncomfortable with the fake eyes and smile of Santa Claus, a plaster look.

Climbing out of bed, holding my blanket and dragging it behind me in the dark, walking to my parent's bedroom located on the other side of the pink apartment. Their bedroom door is closed.

Tap, tap, tap, "Mommy." There's silence. Tap, tap, tap, "Mommy, I'm scared."

Silence fills the air. I hear footsteps. My Mommy wearing her nightgown opens the door.

"Ju maht yeh a? Dim gaai néih mh fun gau a?" meaning, "What is the matter? How come you are not sleeping?"

"Mommy, I'm afraid," I say in an innocent and worried voice. She holds my hand and walks me back to the other unit of the pink apartment. We walk through a small toy room, the laundry room, the small kitchen, Leland's room, and finally into our bedroom.

She helps me climb into my bed. Jason was fast asleep in the other twin bed. Looking up, pointing at the plastic-lit Santa Claus face with staring eyes, "I'm scared of that," I say.

My Mommy looks at the plastic-lit Santa Claus and hits his face to show that he would not bother me anymore. She says, *"Mo päh keuih a. Néih hao fun gau a,"* meaning, "Don't be afraid of him. You ought to sleep." She tucks me in and sits on my bed until I fall asleep.

Chapter 4: Karl's Grand Birth Entrance to Two Years Old

Afraid of death? Fearful of leaving this earth? Being born is the most horrible experience. People welcome in a baby, and everybody is joyful. But for the baby itself, it is torture! Not every spirit goes into the baby's body right away. Some spirits don't come in until the woman is giving birth, pushing out the baby. That's me. I wasn't in the tummy the whole time experiencing that because I had already experienced it plenty of times. I decide to come in as soon as it's my time to show up in the world.

A transition of energy occurs from a very high frequency, and you are suddenly being absorbed. It's like a sponge if you can visualize the sponge being a body, and the water is the soul.

The spirit has energy--an energetic body. The physical body acts like a sponge absorbing the energetic spirit. You get sucked into a body, and your spirit is a higher energetic frequency that doesn't align with the body that has a lower frequency. The body is dense, heavy, and has a lower energy vibration.

Next is the realigning process, where the spirit needs to attach to the body's density. That is extremely painful. On top of that, I get pushed outside of something so narrow. In addition to the mental pain, there's the spiritual pain of realigning to a body with a different density. At the same time, I also have the physical pain of a body squishing through a very narrow passageway.

Eventually, I pop out, appearing in the world. Everything is very confusing at birth. I'm using my third eye to see. Many people think, or the doctors will say, "Babies don't see the first few days because their eyes have to adjust and develop."

But we do see. We use our third eye to see what is going on.

Don't get us wrong; we know what everybody is doing. We see what you're doing, but it can be very disorienting when you're born because there are bright lights. You have the coldness, strangers handling you, tossing you around, and you can't do anything. You have no control over the situation and don't forget, as a baby, we are fully aware of what's going on because we still have the consciousness of an all-knowing, all-connected being to the higher source. **[Ch. 4:1]**

So, I'm this helpless little thing while the doctor smacks me around. "Smack it on the butt," "clean it up," tubes in your nose--all that stuff. I'm lying there, fully aware of what's happening and unable to do anything about it. I have no control. I feel very violated at moments. **[Ch. 4:2], [Ch. 4:3]**

Once we cuddle, I go with my Mommy, and once I go as the spirit in the body, I begin to settle down. I start feeling the connection with the person I have made a contract with in this life. So, I feel at home at that moment, I do. I start adjusting to everything.

I'm feeling my Mommy and my Daddy, and I'm like, "Okay, I'm in the right place. It's okay. We're in the right place. I can feel you and sense you; we're doing all right." I'm a curious baby. When I'm one year old, it's really about adjusting to my family. It's adjusting to their habits, adapting to their smells, and changing to a very confined, restricted area because I do not see the world entirely yet. I'm still very closed off. I sleep a lot.

Why do babies sleep a lot? Babies sleep a lot because we are adjusting to our spirit frequency and our body's frequency. All our cells need to adjust to the frequency of our energetic spiritual human body, which can be very painful. Therefore, we sleep a lot. We leave our bodies a lot so the body can adjust. Even though our consciousness is not in the body, we're still attached to the body. The energy is in the body, but the consciousness is somewhere else. So slowly, we readjust to our energetic spiritual human body's frequency because it would otherwise be too painful. That's why we sleep a lot. We feel, "Screw it. I'm out of here. I'm going to hang out over there."

So, the first year for me is really about getting to know my parents. It is about getting to know my family and figuring out my enclosed environment. When I turn two years old, it is all about me trying to experience the outside world instead of just the family. I want to experience everything, trying to see what my parents would do if I did certain things. It's almost like testing everyone.

My Mommy loves babies. She has a knack for making me smile. My Mommy is with me so much that I feel she is here to guide everyone. She is here to keep the peace. She is here to keep everything stable in the family.

My Daddy loves me as well. I know that, but he is different from me. He is more distant. I'm curious about his journey, and my Daddy is not around much. So, for me, it is almost like a question mark. Like what does he do? Where does he go? What should I be doing? How can I get his attention? I try to get his attention even when I get older. I say that my relationship with my Mommy is entirely different from my relationship with my Daddy. I do look up to my Daddy because he does work very hard.

I come into my life knowing that life is precious and the ability to see details. As a little boy, I could look at the leaves. I can see every individual leaf, seeing the sunshine through it, the small details people ignore. I was born with the feeling that everything is unique. I can see in every person their beauty, whereas people typically see none. I think it is because I have this compassion for enjoying things about living in the moment and seeing the beauty and grasping it as much as possible. It just comes from inside. I feel we are all here for a reason and that it is more important to see the beauty in things than to focus on the negative.

I needed to be born with that quality, so my parents and siblings could grow up with a content kid who is happy most of the time. I can be joyful, and I can be that glue that keeps everybody together. I'm the peacemaker to calm things down. I'm trying to mend things when I'm supposed to. **[Ch. 4:4]**

I grow up in a family with an older brother and two sisters. I'm the baby of the family, the youngest, and very attached to my Mommy. When it comes to a Japanese American family and the Western view of the family, I grew up in a real Japanese family. The Japanese relationship is all about a child and a mother.[1]

When you look at the more Western relationship family, it's all about the husband and the wife. Because I'm the baby, I'm very close, very attached to my Mommy, and she is very protective of me. I have a lot of great memories with her. And I have a lot of great memories of looking up to my brother and sisters.

Starting at two years old, I discover that I can manipulate things by expressing what I want or letting them know I'm not happy. I manipulate things, but I still feel connected to the higher source. I still feel connected to the universe, so I never really feel alone, but I don't feel like an individual. I don't have the sense that, "Oh, I'm just me."

[1] ***Amae*** is a Japanese cultural term that refers to the mother and child relationship that involves the sense of complete interdependence based on a desire to be unconditionally loved, nurtured, and cared for by another. It is a special bond shared between the Japanese mother and her child that is unique and heartfelt.

Chapter 5: More of Mary's Kid Memories

Jason and I always greet our Daddy and Mommy in the morning, *"Ah, Bä Bä, zou san. Ah, Mä Mä, zou san."* One morning, Jason and I are crossing paths with our Daddy repeatedly, and we greet him every time, *"Ah, Bä Bä, zou san."*

After three greetings, my Daddy says in a somewhat scolding tone, *"Hey, Mh saai ai ngou chi chi. Yat chi ho le."* meaning, "You don't have to greet me every time. One time is good enough." Both Jason and I nod to acknowledge our Daddy's instructions.

Television is often our babysitter. Sometimes, when watching TV, we draw pictures of different birds and butterflies from a book—also, place a mirror in front to draw a picture of myself. Other times, we play a board game, *Life*. Jason reads the cards and instructions of the game. Sometimes, I end up doing something to try to cheat to win. Jason always calls me on it.
[Ch. 5:1]

My favorite TV program is *Hobo Kelly*. She enthusiasti-cally greets her viewers, waving and saying, "Hello, Misdemeanors!" She turns on her wonderful magical machine that rolls down presents for a lucky kid who sent her a postcard. She pulls the winning card from her large rotating drum of postcards. **[Ch. 5:1A]**

Always wishing I could win all those toys. I wrote a bunch of postcards to Hobo Kelly and put them in the mailbox. Later I discover that I didn't put the right stamp value on them. Other TV favorite shows of the 60's we enjoy watching are: My Three Sons, Mister Ed, Lassie, The Honeymooners, Ozzie and Harriet, Bewitched, Gun Smoke, Bonanza, Gilligan's Island, Dennis the Menace, McHale's Navy, Leave it to Beaver, Beverly Hill Billies,

My Favorite Martian, The Andy Griffith Show, The Addams Family, The Ed Sullivan Show, The Twilight Zone, Get Smart, Father Knows Best, Dick Van Dyke Show, The Munsters, I Dream of Jeannie, Green Acres, Petticoat Junction, Gomer Pyle, Batman, I Love Lucy, and others. **[Ch.5:2- Ch.5:29]**

I don't like Lucy's husband, Ricky Ricardo. He always has this demeaning tone whenever he says, "Luucccyyy," while pointing and wagging his index finger, giving her the eye. She looks anxious that either she is in trouble for being mischievous or not doing what he says. I often witness Ricky getting angry at Lucy, and he puts Lucy over his knee and spanks her. **[Ch. 5:30]**

That irritates me! It makes me so angry how Ricky treats Lucy in a humiliating way. That's so demeaning toward his wife! He's so wrong! This scene is not comical. It's not funny. Who does he think he is? I feel immense disgust when he degrades Lucy.

I don't care for war movies and cartoons. War movies show Americans fighting against the Japanese and cowboys against the Indians, killing each other, too. On the one hand, I like the animation of the various cartoon characters. On the other hand, cartoon shows are unrealistic, not funny, and mindless.

However, I love the Shirley Temple movies. Shirley, super cute and an incredible talented prodigy. An American icon so loved. I think because I admire Shirley Temple's singing, dancing, and acting like in *The Little Colonel*, my interest grows in entertainment. **[Ch. 5:31]**

I'm watching this scene from her movie, *Bright Eyes*. An aviator Godfather told Shirley Temple that her Mother has gone to heaven. This scene teaches me more about an abstract concept at an early age that people find difficult to talk about--death. **[Ch. 5:32]**

Sitting in front of the TV, Jason and I see this singing band called *Freddie and the Dreamers*. They are funny! Jason and I burst out laughing and giggling as Freddie, the lead singer, jumps around with funny antics and sounds while singing on stage. **[Ch. 5:33]**

Our Daddy is a very thin, serious-minded, hardworking, five feet seven inches tall, with black-slicked comb-back hair. He walks by and stops to see through his spectacles why we're laughing. He does not tolerate nonsense and says in a scolding tone, *"Nei siu maht yeh, le? Mo siu! Soh, soh! ci sin,* meaning, "What are you laughing about? Don't laugh! Silly! Crazy!" We freeze and stop laughing. Our Daddy walks away.

At times, Jason and I entertain ourselves with our hand puppets. Jason introduces his hand puppet creation called Snakey. I imitate his hand puppet, closing my four fingers side by side together as the face, using my thumb as the lower lip, and moving both parts as Snakey is talking. My Snakey is named Little Snakey, and he is called Big Snakey.

In a matter of days, we invented an extensive cast of hand puppet characters. We create Foxy, Doggie, Turtlewie, Big Dinosaury, Little Dinosaury, Wreck-Up Face, and Uni for Unicorn. We have different voices for them. Snakey, Foxy, and Uni have high pitch voices. Foxy has a sophisticated way of speaking. Turtlewie has a slow, low tone voice. Wreck-Up Face expresses himself through different sounds, not by speaking clearly. Big Dinosaury has a lower voice and moves slowly. Small Dinosaury has a higher peppy voice and moves with an upbeat style. **[Ch. 5:34]**

One day, friends of the family come to visit my parents. Their daughter, Wing, who attends junior high school, comes to the pink apartment to play with me. Sitting on the floor in the kid's toy room, she takes one-by-one the nicely organized toys and statues out of a cabinet, scattering them all over the floor.

I'm throwing a tantrum. Wing keeps asking me questions, and I shake my head, "no." She soon realizes that I don't like what she has done. She puts things back to their original position. I calm down. After that, we do something else.

On another day, I'm in the toy room looking in a large box with several plastic dolls. I notice for the first time that all the doll faces have scribbled pen marks. I don't recollect doing that. But most likely, I'm the culprit. Either I got pen happy, or I was frustrated that the dolls are not real and only have one expression.

A pretty music box sits in the toy room that my Godfather and Godmother, Emil and Florence Plasburg, gifted me. When opening the music box lid, the music turns on, and the ballerina in the middle twirls around. The inside music box lid has many half-inch cut mirrors reflecting multiple images of the ballerina and me. I'm frustrated because of the lack of clarity. I want to see one clear reflective mirror image.

I'm a fearless little girl, but probably more mischievous. One morning, I climb up onto the bathtub enamel rim that has enough width for my little feet to walk across and leap around with my two arms and hands in the air, helping me to maintain my balance like a gymnast on the balance beam. As I'm leaping on the bathtub enamel rim, bam! I fall hard, hitting my stomach and mouth on the bathtub enamel rim.

I'm feeling pain in my stomach and my mouth dripping with blood, holding my mouth, crying. Jason helps me up, and we walk to my parents' bedroom. My Mommy cleans me up.

On another day, Jason and I are bouncing on our twin beds parallel to one another. We're having a good time jumping up and down like on trampolines. Jason initiates jumping from bed to bed. I follow him, jumping back and forth. Jason springs too far, completely missing his bed, and crashes on his feet and butt on the carpet floor next to the window.

"Jason, are you alright?" I ask.

He pops his head up, pulling himself up with both of his hands on the bed. "I'm all right," he says. We continue to bounce up and down on the beds until we have enough of that.

Continuing my mischievous nature, wandering into my parents' bedroom when they are at work. Looking through my Mommy's drawers and trying on her jewelry, clothes, and shoes occupies my time. Finding a bottle of red nail polish, twisting off the cap, I begin painting my fingernails and then my toenails.

The following morning, I come to see my parents in their bedroom. My Mommy points at my small fingers and toes and says sternly, *"Tei nei sau ji, guelk ji,"* meaning, "Look at your fingers and toes."

I look at my unevenly painted red fingernails and toenails and the surrounding skin. I have to admit I did a sloppy, lousy, awful manicure and pedicure job! I'm glad I didn't pay for this.

My Mommy begins hitting my legs. Swiftly I tuck in between my Daddy's two legs, protecting me with his hands and arms from my Mommy's slaps of dismay at my naughty behavior. **[Ch. 5:34A]**

One evening, the following week, my Mommy washes my hair, puts rollers on, and fits a plastic bonnet on my head to dry my hair with the portable 1960s hairdryer. **[Ch. 5:35]** I fell asleep while my Mommy paints my nails so perfectly. She is so kind to doll me up on her day off from the restaurant. I look like a Chinese version of Shirley Temple with curly hair.

My Daddy creates a little rhyme and repeatedly sings, *"Moi je si, dai guelk ji,"* meaning, "Little girl, you have a big toe," while pointing to my big toe.

Later that morning, my Daddy sits on the green couch, relaxing before going to the restaurant. I put my pink hula hoop around my waist, saying to him, "Daddy, Daddy, count how many times the hula hoop goes around my waist." As I'm saying this, I feel and can see that I'm outside of my body, observing me pretending to play the role of a little girl. I'm fully aware that I'm pretending and acting like a little girl and saying things expected of how little girls behave. My Daddy cooperates, counting while resting his cheek on his knuckles and fingers with his elbow planted on the armrest.

Later in the afternoon, I'm standing by Leland's large window in his bedroom, watching two sisters next door in their backyard playing in their large plastic swimming pool. It looks fun watching them splashing around in the water on a sunny blue, sky crisp day.

After viewing the sisters playing in their pool, I walk around in my brother's bedroom feeling lightweight, spreading my arms wide at my side, feeling all the space around me. I feel this spacey floaty feeling all around me. I slowly turn around and around, picking up speed and gradually slowing down. I stop and try to keep my balance while standing there, feeling my head spinning, feeling dizzy with closed eyes, and experiencing the room spinning around when my eyes open.

I found a way to get high! It's non-toxic, no cost, nonaddictive, and no lasting side-effects. What a cool trip! However, I caution sensitive kids who may experience side-effects, such as a temporary headache, nausea, or a combination of both, to discontinue. If the side-effects continue, immediately consult with your Mommy, Daddy, or family doctor when necessary.

I'm lying on my tummy on my brother's bedroom carpet allowing my dizziness to subside. My thoughts begin to wander. A thought pops into my mind, muttering to myself, "Do I see any ghosts?" Quickly looking in the air and all around me to see if I can see any ghost. "No, I don't see any ghosts," I mutter, feeling disappointed. With determination and conviction, I say, "Someday, when I die, I will know all the answers to my questions."

At times, I play with Jason and his friend Joey, who visits his grandma now and then, who lives in the apartment next door to us. While visiting Joey at his grandma's home, she pulls out a batch of freshly baked chocolate chip cookies, capturing every tasty, irresistible breath of ours as we greet her.

Soon after, Joey's grandma offers us her warm homemade cookies. Each of us munches delightfully on our heavenly chocolate chip cookie, quickly devouring it. Again, we help ourselves to another warm, freshly baked cookie, satisfying our sweet tooth. Joey and Jason hang out in the living room while I stay in the kitchen with Joey's grandma and the plate of freshly baked chocolate chip cookies.

Chomping my tasty chocolate chip cookie, I curiously peek at the cute hamster in the cage on the kitchen counter. I've never seen a hamster. He's a cute furry creature twitching his nose with his white whiskers moving about. Trying to pet the cute hamster's head and nose between the cage bars with my index finger in a rhythmic circular motion as he stood innocently close.

Observing in slow motion, the quick action of the hamster opening his mouth with big front white teeth attacks my index finger! Chomp! I take a huge gasp, whipping my finger back like a rubber band slingshot. Red blood gushing from my finger! My eyes bug out. I'm in shock!

In a panic, I turn around to show his grandma, startled to see so much blood gushing out from my index finger. She quickly covers my finger with napkins. She sprays *Bactine* on my wound, then wraps my finger with gauze and white tape. Feeling the throbbing pain of my finger under the white mummy wrapped bandages. So much for a cute innocent hamster!

The following weekend, Joey's grandma invites us to her

Catholic church--my first experience. Rows and rows of dark wooden benches fill the large quiet church that slowly reaches nearly total capacity. Sitting in the center pew in the middle of the church, beautiful large color stain-glass windows on the sidewalls contribute to the holy ambiance. On stage, many tall white candles flicker brightly on a long wooden table, contrasting the spacious dim church of people quietly sitting on the wooden pews.

I'm feeling the energy in this ornate scene with a statue of a mother tilting her head, embracing her baby in her nurturing arms. People learn about God here, sensing calm, peaceful, open, and quiet surroundings. I'm in awe, absorbing this new place.

The church service begins with a bible verse, the choir singing, and the priest gives a sermon. The priest wears his ornamental gown performing a ritual. He walks around a large wooden table swinging a metal decorative container that emits a small white trail of incense smoke. Following behind, the altar boys dressed in their religious gowns. Although I don't understand the meaning of the ceremony, I take away an impression of a sense of holiness, God, respect, and peace.

Afterward, Joey's grandma takes us to a shopping center where we sit on Santa Claus' lap. "So, little girl, what would you like for Christmas?" Santa Claus asks.

"I would like a bicycle," **[Ch. 5:36]**

Then we smile for a picture, and I hop down from his lap. On the way out, a woman gives me a spinning tot toy. We return home, and Joey's grandma makes us a tasty sandwich for lunch.

I have to admit, outside of this church experience today, I'm a mischievous little girl. On top of that, I'm a candy addict.

Dragging a chair next to the lime-colored tiled kitchen counter, I climb up on the chair and prop myself on the counter, ready to curiously climb the kitchen cabinets searching for candy. I perch one small barefoot on one shelf, then my other barefoot braces onto the next upper shelf. My little hands grab tightly on each shelf until I reach the top of the cabinet, where it meets the ceiling.

Carefully, I open the door of the wooden dish cabinet. Aha! Eureka! **[Ch. 5:36A]** I successfully sniff out a bag of candy on the top shelf of the dish cabinet! I carefully reach into the open bag, pinch out two wrapped candies.

Cautiously climbing down the cabinet like a little monkey, I gently close the dish cabinet door. Day after day, I find myself returning and climbing up the kitchen cabinet to satisfy my sweet tooth. Fortunately, my Mommy never asks me about the missing candy. Maybe she forgot that she stashed it up there.

The waitresses are fond of Jason and me. Kathy buys two trick-or-treat costumes for both of us. She enthusiastically asks my parents if she can take us trick-or-treating. I have no idea what trick-or-treating is.

My parents don't like the idea but can't say 'no' to Kathy. My Mommy is displeased, but she can't disallow us because Kathy already bought our costumes.

Normatively, in Chinese culture, first-generation immigrants value maintaining group harmony and avoiding offending anyone. I think my Mommy is displeased because she doesn't like the idea of her kids walking house to house asking for candy, like beggars. In China, they don't have this Halloween tradition.

Tonight is Halloween. Kathy dresses me in a Mexican red and green dress with tassel fringes at the hem. She helps Jason wear a black cape with a black mask over his eyes and nose. My mask is a bit oversized for me, and the mask area between my eyes and nose irritates my skin. Kathy folds a napkin piece to cushion my nose from the mask. We are ready to go. **[Ch. 5:37], [Ch. 5:38]**

Carrying our oversized trick-or-treat bags, walking down some blocks of homes near *House of Fong,* Kathy encourages us to go from house to house. We knock on front doors and shout, "Trick-or-treat!" Doors fling open over and over again.

We received plenty of compliments on our costumes like, "What darlings," or "How cute," or "How precious," while home-owners drop candies into our bags. "Thank you!" we shout in chorus. We return to *House of Fong,* and Kathy helps us dump our candy bags onto the table. Our eyes twinkle at the assortment of candy. We could open up our candy store. However, since I'm a candy addict, I plan to eat every piece of deliciously sweet candy to my heart's desire for a whole year!

The following day, our candy bags disappeared, nowhere to be found. "Where did our candy go?" we repeatedly ask—no response from our parents. We suspect our Mommy hid our bags and didn't want us to eat all that candy. I'll have to see if I can sniff it out somewhere in the house.

Six days out of the week, Leland, Jason and I walk about ten blocks to *House of Fong* to eat dinner. While walking, Leland stops and exclaims, "Wow, this is a Rolls Royce!" He peers through the windows of a shiny large car parked along the street. He keeps repeating it while cupping the sides of his face looking through different windows. **[Ch. 5:39]**

I have no clue what a Rolls Royce is. For the longest time, I think a Rolls Royce is a buffalo. The words, Rolls Royce, sounds like a buffalo, wouldn't you agree? My brother marvels over the car's interior and exterior for a minute. Then we continue our walk to the *House of Fong* to eat our dinner.

Every dinner time, we sit in the same booth, closest to the kitchen. Leland hates garbanzo beans, always complaining while picking them out of his food by shoving them to the edge of his dinner plate or onto a napkin. For me, lima beans are not my favorite--too mushy inside and have no flavor. I also shove them aside. Jason never is picky about his food. He eats and enjoys everything.

Sometimes when *House of Fong* is closed, I sit on the lower level of the serving cart while my brothers hold on to the serving cart handle and push and run down the dining area's central aisle. I'm constantly bracing for a thrilling joy ride while tightly grasping the two bars on both corners of the cart. Our parents don't yell at us for once, perhaps because they are in the back kitchen.

Several blocks away from the *House of Fong,* Jason and I sometimes feed a woman's black guinea pig that lives in her front yard. We wait and look for the guinea pig to appear, twitching its nose and whiskers.

One time, the guinea pig pokes his head out of the bushes, and we drop the carrot on top of its head. We chuckle. Although the guinea pig is surprised, it seems happy to get a carrot and nibbles on it.

Every month, our family travels to Chinatown, Los Angeles, on my parents' day off to have dinner and go to the Chinese theatre. In one movie, a Chinese girl entertains a crowd, twirling two small white pom-poms attached to long strings in the air. She makes creative designs in the air with her white pom-poms, captivating the crowd that gathers.

The next night before going home after eating at the *House of Fong,* I'm wearing my little red coat with a long string with white pom-poms attached. I detach them, imitating the Chinese girl in the movie. My parents stop in the kitchen to watch me delightfully twirling my white pom-poms in the air. They smile, laugh a bit, and clap with pleasure.

Before leaving, my Mommy kneels and gives me an Eskimo kiss, which is a rarity. Normatively, Chinese immigrant families don't kiss and hug in public. Kids are touched the most; however, as they become older, touch diminishes significantly.

Before going home, my parents give Leland a couple of rolls of Lifesavers. When we arrive home, Leland separates the variety of lifesavers into three Chinese teacups. Leland likes sitting on the carpet close to the TV, and Jason sits nearby.

I sit six feet in the back of them, chomping on my lifesavers. I'm chomping so loud; both turn around to look at me. Leland turns around, and "Ssh!"

I freeze and look at him. I try to chomp slowly and quietly, but that doesn't last very long. Both of my brothers turn around again.

Leland says, "Don't bite them. Just suck on the lifesavers. They'll last longer."

I stop and look at them, not knowing how to suck on the lifesavers. Leland rests a lifesaver on his colorful tongue and demonstrates sucking. I sit quietly, sucking on the remaining lifesavers in my teacup while watching TV. It's true. I can enjoy the variety of flavors longer.

The family usually eats at the restaurant on my parents' day off. We eat rice for every meal. My parents stir-fry my favorite thinly sliced marinated beef dish in a distinctively sweet, tangy sauce. The aroma satisfies every breath I take, building my appetite. Another favorite dish is canned salmon with thinly sliced white onions stir fry. My Mommy scoops food onto my small plate, and I pick it up with my long wooden chopsticks.

I'm holding my long wooden chopsticks with my fingers and thumb about two inches from the tip for better control. The bowl of steaming white rice uncomfortably heats my fingertips as I scrape the rice with my long wooden chopsticks into my mouth.

It is heavenly when the warm, thinly sliced marinated beef touches my palate. Every chew brings a burst of warm, sweet, tangy juice from the thinly sliced tender and savory beef, satisfying my senses and filling my tummy with joy. The pungent white onions and pink salmon delight my taste buds, too. I'm not a big eater. Usually, when we eat, I get sleepy, so I typically eat just enough to satisfy my hunger.

Once a year, my parents plan a family trip to Disneyland, Knotts Berry Farm, San Francisco, Las Vegas, and the Ice Capades Show. The family sees the Ice Capades at the Long Beach Arena on a Monday evening. During intermission, my Daddy walks me to the restroom while he waits outside in the busy hallway. Coming out of the restroom, I'm glancing for my Daddy. Then a young, middle-aged clean-cut man kneels in front of me and asks,

"Do you know who God is?"

I shake my head.

"Do you know that God loves you?"

I shrug my shoulders.

"Well, God loves you," the man says gently with a smile.

"Maly," my Daddy calls out, waving his hand at me. I look at my Daddy, leaving the man who turns to look in that direction.

"Go a yen, hey bing gwo a?" meaning, "Who is that man?" my Daddy asks.

"Mh jìdou," meaning, "don't know," as I shrug my shoulders. My Daddy holds my hand as we return to our seats before the show starts.

A few days later, at the restaurant, I ask Sherry, the waitress, "Who is God?"

"God is strong and almighty," says Sherry.

"Where did God come from?"

"God comes from dust. We all come from dust."

"Where did the dust come from?"

I keep asking, and eventually, we are going in circles repeatedly. I give up my pursuit of answers to my curious questions.

Shortly after waking up one morning, I see my Daddy and Leland moving swiftly from room to room at home, frantically searching for something. I stand there watching them.

Leland comes up to me and gestures his hand above his tilted head, pantomiming pulling a rope straight above his head. His face grimaces with his mouth stretching wide, showing his teeth and protruding intense eyes. I'm feeling a strong sense of urgency that something is wrong. It has something to do with my Mommy. Later that day, I hear that my Mommy was at the restaurant with a rope around her neck, sitting hopelessly in the restroom contemplating.

It is not until I am much older; that my Mom tells me how she constantly questions why she has lived such an unhappy life for as long as she can remember. She only had three years of schooling because her parents were not supportive, and education was not the norm for girls.

She continuously worked in China ever since she was 9 or 10. Classmates and neighborhood kids were around, but only as acquaintances. Her Daddy was absent most of her life, and her Mom was always sick and not communicative.

Then the difficulties of marriage in a struggling survival existence, raising a family and laboring day in, day out in a foreign country where she speaks and understands very little English.

Although I've never witnessed my parents arguing at a tender age, I feel the energy at home. I feel this density now and then, ever since we lived on Gaviota Street and now at this pink apartment. I rarely see my parents; they work so much. They are very hard-working parents. I rarely see them happy, laughing, or smiling. I rarely see them affectionate toward one another and the kids. I feel this energy of tension, density, thickness, and low vibes in the air.

Chapter 6: Mary Going to Pre-School

Early one morning, Jason asks me, "Do you want to go to school now? I can take you to school?"

"Okay," I say.

We leave home, shuffling our feet down the long flight of wooden stairs from our second-floor pink apartment. Jason holds my hand, standing on the sidewalk on East 4th Street. We turn our heads side to side, back and forth, waiting for a clear path from oncoming cars.

"It's clear. Let's go!" Jason says enthusiastically. We race across the street.

Making it to the other side of the street, I say to Jason, "My shoe fell off," standing there wearing only one rubber zori. Pointing where my other rubber zori sits abandoned in the middle of the street.

"Oh, okay, stay here. I'll go get it."

Jason looks both ways. It's clear. He races to the middle of the street, grabs the zori, and darts back. He drops my zori next to my foot, where I slip it back on.

He holds my hand, and we continue walking to school. He drops me off at my nursery school. **[Ch. 6:1]**

Next door, Jason goes to his first-grade class at Luther Burbank Elementary School. Upon arriving to nursery school, a little boy presents a bunch of flowers in one hand and says to me, "Here, I want to give you these flowers."

"Oh, okay," I say, accepting the bunch of flowers, walking straight to my shoebox located in the children's closet inside the nursery school building. The little boy follows.

Standing on my tippy toes, I raise my shoebox lid, placing the flowers there. I skip outside to the playground.

As I'm playing outside about an hour later, I come across a

wooden playhouse with a cloth covering the doorframe. I pull back the cloth cover to look inside. Surprisingly, I see the little boy who gave me flowers kissing another little girl on the lips. Both stop and look at me.

Quickly pulling the cloth cover closed, I walk swiftly to my shoebox — the little boy dashes to catch up. Standing on my tippy toes, opening my shoebox lid, I pull out the bunch of flowers.

Extending the bunch of flowers to him, saying, "I have to give this back to you." He quietly takes them.

I skip outside to play. I don't cry. I'm not angry. I'm neutral. I feel that it is the right thing to do. Honestly, I don't know the name of the little boy. We never played together. I don't think twice about what happened. I see a tricycle, hop on it, and pedal around the blacktop. **[Ch. 6:1A]**

My Daddy used to drive a pink 1950s Thunderbird. Picking me up from nursery school in the late afternoon, I see the tall nursery school teacher with short dark brown hair and bangs jumping up and down with excitement. She jumps so high seeing my Daddy's new 1964 blue Chevrolet Impala as he parks in front of the nursery school. My Daddy enters the nursery school gates, and the nursery school teacher looks thrilled as if she won a car.

"Your new car is so beautiful!" she exclaims with a big smile, gesturing her hands all around. She reminds me of those fanatical teenagers going wild over their favorite music band.

He smiles and nods. I gather my things together, ready to go home.

During my kindergarten year, I experience a terrifying event. Kids are arriving in the morning class. I'm walking up the stairs, a black dog runs loose. I panic. The dog comes running my way. My heart is pounding, feeling terrified, dashing around all over the green lawn to get away. The dog keeps running after me. I continue to run, feeling petrified.

Somehow, I run up the stairs inside the classroom, and all the kids sit quietly on the large rug. I'm sitting on the teacher's lap, crying while all the kids watch.

"Why are you crying?" the teacher asks.

"The dog," I breathlessly say as I'm crying and wiping my eyes.

"Did the dog bite you?" she asks.

I shake my head, still feeling overwhelmed by the terror.

"Did the dog chase after you?" she asks.

I nod, still crying, and my heart rapidly pounding in my little chest.

"You're all right now. There's nothing to be afraid of."

Soon after, I sit down on the rug with the other kids as we start our day. One fun activity involves the class singing together whenever someone gets new shoes. The kid who wears new shoes can walk around the classroom rug while everyone sings, "Mary has new shoes on today. See them walk, see them talk, look at Mary, go, run and play." Some girls exchange shoes with one another to look like we have new shoes. **[Ch. 6:1B]** Then we tell the teacher, and the entire class sings the new shoe song for each of us.

Kindergartners engaged in a meaningful activity, drawing and coloring a picture of their house on a folded construction paper. The teacher calls each kid in front of the class and asks them to recite their home address.

"Mary, what is your address to your house?"

"Twenty-twenty-six east fourth street," I recite what Leland taught me the day before.

"Good," the teacher says, then hands my little-decorated house to me as I get up to receive it.

I'm brushing my teeth on one sunny, cool afternoon at home. I noticed before that my back molars have big cavities. I brush my front teeth and see blood seeping from my bottom gums. I'm terrified. I'm frantic and rush to the phone to call my parents at the restaurant.

My Mommy picks up the phone, and I speak with urgency, "Mommy, Daddy, come home, come home, right away!" I'm crying. I'm hysterical.

My Mommy speaks with concern, *"Maht yeh?"* meaning, "What is the matter?"

"Come home, Mommy, come home, right away! My teeth are bleeding! Come home. Quick!" I'm agitated and panicking that something is wrong with me.

Within minutes, my parents arrive home. I show them my bleeding teeth. They look at my teeth and check them. They appease me, say I'm all right and put me to bed.

Not long after this incident, I go to the dentist with Donna, a *House of Fong* waitress. This is my first visit to the dentist. The dental assistant greets me and guides me to the dentist's chair to sit down, not knowing what will ensue.

She puts a thick-weight plastic cover in front of me as I sit quietly in the chair. The dentist comes in and greets me. Nobody explains why I'm sitting there.

The dentist fits on a black rubber mask over my nose and mouth. "How does this smell?" the dentist asks.

"It smells! It smells!" I squirm while shaking my head from side to side, complaining.

"Keep breathing. It's all right. Keep breathing," the dentist instructs.

"It smells! It smells!" I keep squirming and complaining. I'm knocked out. After the procedure, I wake up. Donna lifts me to the mirror.

"Open your mouth. Look in the mirror. Do you see, your teeth got pulled out?" she says with a smile.

Looking in the mirror, I see all four of my lower molars gone! I only see red gums with holes in them. I freaked!

"I don't have any more teeth!" I'm crying and kicking with terror. Donna quickly places me down and tries to comfort me.

The next day at the restaurant, Donna mentions to my parents that she has this sizeable black bruise on her leg where I kicked her. She pulls one side of her black pants down and shows me the big black bruise on her thigh. I look at it.

On another day, our family arrives at an office for our appointment. Moments later, the receptionist calls, "Mr. Fong." The family enters a door to the back office, where the doctor momentarily talks to my parents on the side.

Afterwards, Leland sits down, and the doctor asks him to roll up his sleeve. He dabs an alcoholic cotton ball on his arm. The doctor holds a tube with a thin needle up in the air and squirts a bit of liquid out of the needle.

I watch with my round brown eyes wide open, staring at the doctor as he injects my brother, who sits calmly on the chair, looking straight forward. After it's over, Leland gets up and rolls down his sleeve.

Next, Jason sits in the same chair. Jason rolls his sleeve; the doctor rubs an alcohol cotton ball on his arm. The doctor prepares the needle, lifting it above his eyes, and flicks it with his fingers—the solution spurts out of the needle.

I'm standing next to my Mommy, staring intensely. The doctor injects Jason.

After he pulls the needle out, Jason quietly says with a straight face, "Ouch."

Terror strikes when everyone looks at me. A rush of adrenaline pours into my veins. "Aaauuugghhh!" I'm screaming and running in a frenzy around the medical table. My Mommy finally catches me while I'm screaming in horror!

My piercing scream practically cleans everyone's ears out. My Mommy sticks my head under her sweater and repeatedly says, *"Mh tung a, mh tung a,"* meaning, "it doesn't hurt, it doesn't hurt."

I don't know how many people are holding me down. Aaauuugghhh! I feel the sharp needle piercing my skinny little arm while screaming at the top of my lungs! I'm squirming while they hold my arm tight, crying with a higher pitch, "It hurts! Ahhhh!"

Finally, the terror is over. I hate shots! I feel whoever invented shots ought to be in front of the firing squad.

Growing up in the 1960s, my parents feel comfortable in the Long Beach community, allowing me to do things independently. My parents learned to be independent early and instilled independence in my childhood through lessons.

First, I learn how to read the signal lights, walk, and not walk across the street. Second, I learn to walk home by myself. This time, my Daddy instructs me to eat lunch at the diner across the street from *House of Fong.*

Leland writes the word hamburger on the notepaper for me to know what to order. My Daddy gives me just enough money to order a burger and a drink. I put the money and the note in my little pink purse.

The next day, my Daddy walks me in front of the *House of Fong* and instructs me to have lunch across the street at the diner. My Daddy watches me cross the street and enter the diner. I'm wearing a cute pink dress and carrying my little pink purse that hangs at my bent elbow and forearm.

I walk into the diner maturely and independently, climbing up on the green-padded swivel bar stool at the raised counter. Middle-aged and senior customers sit at the raised counter or nearby tables along the walls and windows. The customers glance and smile at me.

The waitress comes and hands me a menu. I can't read a word on the menu. However, I reach into my pink purse and pull out the note with the word, hamburger.

The waitress returns and asks, "What would you like to order, Sweetie?"

"I would like to order a hamburger, please."

"Would you like cheese on it?" she asks.

"Yes," I nod.

"Everything on it?" she inquires.

"Yes, everything."

"Would you like something to drink, Sweetie?"

"Milk, please."

"You got it, Sweetie."

"Thank you," I give her the menu.

I sit quietly on the green padded swivel bar stool, looking straight ahead through the wide rectangle opening in the wall where the cooks busily prepare the food orders. One by one, a plate order pops up onto the counter where the wide rectangle opening is. Two waitresses shout out orders through the wide rectangle opening while clipping new orders on a circular metal rotating carousel, picking up plate orders and delivering them to customers' tables.

I slowly look around at the diner and the people eating. The customers smile at me as I glimpse shyly at them with a grin.

My waitress places a glass of milk with a straw before me. Peeling the white straw paper on one end, gently patting the straw on the counter, and pinching the straw out of the paper wrap, which

I roll into a little ball. I drop the straw into my glass of milk and take a sip. Five minutes later, my hamburger plate pops up on the counter, and the waitress delivers it to me.

"Here you are, Sweetie--enjoy," says the waitress with her ruby red lipstick smile.

"Thank you." She reminds me of Lucy on the *I Love Lucy* show with her red curly fluffy hair and ruby red lipstick smile.

I unfold and expand the white paper napkin, covering my entire chest and lap, tucking it into the neckline of my dress. I pinch the two long toothpicks out of the hamburger. I cup the top bun in one hand, placing it on my dish. I reach for the bottle of ketchup that sits on the counter. Twisting the white cap off, I flip the bottle upside down and shake it up and down like I'm on a pogo stick as the slow-moving thick red ketchup finally plops out onto my bun.

My hamburger includes crispy lettuce, a slice of a red tomato, rings of pungent white onions, and green pickles, along with a secret sauce on a juicy steaming hot marinated beef patty—emitting its scent that blends into an inviting symphonic aroma that captures not only my brown eyes, and my button nose, but my salivating taste buds ready for the rapture. As the symphonic aroma creatively plays, dances, and teases my five senses, I could not move quickly enough to spear back the two long toothpicks into my hamburger.

I'm a hungry pig now, truthfully a hungry bear. I clinch the giant burger in the palm of my hands with my fingers and thumbs tightly wrapped around it. I open my mouth as wide as possible because I'm talking about a serious, gigantic quarter-pounder now held captive in my grip. I chomp my first bite like a shark, ketchup oozing out from the corners of my mouth. I swiftly loosen my grip on my delicious hamburger onto my plate, wiping my mouth, enjoying every chew that bursts the array of flavors, culminating into a beautiful harmonious blend of oneness, capturing my taste buds in ecstasy.

I gently close my eyes, chewing in syncopation, purely savoring every flavor bursting in my mouth as my teeth do their job digesting my delightful burger. I can taste the pungent white onions with every bite, the sour green pickles, the tangy red ketchup, the sweet, creamy, tasty secret sauce, and the marinated beef patty. The crunchy lettuce sounds add textural quality like the percussion section of an orchestra.

Bite after bite, tasting the secret sauce with a slightly sweet, creamy taste. I sip some milk after every bite or two. Licking and wiping my chops clean for the next heavenly bite. My tummy fills up.

The once-hungry bear, now satisfied, transforms back into the not-so-innocent mischievous Chinese American girl experiencing early lessons of independence. I wipe my lips while burping silently with the napkin covering the entire front of my dress.

I peer at my tab on the counter and reach inside my pink purse, leaving the exact amount. I place a tip next to my plate. Rotating my green padded swivel stool, stretching my legs down, and slowly sliding off where my tippy toes touch the floor.

I exit the diner and walk across the street, obeying the traffic signal lights as my Daddy had taught me at least a couple of years ago. Returning to the restaurant, my parents are pleased with my success in ordering a hamburger for lunch at the diner myself. **[6:1C]**

Occasionally in the evening, our Mommy sits at a table with Jason and me in the small kitchen. She teaches us Cantonese using a paperback picture book she bought in Chinatown, Los Angeles. Our Mommy only speaks to us in Cantonese.

Jason and I race to see who could say the Chinese word first when my Mommy turns each page. We learn words like *yàhn* for a person, *sau* for hand, tian for the sky, *shan* for mountain, *che* for car, *gau* for a dog, and so on. We probably have no more than five Chinese lessons growing up since my Mommy can only teach us on her day off when she feels up to it.

Leland spends most of his time doing his homework and school activities. In the sixth grade, he served as student body president of Luther Burbank Elementary School. Although Leland doesn't have time to play with us, sometimes, I sing along with him, playing his steel-string guitar. Two of the first songs I learn to sing are "Bus Stop" and "So Happy Together." **[Ch. 6:2], [Ch. 6:3]**

Sometimes, Leland meets up with his friends, and Jason and I tag along. We walk to the beach about twelve blocks from our pink apartment. **[Ch. 6:4]**

We follow Leland on the sandy beach, where scores of teenagers enjoy the day. Beach goers swim, surf, and wade in the ocean, sunbathing, eating, drinking, socializing, playing volleyball, building sandcastles, or tossing a frisbee. As Jason and I tag behind Leland, we come across a large circle of teenagers standing around, laughing and talking.

We join the ring around a teenage boy's buried body with only his head sticking out of the sand. A talking head on top of the sand looks unusually weird and a bit creepy. Teenagers stand, chatting and laughing with him, pouring water on his face to refresh him now and then. We stay at the beach for a while, following Leland and returning home.

Our Daddy drops off Leland, Jason, and me at the laundromat every other week to do the family's laundry. My Daddy and Leland load the dark and light clothes in separate washers. Jason and I sit nearby, sucking our lifesavers. Peeling a bit of the wrap off my roll of lifesavers, I discover three lifesavers stuck together. I can't separate them, so I toss all three lifesavers in my mouth, sucking and savoring the sweet flavors.

Suddenly, the lifesavers slip partially down my throat! I can't breathe! I hold my throat with one hand in a panic while I try to get Jason's attention. My terrified eyes are bugging out at him. Jason looks at me and yells, "Daddy, Mary has something stuck in her throat!"

Our Daddy drops everything, rushing over. He forcefully whacks me with the palm of his hand on my upper back between my shoulder blades, shooting out the lifesavers to the floor.

"Are you alright?" my Daddy and Jason asks.

I'm nodding while taking deep breaths, feeling immense relief, and feeling my heart still pounding in my chest while swallowing. Tension and panic that once consumed me slowly subsides. Whew! What a close call!

In late 1965, Jason and I tag along with Leland and his friend to see a theatre movie across the street from our pink apartment. It's my first time going to this theatre. I have no idea what movie we're seeing—a long line of girls outside the theatre waiting to purchase their tickets. Finally, we buy our tickets and find four seats together in the packed theatre. Soon after, the lights dim to darkness.

After sitting through a bunch of advertisements, a screaming crowd of teenage girls suddenly goes wild. Ear-piercing screams, girls jumping up and down, reaching toward the big screen when the hottest singing group appears, singing, "Help!" **[Ch. 6:5]**

I'm caught off guard staring with my brown eyes wide open, scoping 360 degrees around. Are these girls crazy or what? I'm stunned. I flip my coat hood on, plugging my ears, blocking the incessant screams. Glancing at these maniac girls crying and wiping their intense, desperate faces, jumping up and down, and reaching for the big screen overwhelms me. No bewilders me, no flabbergasts me!

Chapter 7: Four Years Old is Big for Karl

At four years old, I'm with my Mommy, who is pretty hard working in the house. I think that my father always underestimates what she does. She is always working. She always makes sure everything is just right. She is very organized in everything. She has a specific schedule in her mind that she wants to get this done by that time. The way I see her do things, it needs to be right when my Daddy comes home.

One day, she is cleaning up. I would hide my toys under my bed, thinking that is my best hiding place. Boy, am I wrong. I'm looking for my toys under my bed. They are gone! I can't find my toys, and I think that she has thrown them away. I'm panicking because these are my favorite toys.

I keep searching and looking for my toys. So, I start crying and crying and crying. She doesn't know what is going on. She has no idea. She keeps looking at me, asking, "What's wrong? What's going on?"

I keep crying and pleading, "Don't take my toys away. Please don't throw them away."

My Mommy looks at me with a big smile on her face. She says, "I know what you're looking for." So, she takes them out and shows me where they are. All she did was move them.

She knows she just made a connection with me. In her eyes, I could see the love she feels for me. She has heartfelt compassion for my honest plea. "Don't worry. I won't throw your toys away. I'm going to give them a bath."

She hugs me, wipes my tears away, and kisses my forehead. I feel so warm and safe in her embrace that I close my eyes. In one second, I forget why I'm crying. That is my Mommy's love. I will always carry her love with me. There is this connection that my Mommy will take care of me. My Mommy loves me, and I always feel she sees me for who I am.

That moment she looks inside my soul, and she sees us as the same. We are very compassionate about each other and our family. We would do anything to help them out, and we would do anything to make other people feel wanted because I'm like that too.

That moment is a deep spiritual connection I have with my Mommy. She has always been there. For as long as I could remember, I can feel this energy that flows between us at that moment. It makes me feel wanted. It makes me feel at home with her being there. It feels like I belong.

By the time I'm four, I feel that my Mommy looks at me, not at the universe. Me alone, I feel that individuality. That moment truly creates the sense and the understanding that I am here to have an individual experience, not to have that connected experience. I sense a release from being everything and everyone. I become that individual. It's a special moment for me. It's an intimate moment with my Mommy.

I don't feel like my Daddy ever understands me. He has his mind made up about her and everybody. How everybody should be, he's very structured as well. I'm telling people this story because the smallest experience we have, whether it is your Mommy giving you a lollipop or your Daddy patting you on your shoulder, those moments are invaluable. They are precious and essential in developing your individuality and relational connections, especially when you're a child. **[Ch. 7:1]**

I am a dreamer. I love the ocean. I love nature. I love gazing at the sky, the clouds, trees, and everything else. When I look at a tree, I see the sunlight hitting the leaves. I see that their leaves are transparent and allow the sun's rays to go through the leaves. For me, that is like harmony. It feels beautiful. It feels like home. It feels like love. I see the connections. I see the beauty. I see the energy in everything. I see the different colors around people. I'm sensitive to the energies around me. Everything is connected with love. That's what I see. I think that's what makes me different. I put my awareness in a place where I feel comfort and enjoyment. I have a connection with a higher source. **[Ch. 7:2]**

Chapter 8: First Grade for Mary

I don't have any fears and tears about going to my first day of school that turns out to be a short-day orientation at Luther Burbank Elementary School. Nothing memorable. Miss Henderson, my first-grade teacher, is a tall, pretty, and young teacher wearing a blue suit on the first day. She is pleasant and smiles a lot as she meets her new class this September morning. **[Ch. 8:1]**

Until I'm older, I realize the gravity of the hardship my parents experienced living in a foreign country. Not knowing the language, not having an education, not having a support system, continuously working at the restaurant, taking care of a spouse and three children, a home, and always in a survival mode. An over-whelming existence of survival and being spread so thin. Both of my parents have no time for themselves.

Because of the daily struggles of life, my Mommy musters enough strength to wake up in the only morning to make me a bowl of oatmeal for breakfast. Sitting at the table eating, my Mommy, wrapped in her robe, sits patiently watching. Scooping oatmeal in my mouth little by little, my Mommy says, *"Ni yat gum mahn,"* meaning, "You eat so slow." I keep scooping oatmeal in my mouth until I finish.

My Mommy helps me slip on a pair of hand-me-down black cowboy boots that Leland used to wear. On a rainy morning, wearing my red raincoat, carrying my umbrella as I step one by one down a steep flight of stairs. I wave my Mommy goodbye as she tells me to be careful. Jason does not feel well today. So, I'll walk to school myself.

Walking across the gravel parking lot in front of our pink apartment, I turn right in front of the café, walking down the street. It is pouring rain! My hand-me-down clunky cowboy boots slow me down--three blocks to clunk to school. Clunk, clunk, clunk in the rain, my hand-me-down clunky cowboy boots take me forever to walk. **[Ch. 8:2]** I'm sure not dancing in the rain with my clunky cowboy boots like Gene Kelly! **[Ch. 8:3]**

Finally, I'm half a block from where I can see the cross guard holding her red stop sign. I take my clunky black cowboy boots off to walk faster to school. I get to the corner, and the cross guard says with dismay, "Why did you take your boots off? It's raining!

Put your boots back on!" So, I stick them back on. I'm the last one to walk across the street. I finally make it into the classroom. I like seeing Miss Henderson again. She's friendly, pretty, and has a sweet smile.

Days and weeks go by. None of the girls has played or talked with me on the playground during recess. So, I play alone on the single bar twirling around and around. I like swinging and crossing over on the lateral bars. Hopscotch is fun, too. All this playtime doesn't require having someone to play with. I either play solo or wait in line until it is my turn.

Miss Henderson tells us to bring an object from home for an activity called "Show and Tell." I sneak a pair of wooden chopsticks and a Chinese white porcelain soup spoon from home in a brown paper bag. I don't ask my Mommy. I think she won't allow me because she is a bit strict.

All the kids place their show-and-tell objects on different tables and short bookcases. Our items are displayed for a week. One day, I'm walking to check my objects on the table. **[Ch. 8:4]**

From a short distance, I see shattered pieces of glass on the floor, resembling my Chinese white porcelain soup spoon. I feel devastated. Who did this?

I pick up the pieces and drop them in my brown paper bag and throw them away in the trash can. No one says anything to me, and I tell no one.

One day, standing on the playground, getting ready to line up after recess, three or four boys surround me. The little boys taunt me, bucking their teeth out, slanting their eyes with their fingers, and yelling, "You're a Jap! You're a Jap! You're a Jap! Jap! Jap!"

I stand there, stunned. Pausing and thinking, "Oh, no, you got it all wrong. I'm Chinese."

Scatting the boys away, the playground assistant dispersed the intimidators. I don't cry at school after the taunting incident. I tell no one about this bullying.

I'm absent from school for two weeks after eating a taco at a fast-food place. I keep vomiting. The doctor doesn't know why I'm sick. In bed for a whole week, feeling ill and weak. My parents take me to the doctor again, and the recommendation is to drink 7up soda so the carbonation can work in my stomach. I drink some 7up soda—my Mommy worries.

That night, my Mommy climbs on my bed and straddles me as I sleep on my back under my covers. Holding both my earlobes with her fingers and thumbs, she tugs gently on my earlobes, chanting a prayer that I would get better and live a long life.

In Chinese culture, having long earlobes signifies that a person will have a long life. Look at the Buddha statues. Buddha's earlobes are very long, hanging down to his shoulders.

Eventually, feeling better, I went back to school. Upon returning, two classmates play with me during recess and lunch break for a day.

I think they are welcoming me back to school. However, after the first day, none of the little girls continues playing with me. I wonder why they played with me for one day upon my two-week absence and then never played with me again. Could it be that our teacher asked those two girls to welcome me back and ask them to play with me? It seems so strange that they had never played with me before, and suddenly they do, and then they stopped.

I want my peers to accept me. Instead, they reject me. I feel a need to belong. I'm visibly invisible to them. Visible in that I look different from them. Invisible through their exclusion, nonacceptance, and negative vibes. They perceive and treat me as an outsider.

Not too long after feeling rejected, kneeling on my knees at home on my Mommy's powder-padded bench, I'm looking in the mirror. I feel alone and not accepted. Crying in front of the mirror, tearfully saying, "I don't want to be Chinese. I want to be an American."

Besides not having one friend at school to look forward to seeing and playing with, boys on the playground taunted me. I feel disliked. And why was my soup spoon shattered on the floor? I keep my feelings to myself. Nobody asks how I'm doing in school, so I tell no one. I remember last year, Jason and I were playing together at home.

He said with a sad tone, "You're the only friend I have." Back then, I didn't know what to say. I now sense that we have similar classmates' experiences treating us like we don't belong and are unworthy.

Days and weeks pass, and I want my peers to accept me. I no longer want to be visibly invisible to them. I look ethnically different from them, so they ignore or stay away from me as if I don't exist. I've come to the point of realizing a dream. That someday, my peers will look up to me for doing something notable. Eventually, they will think highly of me. I will treat them like I am no better than them and let them know we are all equal. We are no different as people. I feel a desire to do my best in school and sports. I want my peers to see me in a positive light and that I am worthy. **[Ch. 8:5] [Ch. 8:5A]**

Jason and I always look forward to playing after school on the playground. Playing on the playground means everything to me. I love jump roping like many of the other girls.

Mrs. Norton is 4 feet 10 with short, grey, curly hair in her mid-50s and wears spectacles. As our playground supervisor, she commandingly walks, talks, and blows her whistle energetically. The kids call her Coach. She wears a long durable strap around her neck, dangling her wad of keys and shiny silver whistle. Her organized clipboard lists all the jump rope participants and how much they jump weekly. Coach turns one end of the grey-thick-rope while another girl turns the other end. I'm a pretty competitive single rope jumper.

On another day of the week, Coach has double-dutch, rotating two 10 feet ropes. Coach and usually a sixth-grade girl, turns the rope, alternating and overlapping in a circular motion from one another. Here's the 38th Annual World Double Dutch Championship. By no means do we jump this fast and fancy. **[Ch. 8:6]**

I've never tried double-dutch before. As a first-grader, I'm a beginner, while many girls are in the upper grades. However, that doesn't bother me. I focus on figuring out how to jump with two alternating ropes rotating one after another.

Standing in the double-dutch line, watching intensely, and analyzing how to enter the middle while two ropes turn. Watching and studying each girl jumping into the middle and bouncing on each foot, avoid tangling her feet in the ropes. As I step closer to my turn, I feel my adrenaline pumping through my blood while feeling my heart pound strongly in my chest. Both hands clasp in front of my face, resting on my chin and lips, observing each girl jumping. The shorter the line becomes, the closer and closer I stand at the front of the line. For half an hour, I'm examining this new double-dutch jump rope game never seen or experienced before.

My turn now, position in a stance, heart pounding, eyes hypnotically moving, watching both ropes turning and alternating in two separate circular motions, feeling the rhythm of both ropes smacking the pavement, one after another.

The rope goes up, quickly scooting my body into the middle, lifting each foot up and down, one after another. Both rope turners try to keep up with my quick jumping pace.

"Slow down. You're jumping too fast! Slow down!" yells the Coach. Quickly adjusting my speed, slowing down. Soon, both rope turners and my feet move at a synchronistic rhythm.

Every week, my comfort level and the length of time jumping double-dutch improves. Late spring semester, I receive a yellow ribbon for third place in double-dutch at the award assembly. I nervously stand up when the Coach calls my name. It's my first experience receiving recognition. Returning to my first-grade class, Miss Henderson opens the door and sees my yellow ribbon. She bends down to hold and read it, smiling at me as I peer up at her. **[Ch. 8:7]**

On the first day of class as a second-grader, I go to school with a rectangle shape gift to give to my first-grade teacher, Miss. Henderson. I open her door to poke my head in to see an empty classroom and sitting at her desk.

"Good morning, Mary. Is there something I can help you with?"

"Hi, Miss. Henderson." I walk over to her and say shyly, "I

brought you a gift."

She holds it and looks at the gift of 35 chocolate gold-foil wrapped coins embossed with each U.S. President.

"Ahhh, thank you, Mary. That's sweet of you."

I smiled shyly, turned around, and left her room quickly, ready for my new teacher in the second grade. I felt timid giving my first gift to someone, but simultaneously, a bit guilty. I couldn't resist trying one of the gold-foil coins filled with chocolate. I'm sure she noticed the last U.S. presidential coin missing.

Reflecting, for a candy addict to give up a whole box of 35 chocolate gold-foil-wrapped coins is a significant feat. Well, I'm sure she would have offered one to me if I didn't rush out. **[Ch. 8:7A]**

As a second-grader, looking forward to jumping rope again. Girls from all grades wait in line to jump single rope and double-dutch every week. No longer a beginner but now a veteran double-dutch jumper. Coach responsibly counts how much we jump.

My turn, sliding easily in the middle, lifting one foot, then the other, nice steady alternating rhythm, landing on the front ball of each foot. Coach counting, "Two, four, six, eight, ten, two, four, six, eight, twenty, two, four, six, eight, thirty," and so on. Maintaining my steady pace for quite some time. Coach continuously counts, "two, four, six, eight...as minutes tick away.

Keeping my consistent rhythm, looking and feeling like an EverReady Battery two, four, six, eight. **[Ch.8:7B]** Lightly alternating one foot and then the other. I don't feel tired. I feel pretty good, like a battery, an Energizer Bunny!--Forever hopping! **[Ch. 8:8] [Ch. 8:8A]**

Quickly, Coach pulls back the ropes to the sides of her hips. I stop, standing flat on my feet, looking confused.

"Why did you stop?" I question.

"So, you won't get sick!" Coach says firmly and seriously.

"How much did I jump?" I ask.

"4,000," said the Coach.

"Okay," as I walk off, disappointed.

Feeling mixed emotions of dismay and surprise, I walk about 30 feet to the ball shed, lean my back against it, sliding down to the black asphalt to sit. I'm feeling my heart beating rapidly, at the rate of my jumping pace, feeling my body heat permeating up my moist neck, chin, head, and ears. I sit here, steamy hot, feeling warm energy circulating up and down my feet and legs while, at the same time, feeling fatigued settling into my feet. Thinking, "Wow, I jumped 4,000. That's the highest count ever." **[Ch. 8:9]**

One evening at *House of Fong,* the family is in the kitchen. My Daddy and Leland tell me I no longer can play after school. It's not for punishment. They don't explain.

"After school, you must come home. You can't stay after school to play," says Leland.

"No! I want to play after school on the playground. I want to jump rope!"

"No, you can't play after school. You have to come home right away."

"No!" I scream and start scratching him like a tiger!

Leland grabs both of my wrists as I try to claw him. I try kicking him. He scoots his legs and body back.

My parents are surprised at how fierce I am. Crying and screaming, "I want to play after school!" It's not clear to me why they don't permit me to. I do not know because they do not explain why.

Reflecting, perhaps, it's for my safety. Later that week, I see my Daddy walk next door from the *House of Fong.* Curiously I follow several paces behind. My Daddy talks to the next-door business owner in front of his corner shop.

The owner's wife, hysterically crying and upset, stamping her feet, holding her face, and shaking it side-to-side. Trying to make sense of her extreme distraught, I overhear that someone had stolen her white poodle in front of their business. I've never seen anyone in so much anguish. Feeling terrified and lost within myself and for her.

My parents are home on their day off. I've finished reading the *Cat in the Hat* by Dr. Seuss while sitting on the green couch in the living room. Laying the book aside, I'm thinking of what to do next. I know my two older brothers aren't home from school yet.

I don't feel like playing outside. I wonder what my Mommy and Daddy are busy doing. I walk to my parent's bedroom and stand in the doorway.

My Daddy lies on the bed with one foot hanging on the side of the bed. My Mommy looks concerned and helps my Daddy slowly to his feet. My Mommy holds my Daddy tightly with one arm around his thin waist. Her other hand supports some of his weight at his elbow. My parents slowly walk around the corner of the bed.

My Mom says patiently, *"Mahn, mahn dih...mahn, mahn dih,"* meaning slowly in Cantonese Chinese.

My Daddy shuffles small steps toward the bedroom door. "Aye!" my Daddy yells.

My body stiffens. My heart skips a beat.

A big rush of thick, reddish-brownish substance spurts down my Daddy's pants onto the carpet. Losing his balance and collapsing backwards, my Mommy grabs firmly to his waist urgently. His pants, stained and soaking wet—an immediate foul smell permeates the bedroom. My Mommy supports my Daddy's entire weight.

"Help me to the bed, to the bed," my Daddy says in a weak, monotone voice.

My Mommy holds my Daddy under his underarms and locks her hands together across his chest. She drags him to the bed, and his head rests on the wrinkled white pillow. My Mommy grabs the phonebook next to the telephone and nervously searches urgently for the hospital card. **[Ch. 8:10]**

"I'm all right, I'm all right, I feel better," my Daddy whispers to my Mommy. Nervously thumbing through the telephone book, my Mommy soon finds the hospital card nestled between two pages. Clutching the telephone receiver to her ear, she dials each number with her index finger rotating the dial clockwise, quickly but cautiously.

"Emergency, emergency…send an ambulance to 2026 E. 4th Street. Right away!" My Mommy hangs up the phone. She takes a quick deep breath. Her eyes, flowing tears, holding my Daddy's hands. She kneels beside the bed.

My Daddy whispers reassuringly, "I'm all right."

Within the four walls--complete silence. My Mommy looks at my Daddy, tears streaming down her cheeks. Her eyes trace the wrinkles on his gaunt face. She follows the few strands of hair spread across his forehead. She slowly raises her shaky hand to his weary face, straightening his strands of hair with her fingertips. My Mommy lovingly touches his face.

From a distance, an ambulance streaking siren resounds. My heart beats faster. The siren's wooing sound becomes louder and louder. The siren blasts loud and clear as the red and white ambulance stops abruptly in the gravel parking lot. The siren halts. I see the red revolving light flashing against the window and walls.

My Mommy and I hurry to the front door. The paramedics, dressed in white, hurry up the stairs with the white stretcher.

"Bedroom, this way," my Mommy directs them.

"What happened?" one paramedic says demandingly.

"Bleeding," my Mommy says.

The two paramedics lift my Daddy from the bed onto the stretcher. One paramedic checks my Daddy's pulse, and the other straps my Daddy securely to the stretcher. He covers my Daddy's body with a grey blanket.

My Mommy assures me that things will be all right. She instructs me to tell my two older brothers that she and my father have gone to the hospital.

Looking out the window, the paramedics carry my Daddy down the steep flight of stairs, my Mommy following behind. Everyone moves in the ambulance quickly—the shrieking siren blasts on again as the red and white ambulance speeds away.

Standing, staring at the space the ambulance had occupied. The shrieking siren continues wooing down the distant streets for seconds, until no longer. For the first time, I notice my neighbors returning home one by one. Next-door kids holding their rubber ball against their chest begin bouncing their ball again.

Tears flood, blurring my vision. Walking outside, sitting at the top of the steep staircase. Cold hands, a blue and red vein color feeling a chilly draft pressing on my neck and back. Goosebumps--all over my thin arms and body. Cringe, tucking my head on my forearms that rest on my knees. The abstract word "die" intrudes my head. For the first time, that word seems so close to reality at the age of seven. I never felt so frightened before.

The evening comes, and my Mommy--crying inside her bedroom. Standing in my parents' bedroom doorway, ten feet where my Mommy bends on her hands and knees, scooping a large puddle of smelly brown bloody crap, my Daddy released. I've never seen my Mommy crying so much, sobbing, hopelessly shaking her head from side to side, tears dropping from her face while cleaning up the mess. I feel immense sadness, not knowing what I could say or do. I can only watch.

A few days later, my Mommy and I go to the *Security National Bank* across the street from our home. She withdraws a large sum of money. The bank manager expresses his concern twice if everything is all right. My Mommy says she has to withdraw this amount.

Sitting in a yellow taxi to the St. Mary's Hospital in Long Beach, soon we enter a hospital room where my Daddy rests in his bed. Standing at the foot of his bed, looking at him, my Daddy chuckles and says, *"Nei tei ji ngou. Nei gang ma?"* meaning, "You are looking at me. Are you afraid?"

I don't say anything but keep looking at my Daddy. In an hour, my Daddy discharges from the hospital, and we return home in a yellow taxi.

Not too long after, *House of Fong* is up for sale. A Chinese couple comes to the *House of Fong* and shows interest.

"Why are you selling your business?" they ask.

"I'm not in good health. I went to the hospital for surgery. The business is too much work for us," my Daddy responds.

My parents successfully sell their *House of Fong* restaurant to a Chinese couple.

Chapter 9: Karl's Elementary School Years

I always had a thing for girls at an early age. I think it is because I have a close relationship with my Mommy. I feel safe around girls and even female teachers. When it comes to the male teachers, it doesn't always click for me. At five or six years old, I feel comfortable with girls. Sometimes I feel more comfortable with girls than with boys.

When I'm six years old, I have a crush on Sarah. We don't have a feeling of love, but it's more like a friendship. We see adults kiss and hold hands, and we imitate them. She always makes me smile because she's funny.

I would call her my first love. We didn't have a romantic relationship. However, she's the first girl I play house with, imitating husband and wife. She is my first encounter with the idea of finding someone to spend my life with. I know many people would say, well, that's super early. But we all have that instinct. We're here to find a mate, and we're here to raise a family.

Because we grow up in a family and see how people marry and have babies, it's just part of human existence. It's part of our animal instinct, as well. It's part of the DNA in the human body. We always feel at a young age that boys hate girls. There is an attraction we can't always explain.

Sarah is the one who put the idea in my head when we playhouse for one day. She imitates cooking for me. We hold hands and try kissing each other. It does something to me at that moment. That day, I realized that someday, I would need to find a mate to settle down with and start a family.

We don't have a long relationship. The next day, our relationship play ended, and we stayed friends. However, in a child's life, a day lasts forever. As we grow up, we forget that time seems to speed up. But in a child's mind, a whole day feels like weeks.

So, for me, that relationship is very long. We always stay friends. She will move on from boy to boy to boy. As kids, there is no conception in our minds of a relationship. It's just imitating.

I wouldn't say I like how school conditions us to follow the rules. I don't enjoy the restriction at home, going to school, and being limited there, too. I get into trouble. My relationship with my Daddy does not bring out the best in me. I lash out at others by pushing kids like a bully.

But I do not intentionally try to hurt them. It's an expression of negativity building up inside of me. I want to be seen by my Daddy. I want my Daddy to acknowledge me.

I punched a boy in the nose when I was five or six years old. I don't do it hard, but I just hit him, and he starts crying, runs off, and tells on me. I saw somebody else do it once, and this kid annoyed me, so I punched him.

My parents get upset and don't want me to hurt anybody. My parents don't explain why they are upset. The boy kept annoying me, so I defended myself. He's in my face.

The adults should ask why I do it and do I feel the need that this is the only way to handle the situation. Why don't you talk to him and say, "Hey, I don't like what you're doing." Parents can handle things in different ways to teach and guide their children.

We get along really well afterwards. He stops annoying me, but I also feel guilty. We gradually grow together. He also feels guilty that he made me upset. Then I feel guilty that I punched him. We talk to each other about it. Our parents never ask and explain how we could have taken care of our differences.

Instead, we talk it over. That shows that we sometimes respond better afterwards than our parents at five or six years old. At that moment, I realize that friends come in different ways. It's not always fun, and friends sometimes can annoy each other.

Chapter 10: Mary's Family Moves to Torrance, California

My parents sign the escrow documents to purchase a home in Torrance. Waiting in the escrow office, the mayor of Torrance and a councilman are there, too. Sitting next to a desk, the councilman chats with me a bit. He teases me, swiping my little button nose, lifting his hand in the air with his thumb between his index and middle finger.

"I got your nose!" he says, smiling.

I look up at his gesture with a straight face. Shaking my head, "No, that's not my nose," saying in a matter-of-fact tone.

"Oh, it's not your nose? It's right here," lowering his wiggly thumb in front of me.

"That's not my nose. My nose doesn't have a nail on it," I say neutrally, pointing at it.

"Oh," he looks at it, and puts his hand away.

I'm not a cute giggly girl, actually quite the opposite. At times, I'm serious because of my life experiences.

I can also be quite intense and focused when I do things. I don't smile much. I haven't experienced much joy, happiness, laughter, and affection. Thus far, my family life and school life have not invited me to celebrate these beautiful emotions for any consistent amount of time. I feel a sense of neutrality.

In the second grade, our family moves to Torrance, California, in the latter part of the Fall semester. My parents drop us off earlier in the day at our new home at 804 Kornblum Avenue. The *Bekins* moving truck will arrive shortly, and we'll let the movers in. My Daddy explains which room belongs to which family member. The two movers arrive, and they begin moving boxes into various rooms.

One mover asks me where to put the twin beds. Directing them to place the twin beds proportionately parallel in the rectangle-shaped room, telling them where to put the beds in the other two bedrooms. My parents arrived about a half-an-hour later, pleased the beds are well-positioned in the rooms.

My Daddy says with a smile, *"Nei dim ji dao, je go chuan go dao a?"* meaning, "How do you know where to put the beds?" Raising my eyebrows, I say nothing. I figure placing the twin beds proportionately in the room does not require much thought. My Daddy chuckles a bit.

Jason and I attend Fern Greenwood Elementary School on Torrance Boulevard near Crenshaw Boulevard. I'm in second grade, and Jason is in fourth. Leland attends Torrance High School as an eleventh-grader.

Beautiful towering eucalyptus trees line both sides of Torrance Boulevard. For several blocks, various businesses exist. Conroy's Flower Shop sits on one corner at the intersection of Crenshaw and Torrance Boulevard. Lucky's Supermarket is direct across Torrance Boulevard from my parents' Chinese food-to-go restaurant, *Canton Kitchen.* A couple of shops next door from *Canton Kitchen* is a tempting candy store. *Canton Kitchen* is sandwiched between a T.V. repair shop and a hair salon. A few blocks away is Fern Greenwood Elementary, an easy walk after school. A residential area on the other side of Fern Greenwood Elementary School is where our home resides, about ten blocks away.

My parents cook at their food-to-go restaurant. Leland artistically paints and applies gold leaf lettering on the signage of *Canton Kitchen* on the food-to-go restaurant's glass frontage. Twelve chairs line the sidewalls of the customer waiting room and the large glass frontage of *the Canton Kitchen.* After school, Leland takes food-to-go orders by phone over the front counter and manages the cash register. A Japanese American high school student, Christina works part-time at the front counter. **[Ch. 10:1]**

Sometimes, Leland washes the kitchen pots, pans, and dishes. Jason and I are too young to help out at the restaurant. I'm chatting while Leland washes the dishes.

"Mommy and Daddy told me you gave me my name, Mary. Why did you name me Mary?" I ask.

"You're lucky I didn't call you Lois," Leland responds with a chuckle.

"Lowest?" I question with crinkle eyebrows and wrinkled nose.

"Yeah, Lois, heh, heh, heh," Leland chuckles away.

"Lowest?" I say with a baffled tone.

You know, Superman and Lois Lane?" Leland says with a chuckle again while scrubbing a pot.

"Oh, Lois," I exclaim.

"Heh, heh, heh. Good thing I didn't name you Lois. Heh, heh, heh." Leland chuckles away. **[Ch. 10:2]**

Sometimes, Leland likes to kid me. However, sometimes, I also know that he thinks that I'm a *mung jung* face. One time, he says teasingly, wagging his index finger while smiling, "You're a *mung jung* face," meaning I have a pouty face, either crying, frustrated or displeased.

"No, I'm not," I reply in a disagreeing tone.

"Yes, you are. You're a *mung jung* face," he light-heartedly says while wagging his index finger at the beat of each word.

"No, I'm not!" I stammered back at him.

He continues washing the dishes and putting them on the rack. After that, he dries the dishes and puts them away. I watch him.

One day, I'm enjoying some chewy caramel. It's delicious and sweet. However, the caramel sticks to my teeth. I wear a bridge where my permanent molars have not grown yet since the Long Beach dentist extracted them. I'm wrestling with the sticky caramel with my tongue. Crack! My eyes widen, and I freeze. I pull out my bridge, and it's broken in half! I burst out crying.

My parents in the restaurant kitchen come quickly and ask why I'm in a panic. Opening my palm, I show them my broken bridge. I cry in fear, saying, "Oh, no, we're going to be poor!"

I know the bridge costs $100 when I first got it. For me, $100 is a lot of money in the late '60s. It's worth one day of work for my parents, who make something like $75-$100 at the end of the day at the restaurant. My parents pay for another bridge.

No, after-school playground sports and activities are avail-able at Fern Greenwood Elementary School, unlike Burbank Elementary School. Instead, Jason and I walk a few blocks to our parents' restaurant. We do our homework when we have some. I enjoy reading my favorite Charlie Brown or Peanuts comic books. Sometimes, we like playing outside in the back parking lot with the plastic ball we bought across the street at Lucky's Market.

After school, one pouring rainy day, Jason and I are relaxing in our parents' car, parked in the back of *Canton Kitchen.* Screaming at the top of our voices for fun as the rain falls harder and stronger. We chuckle in between screams. On dry days, we use chalk to create our hopscotch on the blacktop parking lot.

One afternoon, I'm looking to satisfy my boredom. My mischievous and curious nature gets the best of me. To fulfill my self-entertaining endeavors, I mischievously crawl under the restaurant's large kitchen steel tables where items like chopping boards, cookware, containers, can foods, etc. are placed.

Crawling around, I come across a white plastic gallon container. Curiously, I unscrew it and take a huge whiff. My head whips back, nose flares open, face contorts, knowing that I inhaled powerful bleach! Boy! That's a big mistake!

Quickly, turning my head to exhale, breathing several times to detox my nose, head, and lungs while screwing the white cap on the bleach container. Quietly gasping under the kitchen steel table, I continue crawling around. Nearby I see my Daddy standing in his black shoes and long white apron wrapped around his white shirt and tan trousers, busy cooking at a professional four-wok stove.

Does that horrible whiff of bleach stop me? No. I continue to slowly and quietly crawl under the kitchen steel table while watching my Daddy cook. He places the cooking utensil down and turns around toward the kitchen steel table to pick up his cigarette from the ashtray, taking a puff. He returns his cigarette to the ashtray on the corner of the long steel table five feet behind him. He doesn't notice me. He turns back toward the stove to continue stir-frying.

I quietly and carefully crawl over to my Daddy's white cigarette, curious about what my Daddy puffs on—watching my Daddy cooking for seconds. Mischievously, I slowly and carefully reach from underneath the steel table to the ashtray where the white cigarette innocently rests. I gently clinch the white cigarette with my small fingertips and thumb, quickly abducting it, not even dropping one ash. Oh, how smooth I am as I pull the white cigarette to my lips, imitating my Daddy, pressing my lips on the end tip. I inhale.

A rush of smoke enters my nose and lungs. My eyes bug out, quietly gasping while covering my mouth, muffling my coughing puffs of smoke that seep between the cracks of my cupped hand. Boy! That's another big mistake again!

Quickly returning his cigarette to the ashtray, I duck underneath the long steel table, crawling back while gasping quietly. That's two big strikes! I'm on the verge of strike three at the rate I'm going. My curious and mischievous behavior comes to a halt.

Mrs. Lathrop is my second-grade teacher, a fairly tall, medium-built woman around 60 years old with short curly brown hair. She reads a favorite book, *The Boxcar Children,* to the class. Spectacles perched halfway down her nose, a chain on both sides that drape down to the sides of her face. Day after day, she reads aloud a chapter while habitually flicking and playing with her fingertips. It's interesting to listen to the adventures of a family of homeless children, without their parents, finding ways to survive outdoors while living in a boxcar train.

The teacher assigns the class to small reading groups. One time in our reading group, I'm designated to sit in the center and lead the group. Before Mrs. Lathrop comes to our group, each student takes a turn to read aloud. My group members keep clowning around, and I try to get them back on task, and I accidentally say to them, "Shut up."

Group members stop, eyes wide open, their mouths shaped like a cheerio while gasping. One boy got out of his chair, walks swiftly to Mrs. Lathrop, and tells on me. She instructs our group to return to our seats and put our heads down.

Mrs. Lathrop eventually sits with our reading group that gathers. Each student reads a paragraph. After we read, she selects one student who read the best in our group and rewards the student with a green leprechaun doll to sit on the student's desk for the rest of the day. Mrs. Lathrop awards the little leprechaun to me. It feels good to receive it for a day, sitting on my desk.

Another small group activity involves flashcards with a word on them. A row of five students sit and one rotates, standing behind each sitting student. Whichever student shouts out the correct word when Mrs. Lathrop flashes a card wins that competition. If the standing student is the winner, they will move and stand behind the next student sitting.

This word activity is stressful rather than a learning experience. It's a challenge to see who can say the word faster, which I find to be a competitive, nerve-racking, and heart-pounding experience rather than a fun and enjoyable learning game.

As an outdoor activity, Mrs. Lathrop has the class run a race on a large open grass area on the playground. She blows her whistle, and all the students run the grass field to the school fence, tagging it, turning around, and racing back. I'm the fastest runner in the class.

Another day, Mrs. Lathrop decides to have her top fast runners do a run-off. The finalists are set on our mark, ready to go. Mrs. Lathrop says, "On your mark, get set," and she blows her whistle.

We dash off running. I'm leading the pack. My feet fly up into the sky, and I land awkwardly on my back. I'm lying there on the wet slippery grass, crying. Mrs. Lathrop and the entire class rush over to me.

"Are you alright?" Mrs. Lathrop asks.

Crying, shaking my head, replying, "I ran too fast for my age."

"Take your time. When you're ready to get up, we'll be waiting for you," Mrs. Lathrop says.

She waves at the class, directing them back to where the blacktop playground meets the open grass field. A few moments lapse, and finally, I stop crying. No one helps me up. I slowly get up and walk over to the class. Mrs. Lathrop and my peers don't ask how I'm doing. She doesn't report it or contacts my parents.

I can feel the soreness on my side and hip for a week. Eventually, the tenderness goes away. Our class never race again on the wet grass.

At recess, I notice a 5th-grade girl named Rhonda who has long, dirty blond hair and often wears it in a ponytail. She is good at playing tetherball. She knows all the right moves--smacking the tetherball with her palm, hitting the tetherball with her fist with confidence and strength. Watching her technique, competitiveness, and confidence--winning all her games. She's the one to beat. She never loses--the tetherball champ.

Every morning, all the children line up outside on the blacktop playground. Rhonda carries the American flag and our right hand over our hearts, pledging allegiance. Then, the Star-Spangled Banner anthem plays on a record player over the school's loudspeaker. Rhonda holds the flag very still throughout the ceremony. Her confident movements are worth observing, and she isn't girlie.

My family lives in a middle-class, single-story, three bedrooms, one-bath house. We have a beautiful backyard with a green lawn and a tree next to the house. Leland and my Daddy install a tetherball in the yard. Jason and I enjoy playing.

One day, we happen to see some dirt mounting on the backyard green lawn. We don't have a clue why the soil continues to kick up. I guess it's a snake. All of us are watching for a while. A little furry head pops up.

"He looks like a little beaver," I say.

"It's a gopher," Leland says.

We think the gopher looks so cute. I name him "Henry." My Daddy, not pleased, goes to the store to buy something to get rid of it. The gopher is now in heaven.

I meet a few friends in the neighborhood. A long blond-haired girl a year older than me lives across the street. She's tall and slender, named Kimberly. Friendly and attractive, she invites me over to her house. Her backyard has a nice-size swing set, and we jump on it, swinging back and forth.

Her Mommy welcomes me, giving each of us a small bag of potato chips, a snack I've never tasted before. I pinch a chip and begin crunching while chatting. Hhhmmm, these potato chips are sure crispy and amazingly delightful to munch on—crunch, crunch, crunch, devouring chip after chip. In no time, we've finished our tasty, salty, crispy chips. Licking my salty fingertips to savor the last remains of my first pleasurable, delicious potato chip binge. I'm now officially a potato chip addict. Move over, sweet tooth!

Two other neighbors, both sisters named Carrie and Sherrie, enjoy roller skating. Jason and I asked our parents if they could buy us roller skates. We're excited that our Daddy takes us to buy our roller skates. Our parents love to watch *Roller Derby* on T.V. When we lived in Long Beach, I practiced on pink plastic roller skates for kids. Jason and I used to skate in the back of *House of Fong* on a long concrete walkway.

Carrie and Sherrie show me how to turn, stop, and skate backwards. They also teach me to skate forward on one foot, hop while doing a body turn in the air, land on both skates, and continue skating backwards. Carrie and Sherrie also share their bikes with me so that I can learn and practice. They make good friends, sharing and teaching me new things.

One afternoon in 1968, Carrie and Sherrie tell me their Momma threw a shoe at the TV set that morning, smashing the TV screen and cursing at Martin Luther King Jr. I met their Momma before when I occasionally visited their house. I never knew she had this rage inside of her.

Besides my experience in the first grade of being taunted by little boys on the playground and girls in my class not playing with me, this is the first time I have heard someone disliking African Americans. Up to this time, I've never interacted with an African American person before or seen one in person. I only have seen African Americans on TV, like in the Shirley Temple movies. I don't understand why their Momma would have so much hatred for King Jr. It doesn't make any sense. **[Ch. 10:3]**

Years later, I learned that Martin Luther King Jr. was known as an American Baptist minister and civil rights activist who became the most prominent spokesperson and leader in the civil rights movement from 1954 until his death, assassinated on April 4, 1968 in Memphis, Tennessee.

King is known for advancing civil rights through nonviolence and civil disobedience. His ideas and words resonate deeply with me. He states all people are created equal. Not to judge another by their skin color but by the substance of their real character. King's words are powerful and wise: "Darkness cannot drive out darkness; only light can do that. Hate cannot drive out hate; only love can do that."

Other times, Jason and I are together when we are not in school or playing with other friends. Jason knows how to roller skate too. We skate in the backyard from the tetherball area, speeding down a sidewalk strip along the edge of the green lawn onto the patio. Jason is a fast skater.

One time, Jason and I decide to have a roller skate race. Jason skates on the sidewalk across the street, and I'm on the sidewalk in front of our home. We count, "One, two, three, go!" We skate as fast as we can. As I'm racing, I lose control of my roller skates and fall! I'm crying—Jason skates across the street to help me up.

Later that day, two scary movies are on TV. One involves a man who turns into a giant blob. The other horror movie has a young, attractive woman who transforms into a cobra. I'm so engrossed in watching I notice my heart beating rapidly and feeling intense. I'm getting sucked into the reality of the scary movies that lure me deeper and deeper into hypnotic fear. To escape and maintain my sanity—mentally, emotionally, and physically, I snap myself out of the hypnotic terror, consciously distancing myself. I realize I'm only watching a movie and must separate from it, helping me calm my nerves, wipe the sweat off my brows, and not be hypnotized and pulled into the gravity of the drama.

Annually, the City of Torrance has a parade that marches down Torrance Boulevard, where we have front-row seats at *Canton Kitchen.* Leland, an excellent student, engages in activities throughout his education. He's been the yearbook editor at school and has professional calligraphy skills. He entered an art contest to design a US postal stamp. He wins first place, and a vehicle rolling in the parade displays his stamp design. Leland is artistically talented. While in high school, *The Yellow Pages* company hires him to create artwork for some advertisements.

Leland is also in ROTC. He practices his rifle drills like saluting at home, being at attention, at ease stance, and twirling his rifle. The ROTC high school cadets march uniformly in the Torrance parade. It's impressive watching the front row marchers toss their rifles to the back row, and the cadets in the back row catch the rifles without skipping a beat in their march: the crowd claps and cheers after the ROTC demonstration.

Growing up in the 1960s, I was unaware of the Vietnam War fought between 1955 and 1975. My parents and school teachers shelter children from knowing about the Vietnam War, probably not to create fear in kids. I do not know how I first heard about the Vietnam War, but I vaguely recollect hearing about it in the 1970s.

Officially the war occurred between the North and South Vietnam governments. The U.S., Australia, Thailand, and other anti-communist allies support South Vietnam, fighting for democracy. The Soviet Union, China, and other communist allies support North Vietnam. In 1965 the mandatory U.S. Draft of men rose from 5,400 to 45,000. The monthly draft call increases from 17,000 to 35,000 in which civil disobedience occurs. Many Vietnam veterans say they like and identify with the lyrics of this song: **[Ch. 10:4], [Ch. 10:5]**

Weeks later, a Hippie parade occurs on Torrance Boulevard. Standing in front of *Canton Kitchen,* watching many Hippies walking down the boulevard. I have no idea what the hippie movement represents.

I understand now that the hippie movement in the 1960s and 1970s is a counterculture against society's mainstream mores. The hippie movement becomes nationally widespread across college campuses supporting harmony with nature, communal living, artistic experimentation with music, recreational drugs, peace, no war, and so forth. The three-day Woodstock Music Festival beginning on August 15, 1969, brought half a million people to enjoy top music acts performing, symbolizing peace and love during the era of the Vietnam War. **[Ch. 10:6], [Ch. 10:7]**

Standing outside *Canton Kitchen* watching the Hippie Parade, I witness a commotion. A Caucasian male spectator hits a tall, long hair bearded hippie in the face. The hippie startled and held his face. He walks rapidly toward me with gigantic steps. I'm frightened. The tall long-hair bearded hippie is ten paces away.

My heart rapidly pounds as I dart back into the restaurant. Quickly lifting the movable hinged counter, opening the small swinging door, immediately closing it, and bringing the hinged counter-table down at lightning speed.

I run behind the kitchen wall, hyperventilating while collapsing into the chair next to the table. My parents in the kitchen see me and ask, *"Ju maht yeh a?"* meaning, "What is going on?" Slouching in the chair, hyperventilating, hardly able to speak.

The hippie pushes the front door open of *Canton Kitchen* and asks urgently, "Please, someone, help me. Can I use your telephone? Someone hit me outside. I need to call the police."

My Daddy cautiously peers through his spectacles around the wall at the tall, long-haired, bearded hippie. My Daddy nods and says, "All ligh," and pulls the phone closer to the front counter so the hippie can dial it.

After making his call, he says, "Thank you," and leaves the food-to-go restaurant.

The school year ends in June, and I've completed the second grade. Mrs Marshall, my summer school teacher in her mid-fifties with reddish-brown curly hair, helps every child create an art project. For each student, she cuts the shape of a fish from perforated brown cardboard.

One by one, every student assists Mrs. Marshall, who does most of the decorating by gluing uncooked, straight noodles for the tail, top and side fins. She glues several shell-shaped-pasta on the body of the fish. Lastly, she sprinkles thin short noodles on the head of the fish.

After helping her students glue the various pasta shapes on their fishes, she let the art projects dry overnight. Over the weekend, Mrs. Marshall spray-painted turquoise on the fishes and sprinkled glitter on top. She sprayed black on all the rectangle cardboard backing where she attached the fish. Mrs. Marshall created a beautiful art project for her students to take home.

I take my beautifully decorated fish home to show my parents. They are delighted. That weekend my parents tack up my beautiful fish artwork on the wall right above a broad set of mirrors in the dining room.

My Daddy stands on the chair, holding a hammer and nail, while my Mommy directs him toward the center of the wall. My parents smile. They don't say anything to me, but they look happy. It's a rare occasion to see my parents looking very pleased.

The beautiful fish is symbolically meaningful to my parents, and having their youngest daughter bring home the creative artwork delights them. I learned many years later that fish in the Chinese culture symbolizes abundance and prosperity in life.

I always look forward to the *Helms* food truck that drives up and down the neighborhood streets during summer, honking midmorning. Jason and I run outside, look at all the yummy snacks, and pick something to buy.

Excitement fills the air when the ice cream truck's musical tune plays in the afternoon. All the kids on the block race outside their homes to buy their favorite ice cream.

One day we buy a kite, and I watch Jason construct it at home. He is talented at making things with his hands. I watch him do the finishing touches, tying a whitetail on the end of the kite to help it fly better. "Finished, we're ready to go," says Jason.

We walk across the street to the open field. It's a sunny clear blue sky with a gentle breeze, perfect for flying our kite. We see our kite soaring higher and farther in the atmosphere for almost two hours. We release the entire roll of kite string to the point that it's so far and small. As the sun sets, it's time to return home for dinner. We don't want to reel the kite down. So, we keep the kite flying, tying it to a post in the open field to keep it alive.

The next day, Jason and I return to see if the kite is still flying. It's no longer there.

Mrs. Marshall throws a class party with a Hawaiian luau theme on the last day of summer school. I don't remember her telling us to wear Hawaiian style clothing. Perhaps I'm not paying attention or don't understand her.

Maybe a note was sent home for my parents to consider dressing me in Hawaiian clothes. I do not know what Hawaiian clothing and luau mean, and I don't know if my parents know, either.

On the day of the classroom party, I wear my yellow princess party dress that has been rescued and liberated from that eight-legged hairy black spider that used to sit on the sticky, silky web. Luckily, the dress still fits, since my parents bought it oversized.

Mrs. Marshall lines up all the chairs in a large oval circle. Sitting in a chair, a little boy walks across the circle toward me. However, the teacher redirects him to sit elsewhere.

"I want to sit next to Mary," he says.

"She's not wearing Hawaiian clothes," says Mrs. Marshall as she guides the little boy to sit elsewhere.

Glancing at my classmates, I get a better idea of what

Hawaiian style clothing looks like. I'm the only one dressed in a fluffy party dress. I don't feel different until Mrs. Marshall makes that response. But her comment doesn't bother me. I feel good wearing my yellow princess party dress.

I never interacted with that little boy before in Mrs. Marshall's class. I don't know him.

Walking with my brothers to the restaurant one day, we pass a house with a wooden stand signage indicating that the Mayor of Torrance lives there. Standing outside with his siblings is the little boy who wanted to sit next to me.

As we walk by, he sees me. "Hi, Mary," he calls out to me.

I look surprisingly at him with shyness, looking away. I'm slow to recognize him from the summer luau in class.

Upon reflection, he probably knows of me because his Daddy, the Mayor, had met my parents before when we first moved here. And maybe they have ordered food-to-go at *Canton Kitchen,* too.

Chapter 11: Third Grade for Mary

A week before the new academic year, our Daddy drops off Leland, Jason, and me at a large White Front department store. We shop for new clothes, shoes, and accessories for a few hours. Every new school year, I never sleep a wink the night before the first day of class because I'm so excited about wearing my new dress.

Mrs. Lewis, my third-grade teacher, looks about 65 years old, has a petite frame, and wears glasses. She has the best penmanship. She teaches us cursive writing, and we no longer handprint our work.

On Fridays, we turn in our weekly science reports and read them in front of the class. Fortunately, Leland has a set of science encyclopedias in his bedroom, where I sit on top of his desk and look up different topics. I write about meteorites, comets, the sun, the moon, stars, Saturn, Jupiter, Pluto, Mars, Uranus, Mercury, volcanoes, and types of rocks like igneous, sedimentary, granite, petrified wood, and metamorphic.

Other class projects include writing about Torrance, California's history and "What do I want to be when I grow up." I have no idea what I want to be when I grow up. Two of my classmates say they want to be a nurse. So, I write this, too. Two classmates, Beth and Elaine, help me with my projects. A couple of times, I go over to their house after school. They give me some helpful suggestions.

Sometimes, Jason and I come across friends to walk to school. The kids dress in raincoats, boots, and umbrellas on rainy days. Four-inch earthworms noticeably worm their way on the sidewalk. We carefully maneuver around them to avoid stepping or squishing them on a rainy day.

One morning, I'm walking with my neighbor, Kimberly, who shows me what she likes doing to earthworms. "Watch this," she says.

I stop and stand back a bit to watch what she's going to do. She positions her shoe edge and squishes the tip of an earthworm that jumps about a half foot in the air, landing on the sidewalk.

Grimacing my face, I feel yuck and gross. Turning forward, I continue walking to school.

Many girls like Elaine, Beth, Kathy, Sheila, Yvonne, and Eileen wear their girl scouts, blue jays, or brownies uniforms on particular days when they have meetings or activities. I wish I'm in one of those clubs, but I don't know how to ask my parents. I also wish to take dance classes, but I never ask.

One afternoon, a classmate across my table asked me to borrow my pink eraser. I let her use it. She keeps my eraser for a while, and I ask for it. She opens her mouth showing that she's chewing and sucking on my pink eraser. I tell her that I want my eraser. She refuses to return my pink eraser and keeps moving it around in her mouth.

"I'm going to beat you up if you don't give me back my pink eraser," I sternly say. She ignores me and keeps playing with my eraser in her mouth.

The end of the school day draws near. Mrs. Lewis selects quiet students, sitting upright with hands folded on their desks to stand in line to go home. I'm upfront in the line with the girl still chewing on my pink eraser.

Again, I threatened that I would beat her up after school if she doesn't give me back my pink eraser. My threats don't bother her one bit. She keeps playing with my pink eraser in her mouth. The bell rings, the teacher opens the door, and we all exit the hallway. I say nothing to her. She walks away still chomping on my abducted pink eraser, never to return.

I'm still a candy addict. I save my cafeteria lunch money to buy candy after school. Many students take their lunch boxes. It is cool to take a lunch box to school since I've never done so before. There's a lunchbox at home I could use. I bring that lunch box with not much in it.

Classmates invite me to their lunch table to eat. They are curious to know what I brought to school to eat. I'm feeling very embarrassed because I don't have much in my lunch box. A couple of girls share their food. I won't let them see inside my lunchbox.

After school, I look forward to the candy store, just two businesses next to *Canton Kitchen.* I have a turquoise octagon plastic carrying case where I put my notebook, supplies, and candy. I took my lunch box to school a few times and went back to buying my lunch at the cafeteria.

One evening, sitting at the small table in the restaurant kitchen, I'm starving to the point of shaking and perspiring. Incredibly hungry, I didn't eat much the entire day. My parents, busily working, have another hour left before closing. Seeing that I'm not looking well, my Mommy comes to me. She touches my hands, arms, and forehead. She puts together something for me to snack on.

Our family eats late every night when *Canton Kitchen* closes at 9. I'm tired and hungry. I find it easier to swallow my food when I drink water. I don't eat much.

On another evening, around 8, an hour before the closing time of *Canton Kitchen,* my parents have a few Chinese acquaintances drop by unexpectedly for a visit. They probably only stayed for about half an hour or so. At closing time, Leland and my parents discover that the brown money bag from the cash register is missing.

Those unexpected Chinese acquaintances find the money bag near the cash register and steal my parents' one-day earnings. My parents suspect that one of the men had taken the money bag, hid it under his coat, walked outside, and sat in the car. The man and woman remain in the restaurant, chatting with my parents while busily cleaning up. They stole about $100 from the money bag. A whole day of earnings is gone.

Every other Monday, my parents, Jason, and I travel to Chinatown, Los Angeles, to have dinner and see a double-feature movie. Leland, an undergraduate at USC, lives on the campus. Jason and I always look forward to munching on a box of Cracker Jacks and what little prize we get inside.

One movie is typically a romantic comedy. The other is a sword fighting or gung fu movie. There's one movie I find so scary; it's called "The One Arm Swordsman." At the film's beginning, a Chinese swordsman talks to a swordswoman in a snowy mountainous area. Conversing with him, she throws her sword into the snow directly in front of her.

"Aauuugh!" the swordsman yells in great agony. The swordswoman accidentally severed off his arm! I jump at the loud and dramatic music, quickly sticking my head under my Mommy's sweater.

The swordsman's face shows extreme anguish and pain, clutching his upper arm, staggering back, bleeding profusely, and dripping blood onto the white snow. The swordswoman, shocked seeing what she has done, as he stumbles backwards and away from her, leaving a bloody trail in the white snow. She desperately cries out to him.

I'm horrifically terrified, scared out of my wits with my heart pounding while peeking out from my Mommy's sweater. I lost half of my Cracker Jack popcorn in the dark. Fortunately, the romantic comedy movie rescues me from this action-packed terror.

Other evenings, the family enjoys watching the *Smother Brothers*, where they open up their variety show with comic exchanges, music, and singing. Here's a clip of the Smother Brothers on the Judy Garland Show. Also, other favorite variety programs are the *Glen Campbell Show, Red Skelton, Carol Burnett Show, and Laugh-In.* TV drama shows we watch are *Mannix, Mission Impossible, Star Trek, and Hawaii-Five-O.* **[Ch.11:1 - Ch.11:9]**

Once a year, our family goes to the Chinese New Year celebration to watch the Chinatown New Year's parade that proceeds down Hill Street for an hour. The LA City Mayor waves from his escorted vehicle. Miss Chinatown and her court of princesses are wearing beautiful sequined Chinese gowns, smiling and waving their hands covered with long white gloves that reach above their elbows. **[Ch. 11:10]**

The local high school bands march down the parade route playing their tunes. The long dragon with twelve young men underneath, running and dancing down the street. The LA Drum and Bugle Corp. are musically powerful and robust while playing and marching precision down the parade route.

The lion dancers usually have one boy at the back end, and a young man dancing, lifting the lion's head up and down while flapping the lion's mouth and eyelids for amusing animation. After the parade, firecrackers pop down the parade route to ward off evil spirits. Continuous sharp, ear-piercing pops and sparks of firecrackers explode, whipping and bouncing about on the streets.

[Ch. 11:11], **[Ch. 11:12]**

Flipping my coat hood over my head, I turn away from the loud pops and sparks toward my parents. My Daddy chuckles at me, taking cover. My Daddy chuckles at me for taking cover.

One day, my Mommy trims my hair that flows past my shoulders. After she finished, I realize I have a rice bowl hairstyle, just below my earlobes! I'm crying and pouting that she cut my hair so short to my chin! Picture day is this week at school. **[Ch. 11:13]**

Two months pass, and our class pictures arrive. I take my class picture home and show my parents. When my Mommy sees it, she smiles and says, *"Te nei a sheung, gum hao te,"* meaning "Look at your portrait. It looks so good."

I don't say anything. My Mommy also adds, *"Nei tau fat hao tei a,"* "Your hair looks good." The first time my Mommy ever gave me a verbal compliment.

She tries to make me feel better about my strong disapproval of the rice bowl haircut. Compliments are rarely voiced, if nonexistent, in my family. I later learned that praise-giving, sparingly communicated in Chinese cultures abroad, Chinese immigrants in America, and sometimes second-generation Chinese Americans. Denying a compliment is normative for these Chinese communities to maintain modesty. However, some Chinese people adopt Westernized ways of complimenting, depending on their adaptation.

Third grade comes to an end. Mrs. Lewis awarded some students with good penmanship certificates. I receive one. Our teacher has the most beautiful penmanship.

That summer, my family goes to Long Beach to check on my parents' four-unit pink rental apartments. While at Long Beach, our family visits Judge DeVries and his wife, Ann. They sponsored my

Mommy and Leland to the U.S. and rented their Gaviota Street house to us.

The first time meeting them both, they are kind people. The retired Judge DeVries sits in a wheelchair from a railroad accident with a severed arm near his shoulder and both legs at a young age.

I've never met a person with disabilities who achieved a successful career as a judge. Our family brings a small gift of tea and Chinese cookies to them. Ann makes a delicious homemade lunch for us, sitting around their dining room table chatting.

During the ride back home to Torrance, I overhear my parents talking about a former dishwasher employee of the *House of Fong*. His name is Skip, a Caucasian American young man in his late teens. My parents heard from someone at Long Beach that Skip had hit a senior man in the bar during an argument. Tragically, the older man died. Skip was convicted and sentenced to death row at San Quentin.

Hearing the ill fate of Skip, memories flood my mind. He was a 6-feet slender build, red hair slicked back, fair skin, and walked with a relaxed rhythmic stride. My parents asked Skip to walk me home from the *House of Fong* one day. I'm around three years old, clasping onto Skip's pinky finger. We walk ten blocks to my parents' four-unit pink apartment.

Looking back, I don't see or sense any mean streak in Skip. I feel his innocence and a teenager with no direction in his life. He grew up as the only child with alcoholic parents who smoked. He, too, has both addictive behaviors.

Now and then, I wonder about his tragic life, sitting on death row. I question why he grew up with dysfunctional parents, not having love, care, and guidance, while others grow up in a functional family with love, care, and guidance influencing their school success and well-being.

I wonder how people's life circumstances are vast and different in terms of health, well-being, personality, attractiveness, intelligence, emotional well-being, happiness, character, wealth, support, care, love, family life, treatment from others, etc. I feel sad for Skip, someone sitting on death row, or perhaps his time expired.

I know he never had a chance to dream a happy life. Instead, he is a person who feels sad, lonely, lost, and has little sense of self-worth. What's the point of living?

My parents have old-time friends, Emil and Florence Plasburg, the hotel owners in Healdsburg, California. My parents had a café in their hotel in Northern California before 1959. Emil and Florence sold their hotel and retired. Afterwards, Emil and Florence remain in touch every Christmas sending a package of gifts to our family. My parents tell me that Emil and Florence are my Godparents.

Emil and Florence visited our family when we lived in Long Beach. Since then, Florence died of a heart attack. My Daddy flew up to Santa Rosa for her funeral. Later that year, Emil comes down to visit our family in Torrance. He brings Heidi, his German Shepherd, and both stay with us during their visit.

Over the years, I received Christmas gifts like a Barbie doll, a fancy 60s vanity set with a comb, brush, mirror, a music box with a rotating ballerina dancing inside, and more dolls. Looking back, Emil and Florence have been thoughtful, kind, and generous in giving our family Christmas gifts yearly.

Both of my parents hardly speak English, if any, it is broken English. Yet, Emil and Florence keep in touch with our family. Emil drives from Santa Rosa to visit our family as one of his visits to the Southern California area.

In the Fall semester of fourth grade, we have class officer elections. A few nominated students wait in the open student closet at the back of the classroom. We sit leaning against the hanging coats and jackets for a few minutes. We come out after the vote count identifying the class President.

I'm voted class President. Quietly stunned, I don't think any of my classmates know me. I don't feel I have a group of friends. I have no clue why they voted for me. At home, my parents look pleased, although they never say anything to me.

My parents have a profitable business at *Canton Kitchen.* Somehow, my parents enter into a partnership with a relative. They remodeled a nice-sized restaurant on Crenshaw Boulevard, just down the street from El Camino Junior College. The ceiling is beautiful with elaborately sculpted dragons. They have beautiful lanterns similar to the *House of Fong.* My parents invested quite a bit of their savings into this joint venture.

Before the restaurant opened, my parents had many disagreements with their partner, who had never operated a restaurant business. I do not witness the conflicts, but I overhear my parents complaining.

Reflecting on the Chinese cultural ways, normatively, they do not directly confront people. They avoid face-to-face conflict to maintain harmonious relations with people. Culturally, they use intermediaries who try to directly help resolve significant differences and issues as an indirect way of communicating between both disputing parties.

For several days, I notice my parents are at home. My Mommy does not look like she slept last night, looking miserable, walking in an unbalanced way in her robe across the living room. My parents severed their restaurant partnership. They lose all their money invested in the creation of this new restaurant.

Midway through the Fall semester of my fourth-grade year, our family moves from Torrance to Sun Valley. The *Bekins* movers come two-and-half years later. My Daddy gives our box of toys away to the movers again. Jason and I watch. We do not understand my Daddy's generous offer to the movers--hesitant to take our toys. Jason and I say nothing. Years later, looking back and understanding that it was a generous Chinese offer to give the two movers gifts for their help by sacrificing our toys. Jason and I experience the lesson of detachment from material things.

Chapter 12: Mary's Family Moves to Sun Valley, California

Our family moves to a two-bedroom apartment on Ensign Avenue in Sun Valley, California. A large sparkling blue pool in the middle of the apartment complex right outside our second-floor balcony interests me in learning how to swim.

Walking across the parking lot behind our apartment, Jason and I visit our parents' Chinese restaurant, Ming's *Café,* where a bar and a liquor store hold business a few doors away. Booths lined both sides of *Ming's Café* walls and a breakfast counter with green swivel chairs. *Ming's Café* does not have a Chinese décor style.

Jason and I transfer to Camellia Elementary School in North Hollywood from Torrance. I'm in the fourth grade, and Jason is in the sixth. We walk ten blocks to school every morning. Middle-class homes line the streets, and a junior high school is located mid-way on our walk to Camellia Elementary School.

Meeting the principal on my first day, he says I'm joining Mrs. Tobbin's class, a bright group of students. My teacher is Japanese American, middle-aged, short, plump, and strict. In class, she says she will kick her son from room to room if he misbehaves. That doesn't sound pleasant at all.

I noticed quite a few intelligent classmates--articulate, outspoken, and confident. I've learned many of my classmates' names like Mitchell, Vern, Ronnie, Cindy, Steven, Joey, Roger, Melody, Anita, Laurie, Annette, Shelley, and Kathy--all Caucasian American peers.

A boy with a crewcut loves girls and flirts with them. One time, I looked in his direction during the class and noticed him looking straight at me from the next table, flexing his nostrils in and out, batting his eyelashes, and smiling. I turn away from his flirtatious unappealing odd antics. I wonder where on earth did he learn how to flex his nostrils like that? Such a peculiar and confident kid, flexing his nostrils and batting his eyes while resting his chin on his hand during class. **[Ch. 12:1]**

Mrs. Tobbins instructs me after lunch that I need to go to the Principal's Office to do something. Arriving there, the secretary invites me into the office to sit down. The principal comes in, along with two other adults. They look at me, but I don't know why.

The principal tells me that I can no longer wear my gold necklace to school. They don't tell me why. Then the principal calls my Daddy on the phone that I could no longer wear my gold necklace to school.

Jason and I arrive home. We greet our parents at *Ming's Café*. Both of them tell me I can no longer wear my gold necklace to school. My Mommy helps me to take off my jewelry. I start crying. I've been wearing that gold necklace since my parents gave it to me in the first grade. I don't know why. No one explains. My parents say the school will not allow it.

Years later, I figured the concern was related to my safety. Commonly in the Chinese culture, a jade bracelet or a jade or gold necklace is believed to provide good health, balance, and protection.

On another day, Jason and I arrive to greet our parents, entering the restaurant kitchen door seeing a box of live turtles on the floor. The next day, I no longer see the live turtles and wonder where they went. My Daddy lifts the lid on a large metal pot boiling on the stove. I peek inside and see the floating turtle shells. My Daddy says he's making turtle soup. I'm stunned and speechless.

In Mrs. Tobbins' class, we learn a variety of subjects. For the Christmas assembly, ten classmates recite an amendment of the Constitution, known as the Bill of Rights. I recite the introduction saying, "Ladies and Gentleman. We are proud to present the first ten amendments of the Constitution of the United States of America." I also recite the second amendment concerning the right to bear arms.

The class also learns about the human ear. I draw the parts of the ear on a large white poster board, from the outer ear and the ear canal, the middle ear where the eardrum, the hammer, anvil, and stirrup; and the inner ear consists of the cochlea and the eustachian tube.

After studying the human ear, we learn about the four main islands of Japan. We learn some words in Japanese, such as *Konichiwa* (have a good day), *do zo* (sorry, please excuse me), *arigatōgozaimasu* (thank you), *ohayōgozaimasu* (good morning), *oyasumi* (good night). The students write a report on various aspects of Japan, submitting a folder. Japan is known as the land of the rising sun.

Our class goes on a field trip to tour the Jet Propulsion Lab (JPL) in Pasadena. Later that week, two men from JPL come to our class and talk about the moon. We're assigned to write an essay responding to this question, "How can we put enough oxygen in the atmosphere of the moon so that people can live there?" My answer is, grow plants there, so they produce enough oxygen while using the carbon dioxide that humans exhale.

During our fourth-grade year, Mrs. Tobbins walks all the students outside onto the playground to take a California state test on our physical abilities. The teacher timed on how many sit-ups, chin-ups, push-ups we could do.

In the black rubber matted area on the playground, we each have a partner responsible for counting our sit-ups while holding our feet down. I've never done sit-ups before, but I remember seeing Jack LaLanne on his exercise TV show in the 60s. I mimic him and do 40 sit-ups, the most of anyone in class in one minute.

We play handball during recess, hitting the rubber ball against a tall backboard but within the boundaries. Two players play against each other. My favorite apparatus is swinging on the rings. It requires the right timing, swinging and gliding in the air from ring-to-ring, alternating one hand and then the other, grabbing onto the next ring. I love playing on the rings, soaring and gliding through the air--quite liberating. If I can do this smoothly from ring-to-ring with perfect timing and ease, it's a feeling of flying like a bird--effortlessly in the clear blue sky without a worry or a care in life, enjoying the present mood being free.

However, all the girls get blisters on our upper palms. They burst eventually. We let the skin from our blisters dry, and we pick on them to peel off our dead skin. We lose layers of skin on our upper palms. Besides that, it's just fun, liberating, and enjoyable gliding and swinging from ring to ring. It's addicting.

My favorite game is tetherball. I sign up for the tetherball contest at the school playground. I sit, waiting in line for my turn on the rings. Hearing loud and clear, "Mary Fong, it's your turn on the tetherball!" the playground coach yells out with both of his hands cupped around his mouth. I run across the playground to the tetherball area, where many kids stand and watch in line to take their turn.

I'm up against a tall, sixth-grade, dark-haired boy. I'm at least a foot shorter than my competitor. He's wearing an all-black t-shirt, jeans, tennis shoes, and black leather gloves with openings for his fingers and thumbs to move freely.

The playground coach bounces the tetherball in the middle of the pole to start the match. The sixth-grade boy gets a hold of the ball first. He starts whacking the tetherball around and around the pole, flying high above my head. The rope gets shorter and shorter as I stand next to the pole, looking straight up at the revolving ball flying around and around the pole.

The tall, sixth-grade boy grins, having a good time hitting the tetherball around and around, feeling what an easy win. I'm still standing there, looking straight up at the pole as the tetherball flies around and around. I don't even have a chance to touch the tetherball. Only two feet of rope left, everyone thinks the end is evitable--the game is over.

Springing up, I hit the ball my way! I'm in control, hitting the tetherball. **[Ch. 12:2]**

Caught off guard, the tall, sixth-grade boy frantically runs back and forth, jumping up and down, trying to get his black-gloved hands on the fast-moving tetherball as I'm whacking it around and around. I maneuver, hitting the ball with an upward slant while backing away from the line that divides us. The ball goes over his black-gloved hands as he intensely jumps up and down next to the boundary line. He's unable to inhibit the lightning-speed path of the tetherball, a blazing comet to its final destination.

I keep hitting the ball with force. Around and around, the ball flies faster and faster as it unravels into a long, fully extended rope. The tetherball whips around at torpedo speed, jetting toward the ill-fate of my opponent. Chaotically running back and forth, his flailing arms and black-gloved hands trying to stop this unexpected turn of events.

I maneuver my body position and angle my hits higher according to his competitive positioning in the space within the tetherball ring. Shorter and shorter the rope becomes as the tetherball zips, wrapping high around the tall pole towards my competitor's demise. I'm focused and determined to win the battle. I remain calm, steady, concentrated, and consistent to finish him off. Game over! I win!

"You stink, Fong, you stink!" the tall, sixth-grade boy yells in angry disgust, ripping off his black-gloves before stammering away.

I ignore him. I turn to the Coach and calmly ask for permission, "Can I go back to the rings?"

"Yeah, go ahead," the Coach responds.

Eagerly running back across the playground blacktop, I sit on the bench filled with girls in line waiting for their turn. I act as if nothing happened. I don't think twice about how I crushed the ego of that tall, sixth-grade boy—what a drama king. Never underestimate fearless Fong. **[Ch. 12:3]**

Reflecting, they didn't call upon me to play another tetherball match. I wonder why? Oh well, it's just a game.

It's springtime, and Jason is outside on the apartment balcony. Flying from the sky, a green parakeet lands on Jason's hand. He comes inside with the green parakeet and says, "Mary, look what flew to me. It's a bird."

"Really? How did you get it?" I ask with amazement.

"It just flew and landed on me."

We keep the parakeet in the apartment. It perches and flies back and forth between curtain rods and lampshades. **[Ch. 12:4]**

We tell our parents what occurred when they arrived home.

They like the idea of keeping the green parakeet. That weekend, our parents take us to a pet store and buy a birdcage with a swing in the middle, a bird feeder, a bathtub, and bird seeds. We name him, Chipper.

A week later, a man looks for his green parakeet. We show him the green parakeet that flew to Jason. The man looks at the green parakeet and says it belongs to him because he can see the birthdate ring on one of his feet. The original owner had named his green parakeet, Sleepy.

The kind man gives us his green parakeet since we have already bought a birdcage and accessories. He also knows that Jason and I would like to keep Chipper.

In another adventure, Jason and I play in the shallow end of the beautiful sizeable sparkling pool in the center of our apartment complex. For some weeks, Jason and I, wearing our innertube around our waist, we play in the deep end.

One afternoon, Jason says excitedly while in the shallow side of the pool, "Hey, Mary, look, I can swim." He puts his head underwater and pushes off from the pool wall with his feet, jetting forward, kicking his feet while stroking the water with his arms and hands across the pool. He pops up from the water and says, "Go ahead, try it, Mary."

I take off my innertube and imitate what he did. Magically, I'm swimming like him too! Cool!

Every day, we keep improving and learning new ways to swim, like backstroke, breathing, diving, treading water, and swimming to the bottom of the 7-foot pool. Jason and I enjoy swimming daily in the pool for the entire summer, right after lunch until late afternoon.

One time, I'm swimming in the deep end of the pool. Out of nowhere, I see my neighbor's kids, 2½-year-old Jeffrey and his younger brother Brian who is 1½ years old, going around the pool, clinging onto the edge. I'm nine years old, and I ask them, "What are you two doing over here?"

Both of them only make baby sounds. I wrap one arm around Jeffrey and my other around Brian, holding them, treading water to stay afloat to get to the shallow end of the pool. I tell their Mom that I encountered both at the pool's deep end and brought them over.

During another week in the summer, Jason and I sit at the booth having our lunch at *Ming's Café.* We're goofing around, jabbing each other in the ribs with our elbows. My parents see us. My Daddy angrily scolds us, "You can hurt or kill someone that way." We freeze.

Our Daddy grounds us from swimming. It's tough not to swim today. We always feel anxious and excited to gobble lunch and have fun swimming. It's not happening today. We're bummed.

The next day, we both apologize to our parents and ask if we could go swimming. They allow us. We're thrilled! We're back to our summer fun in the sun in the sparkling pool. How cool!

Reflecting on my childhood years, Jason and I have never argued or fought with one another. As an older brother, he has always been helpful, compassionate, and caring toward me. It's not until I reflect on how much we played together—looking back, wishing I could have reciprocated his positive qualities.

Summer, finally comes to an end. September arrives, and we're back in school again. One day after school, I hear my Mommy crying in her bedroom. I inch over in the hallway toward my parents' bedroom to peek inside. My Mommy is lying on her stomach, weeping with her face buried in her pillow. She's grieving for hours. I don't know why my Mommy is crying.

A couple of hours later, one of the Chinese cooks from *Ming's Café,* named Bing, comes to our apartment. He sits by my Mommy's side and talks to her, trying to console her. She continues to weep.

My parents never disclosed or let the children know how their restaurant businesses were doing throughout my young life. They rarely talk about their experience of hardship. They work long days. I never hear my parents complain. Perhaps they do it in private. My parents have owned four Chinese restaurants for ten years.

One evening, my parents come home to the apartment with a sense of hope. A potential Chinese couple has an interest in taking over *Ming's Café.* That evening, my parents instruct Leland and me to scoop rice bowls from a 25-pound burlap bag into another empty large burlap bag.

Our parents firmly say to carefully scoop the rice over to the other bag and not drop one rice grain on the floor. Leland and I cautiously scoop bowls of rice, one after another. I don't know why we are doing this. However, upon reflection, I think this is a symbolic gesture of desiring a successful transfer of *Ming's Café* to a new owner.

Chapter 13: Mary's Family Moves to Chinatown, L.A.

The transition from Sun Valley to Chinatown, Los Angeles, seems smooth. We traded places with the Chinese family who lived in Chinatown. They took over *Ming's Café* and moved to the Sun Valley apartment.

In the early Fall semester of my fifth-grade year, I transferred to Castelar Elementary School in the heart of Chinatown, Los Angeles, in 1969. In our first week living in a two-bedroom, one-bath apartment in Chinatown, a few of my parents' Chinese friends invite our family to lunch. We sit around a large round table, enjoying a delicious Chinese meal.

After completing our meal, the waiter comes by to drop off the bill. Each male waves and calls the waiter to give the bill to him. The waiter experiences a dilemma. However, the waiter knows the Chinese ritual, "I'll pay the bill," which dramatically unfolds.

Face-saving is considered an honor for the one who pays the bill, providing for others. Some waiters have different ways in how they deliver the bill. Some may drop the bill in the middle of the table, and those who demand it will grab for it. Others may give it to the person who convinces the most or who sits the closest to the waiter or the one who asks in advance or made prior arrangements.

Amuse like other occasions I've witnessed, the "I'll pay the bill" ritual. One of the men stands up and grabs the bill, while the other men attempt to persuade the one who has the bill to hand it over. A few rounds of persuasion occur amongst them.

Finally, the person with the bill places his credit card on the bill tray and waves the waiter over to whisk it away. The other two men, including my Daddy, have serious faces, shaking their heads, looking like they lost the battle. Leaving the restaurant, everyone thanks the person who ultimately pays the bill.

Our family arrives back at our apartment, and my parents are chatting. My Daddy says, "I'm so glad someone else paid the bill." My Mommy smiles and nods.

"I was so worried. I only had forty dollars in my pocket. That's all I had when we moved here," my Daddy says with relief. "I don't know what I would have done if I was stuck with the bill."

"Ho choi," meaning good luck, my Mommy responds.

"Ho choi," my Daddy says with a smile while slapping his leg and shaking his head.

I sense from this brief exchange that my parents are financially rock bottom--barely surviving. My Mommy stays at home for the first year living in Chinatown. She starts waitressing at *Ling Nam* restaurant the second year, only a few blocks from our apartment. Shortly afterwards, she begins waitressing at *Pearl Dragon*, where my Daddy cooks in Highland Park. They commute together and return home at about 10 p.m.

Castelar Elementary School is conveniently one block away; I see it from my front-door apartment. Right across the street is Alpine Playground, where I play quite often, especially during the summertime. There's no recreational coach or supervisor who organizes activities at Alpine daily.

Mrs. Sherry, our fifth-grade teacher, stands 4 feet 10 and is a small-framed, middle-aged, blond pixie hairstyle Caucasian walking with a significant limp due to one short leg. A strict teacher keeping control of the class with her straightforward teaching style is unnecessary because Chinese American and Mexican American students behave well and act like perfect angels in the classroom. Everyone is well-behaved, quiet, and does our work.

On the first day of class, I notice almost all of my classmates are Chinese. Some Mexican American classmates are Aida, Isabel, Theresa, Virginia, Maria, Jose, and Sammy. For the first time, I have Chinese and Mexican classmates. I'm experiencing culture shock, feeling different and unfamiliar with them. I want to move again right away.

Almost all my Chinese classmates have parents who work either in the restaurant business, grocery stores, or sewing factories.

A majority of my classmates have immigrated from Hong Kong. One boy from Italy, Alfredo Maguchi, speaks English with an Italian accent. Jackie is the only Caucasian girl. Three students like me are ABCs, meaning American-born Chinese. Only three classmates have parents who have an education. Susie's dad is a medical doctor. Calvin's dad graduated from USC in business; now an owner of a Chinatown grocery store, and Tammy's Mom works at Cathay Bank in Chinatown.

At first, I felt different from my Chinatown classmates. I don't know what being Chinese is. My parents speak Cantonese at home. We eat rice every night with chopsticks and use a Chinese soup spoon that differs from American culture. I know the Chinese language uses Chinese characters and not an alphabet. We physically look ethnically different from Euro-Americans. My family eats Chinese cuisine at home, whereas we eat American food for lunch in all the schools I've attended.

During the first week of class, the students work on fractions. I haven't learned fractions at my previous school. I need help. I sit at a group of tables that seats six classmates. I say to my group of classmates, "I need help. I don't know how to do fractions.

Can someone help me?"

The Chinese students look at one another and respond giggly, shyly. One student says to the other student, "You show her."

"No, you show her," the other replies. They shyly giggle.

"Will someone just help me?" I say with a frustrated tone.

Soon I begin developing friendships, particularly with two Chinese girls born in Hong Kong. Ruby has a pixie haircut and a cute smile. She's not interested in sports. Her best friend, Grace, has a sweet smile too, and always wears a ponytail, tied at the back of her neck and resting between her shoulder blades.

The other kids actively play ball during recess. Ruby and Grace invite me to stroll around the playground for the first few days. This speed is too slow for me. I engage with the other Chinese kids playing actively on the playground, whether team handball, four-square, or tetherball. I continue playing my game of tetherball, and well, yes, winning every game.

I learned a lot from observing Rhonda beat everyone in tether ball at Fern Greenwood Elementary School in Torrance. It sure paid off when I beat that tall 6th-grade boy in Camellia Elementary School's tetherball contest. I call this observe, analyze, and apply.

My initial impression of my classmates as perfect angels in the classroom soon turns into a surprising reality. Some of my Chinese classmates show another side of their nature and personality during recess. Playing four-square, the little boys especially would say, *"Säät a nei! Säät a nei,* meaning, "Kill you! Kill you!" as they hit the red rubber ball forcefully.

"Wow, pretty violent words," I'm thinking. We use various techniques like the knuckle spin, karate chop spin, or the double hand twist spin of the rubber ball. These spin techniques create an unpredictable ball bounce that catches the recipient off-balance in returning the ball. We also use sheer forceful hits or strategically hit the ball far from the player in their square to get them out.

A Chinese classmate named Willie Wong loves to shout out to his good buddy, Eugene, who has a crew cut, is easy-going, and likes to smile. Willie loves to call with great vitality to Eugene on the playground, "Hey, Bald Eagle, come over here!" or "Hey, Bald Eagle, hit the ball far and make a home run!" Willie likes to give orders and shout on the playground.

There's tall Nancy Dang. She's quiet but can whomp that red rubber ball like a torpedo out of the playground and hit a home run every time. As I say, the cute, sweet angels in the classroom behave as complete opposites on the playground. Instead, many behave with expressive, active, competitive, and outspoken styles.

Since the new academic year recently began, the election of class officers occurs. Ruby is elected President of our class. Jacquelin, Willie, and I are the vice presidents. Every day, I'm responsible for giving out the free lunch tickets.

Lunchtime is the highlight for all of us. Most of us are on the free lunch program. Once released in an orderly way from our classroom at noon, we walk rapidly through the hallway, down the flight of stairs, pushing the doors open, and bursting outside the main building onto the blacktop playground.

We're not allowed to run, but we certainly speed walk fast like in the Olympics. We're bouncing on every rapid step we make with energy, consistency, determination, and competitiveness to get in the lunch line early before the crowd. Jacquelin and I lead the pack every time as speedsters. My favorite dessert item is the ice cream sandwich. We sit together either inside the cafeteria or outside at the lunch benches.

Every day after school, my typical routine involves fixing my bed, changing into my home clothes, cleaning Chipper's parakeet cage, and doing my homework. Every Monday, the class receives our new spelling words and paragraphs of sentences containing the new spelling words. Mrs. Sherry tests us weekly by reciting each spelling word and then sentence dictation for us to write. I'm an "A" speller, diligently studying every day after receiving our new weekly spelling list and dictation paragraphs.

Chipper's cage stands next to my desk. Every day, I talk to Chipper and teach him how to speak. Chipper knows how to say, "Ah, Chipper, what a pretty, pretty, pretty, pretty bird," *"Zou tau,"* meaning "goodnight." I say to Chipper before covering his cage to tuck him in bed every night.

Sometimes we let Chipper fly in the apartment, from the curtain rod to the curtain rod. When we nod and make a sound, Chipper flies on our heads. We return Chipper to his cage when he lands on the hand mirror. I slide the mirror inside his cage door, and him standing on it, looking at himself in the mirror. I think he feels companionship, seeing his reflection in the mirror.

Our fifth-grade class participates in the Partners In Education (PIE) program with the intent to socialize and share Chinese, Mexican, and African American cultures. We go on field trips with fifth-grade students from *Grape Street* Elementary School, a newly built school in the Watts area of South LA.

We visit their new school, made with fresh carpet, modern desks, chairs, and everything. Visiting Grape Street Elementary School, we also explore Watts Tower. **[Ch.13:1]**

Simon Rodia, the creator of Watts Towers, used trash remnants to build this beautiful site. Indeed, it is a creative original. Students paint on a large construction paper whatever we like about our visit. I paint Watts Towers. **[Ch. 13:2]**

Throughout the year, we go on more trips together. The Grape Street School students also come to Chinatown to visit us. We also venture to Olvera Street, next door from Chinatown, Los Angeles. Another time, we travel to Santa Barbara to look at the missions. We go to the mountains when it's snowing and the beach when it's sunny. **[Ch. 13:3], [Ch. 13:4]**

One day in class, Mrs. Bishop plays a recording with multiple messages that The Grape Street School kids expressed. I'm surprised they remember my name and say, "Hi, Mary, we love you!" I'm surprised.

Culturally, Chinese people do not publicly and openly express, "I love you." Their open expression surprises and embarrasses me because of the directness and strong adjective. That's too heavy for us! However, I think the more intercultural socialization of Chinese Americans in Western society today, they may adopt or become more open to the public expression of affection toward one another.

I have observed a difference in communications between the African American students from Grape Street and the Chinese American and Mexican American students from Castelar. The Grape Street students are expressive, talkative, and look comfortable touching one another, if it's hugging, bumping into each other, or holding hands.

Whereas the Castelar students typically keep to themselves, talk quietly, or not talkative. They respect everyone's physical space by allowing less physical contact. Good friends who are comfortable with one another would talk and sometimes kid around with each other.

Ruby and Jacquelin are two friends I interact with the most. They both come in the morning to pick me up to go to school. Sometimes, I oversleep, and I'm not ready when they come to the door. So, I tell them to go ahead to class, and I'll be coming soon.

One Saturday morning in January, Ruby, Jacquelin, and I decide to meet at Alpine Playground's benches. As I step out of the front door, walk down the flight of stairs, I see Ruby and Jacquelin preparing a gathering on the park table and benches. They have prepared a surprise birthday party!

I never had a surprise birthday party before. I don't know how to react. How super thoughtful and kind of them to celebrate my birthday! Aren't they the sweetest? At school, Mamie, another classmate of mine, gives me a birthday gift, too! She thoughtfully selected a variety of chewing gum in a rectangular box. What a neat gift that appeals to my candy addiction.

Many Saturday mornings, my Daddy drives Ruby, Jacquelin, and me to the downtown L.A. Public Library before he drives to work in the opposite direction toward South Pasadena. This library has extensive resources to help us gather information to do our class projects and reports. My friends, always polite when-ever my Daddy picks them up. They say, "Hello Mr. Fong" or "Good morning, Mr. Fong," and "Thank you, Mr. Fong, for driving us.

We check out books on the assigned U.S. President in order to write a report. I'm assigned to study Richard Milhouse Nixon, Ruby has Dwight Eisenhower, and Jacquelin has John F. Kennedy. It was not until this report assignment I became aware of President John F. Kennedy's inauguration in 1961 and was assassinated in 1963. It was a tremendous tragedy and loss for the Americans to witness this violent crime. His son, J.F.K, Jr. was only three years old when his father was assassinated. **[Ch. 13:5]**, **[Ch. 13:6]**

After this assignment, we are each given a U.S. state to create an informative project. I'm learning about Minnesota. I write to the Chamber of Commerce of Minnesota. They send pamphlets of information that I include in my project. I create a theatre where I paste pictures and information on several lengthy rectangle cardboards. I get a large cardboard box and decorate it, stapling fiberglass burlap on the exterior. The viewer slides it through two slits on both sides of the theatre walls while sitting at the open side and reads the informative presentation.

Typically, after going to the L.A. Public Library, we always look forward to shopping downtown to buy 25-cent slices of freshly baked delicious pizza with tomato sauce, cheese, and pepperoni at the *Newberry* department store. There's always a crowd, not a line. We slowly and patiently squeeze our way up to the front glass counter as hot oven pizza comes sizzling out of the oven. There's nothing better than tasting the freshly baked cheesy tomato sauce and pepperoni pizza that hits our hungry palate. There's nothing better than tasting the freshly baked cheesy tomato sauce and pepperoni pizza that hits our hungry palate.

After we eat, we browse around to see if we like anything on sale. We particularly enjoy going to the end of the month clearance sales. After an entire day out, we catch the bus home, returning by 5:00 p.m.

Sometimes, my friends come over, and they meet my Mom. My friends tell me, "Your Mom is pretty." Jacqueline loves chatting with my Mommy about cooking and recipes. My Mommy smiles and enjoys chatting with my friends, too.

While at work one day, the stove pilot light goes out. My Daddy strikes a match. Boom! An explosion occurs! Both of my Daddy's hands and arms suffer burns. Too much gas from the stove leaked. He's rushed to the hospital.

My Daddy's hands are treated with a layer of clear ointment to protect his hands and part of his arms. Release from the hospital, the ambulance returns my Daddy home. Paramedics carry my Dad on a stretcher and placed in his bed.

His hands and arms have burns that eventually develop a reddish crust. He does not have any scarring, but he does have skin discoloration of pink and white patches on his tan skin as he is healing. In time, my Daddy's skin heals, but patches of discoloration remain for many years.

A few months go by, and I begin acclimating to my new cultural environment in Chinatown with new Chinese American friends who befriend me. One day, Jacquelin explains the dos and don'ts during the Chinese New Year week-long celebration between January to February, depending on the lunar calendar year.

"Don't wash your hair on Chinese New Year's Day," Jacquelin says.

"Why?" I ask with a puzzled look.

"It makes you look like a white lady or a white ghost. It's bad luck.

"Oh, really."

"Imagine a dead white lady with wet straight hair hanging on both sides of her face. Do you see?"

"Oh, I see."

"Also, we don't clean our house, throw out the trash, or sweep the floor on the first day of Chinese New Year."

"Why?"

"It's bad luck. It's like throwing your money away or sweeping your riches away."

"Oh, I see."

This brief conversation strikes me as odd but, at the same time, mystified, intrigued, and unfamiliar. I have heard my parents say, *hao choi,* meaning good luck. Our parents give Leland, Jason, and me a Chinese red envelope called *lai see* or *hóngbāo,* which is good luck money to spend. **[Ch. 13:7]**

Walking through Chinatown during the month of preparation and the actual week of festivities, vendors sell red ornaments like hanging firecrackers, lanterns, live flower plants, Chinese red envelopes, and pictures of the horoscope animal representing the incoming new year. I was born in the year of the dog based on Chinese astrology, having characteristics reflecting the qualities of a dog. I'm loyal, helpful, honest, and can tell the difference between friends and foes. I'm also born in the hour of the snake, resonating with the qualities representing wisdom and a deep thinker.

During the Chinese New Year celebration, Chinatown has its one-hour parade with local school marching bands, a dragon dance, Miss Chinatown and her court, the LA mayor, other local dignitaries, local community organizations, and so on.

I always enjoy the three-day Chinatown carnival only three blocks from my home. I like the booth with many jars of goldfish displayed on a table. Winning a goldfish requires successfully tossing a white ping pong ball into the jar.

I pay 75 cents to the booth worker. He gives me three ping pong balls. Standing there, intensely focused on the fish jars, holding my three white ping pong balls. I examine the distance for 5 to 10 minutes and how to toss my ping pong ball into a jar. I feel my heart thumping.

I'm ready to try. I get into position, holding one white ping pong ball with my fingers on the side of my face. I toss. It's airborne and bounces on the rim of a jar. The booth worker retrieves it. He's watching me. I reload my right-hand fingers with another white ping pong ball, holding it close to the side of my face. I'm pausing, evaluating, and calculating how I did with my first ping pong toss and how to adjust my next toss.

Another few minutes elapse. I'm patient, focused, calm, and aiming. I toss the second white ping pong ball. It flies! It bounces on the jar rim, shooting straight up, and off the table, kerplunk! "Rats! Okay. It's all right. Keep calm," I'm thinking while taking a deep breath. The booth worker picks up the second time.

I'm refocusing, analyzing my two tosses, and adjusting my final ping pong toss. A few minutes tick away. I feel ready now. Using my eye-hand coordination, I toss the ping pong with a perfect arc into the air. Splash! Bingo! I'm happy! **[Ch. 13:7A]**

The booth worker smiles and picks the white ping pong ball out of the fish jar. He lifts the fish jar, pours it into a clear cellophane bag, and knots it. "Good job," says the booth worker as he hands it to me. I'm smiling, a bounce to my walk home, holding my clear plastic bag with my beautiful goldfish swimming around.

Leland comes home from USC to visit us now and then in our Chinatown apartment. Jason and I jump up and down and kiss Leland when coming through the front door. During his weekend stay, I give Leland the saved money I keep in my white sandwich box. He could use it since I'm at home and don't need to buy anything.

Sometimes, we go to the laundromat to do the family laundry. Leland drives us in his hand-me-down 1964 blue Chevrolet Impala from our Dad. Otherwise, Jason and I carry four shopping bags of laundry to the local laundry mat.

Leland has the car radio tuned to the USC Trojan football game on Saturdays. Leland introduces us to football, and it's exciting to listen. USC eventually has three national championship-winning teams with Mike Rae, the quarterback, in 1972. In the following years, Pat Haden, the quarterback with his high school buddy, JK MacKay Jr., as his favorite receiver, and the son of the USC head coach, John McKay, Sr., continues the winning streak. Also, Lynn Swann, wide receiver, Sam "Bam" Cunningham, the fullback, and Anthony Davis, the running back, making electrifying runs.

The football games are exciting because Tom Kelly makes it thrilling as the radio football announcer for USC Athletics. I become an instant USC football and basketball sports fan. **[Ch. 13:8]**

Every weekend, I faithfully watch the football games on TV and listen on the radio. I also purchase *Sports Illustrated* and the *LA Times* Sunday newspaper, cut out the USC sports stories, and watch the John McKay football coach show. I'm a USC sports fanatic! **[Ch.13:8A]**

My oldest brother Leland is a junior at USC, majoring in East Asian Studies. USC is eight miles from Chinatown. Leland is very active as President of the Chinese student club on campus. He has many Chinese friends from USC, UCLA, and CSULA, whom he meets at intercampus Chinese American student activities.

Leland received complimentary tickets for our family to see the ping-pong players from the People's Republic of China play a friendly competition with the US ping-pong team at USC. During President Nixon's term, this 1970s event is one of the tour locations for ping-pong diplomacy. This successful historical event steps toward helping Sino-American relations. **[Ch. 13:9]**

Jacquelin is the biggest UCLA and Laker basketball fan in our class. Born in China, she speaks *Sei-Yup Wa* or *Toi Shan Wa,* the fourth Chinese dialect. Her personality is most different from the Chinese girls in Chinatown. She is expressive, outspoken, blunt, bold, assertive, and competitive. She has beautiful long healthy hair and loves to say "aaayy" with a smile whenever she's kidding around.

Jacquelin comes to school wearing her first pair of high heels. She parades around with her new pair of blue heels, feeling taller, prouder, and mature. A group of girls chat on the playground, and she slightly lifts her head and nose in the air with her eyes looking down at me and says, "You look short."

I don't know how to respond to her unexpected comment that reflects her attitude. So, I say nothing. I don't think about her statement and allow it to go in one ear and out the other.

Jacquelin easily expresses her disgust or dismay at three boys—a Chinese boy named Bruce, the Italian boy Alfredo, and the Mexican American boy, Sammy. She complains about Bruce and says, "Look at his small crescent shifty eyes. Yuck!" She doesn't like it when he looks at her and the other girls in the class.

Alfredo, who speaks expressively with his hands, challenges Jacquelin's unpleasant facial expressions, gestures, and comments toward him. Sammy has long straight hair to his shoulders, bangs long enough to cover his eyes, is a bit shy and quiet, and has a double row of teeth on the top and bottom. Jacquelin sometimes shows her bold disgust through her facial expressions and sharp comments. No doubt, she is one of a kind.

Another Chinese classmate is Rachel, who has a shiny rice bowl haircut. Her grandmother from her father's side has a strong personality. The domineering grandmother lives with Rachel's parents and the rest of the family of six children in a cramped one-bedroom apartment in Chinatown. Their apartment has one semi-large bedroom and a small living room with only room for a couch, TV, and a factory sewing machine. Visiting Rachel, it's crowded, with loud voices and yelling.

Standing next to the front door, I'm quite surprised while observing almost everyone yelling at each other and tempers flaring. They don't feel a need to tame their behavior when I'm there as a visitor. I'm like a fly on the wall.

Rachel has two younger siblings. Her youngest brother is in the second grade and stares at me one of the first few times I've seen him. He curiously asks me, "Mary, why do you have such big teeth?"

I don't know how to respond to a question like that. However, Rachel yells, "Shut up, stop asking such stupid questions!"

Another friend, Linda, also yells sometimes when I visit her home. Direct bossing occurs amongst their siblings according to the pecking order. I rarely see Linda's parents, usually sitting in another room.

Melissa is a classmate with shoulder-length-shiny hair. She matured the earliest, and visiting her family's apartment, she, along with her younger sister and brother, sometimes engage in a yelling match. However, I don't think they are mean-spirited. They like ordering each other around, especially playing outside. It's surprising to visit three of my Chinese friends' homes, where yelling is apparent in their family interactions to varying degrees.

Among my siblings, we do not have the yelling mode of communication. Perhaps, because there is a ten-year difference between my oldest brother and me, Jason and I are almost two years apart, and we share our time growing up together.

Living in Chinatown in the early 1970s, many Chinese immigrant parents had limited educational opportunities growing up, particularly in Mainland China and other Chinese populated regions abroad. Boys in China typically have more schooling than females.

My Mommy tells me that beginning at nine years of age, she got up in the early morning hours to join with other villagers to climb the mountain to gather sticks to use as firewood to cook. She says, "Lucky if you have an old bicycle tire to cut and stick your foot in it as your shoes." Otherwise, people walk barefoot or wear their *taw hai,* a Chinese slipper or sandal.

My Mommy did not have running water growing up. Every day she fetched water, cooked, and cleaned the house. There were no conveniences like a toilet or bathtub. Instead, a hole in the ground where they crotch and relieve themselves. Instead, everyone used their hand towel to *mät sun,* a sponge bath every evening.

Her Mom never talked to her but told her what to do. Her Mom was always tired and not well. She gave her Mom massages every day. Her older brother works on the farm and also attended school. He eventually married and had children and remained in Guangdong, China, throughout his life.

Her Dad went to Canada for work and was absent from the home for most of my Mommy's life. Her Dad returned home when she was 17 years old and was told to get married. My Mommy's existence beginning at a very young age is work, work, work.

My Mommy grew up in a survival upbringing, beginning in the mid-1920s in Mainland China. Similar to her parents' childhood, she receives no display of affection and love from either of her parents. She did not experience much fun, celebrations, or happy times. My Mommy never tells me about these aspects of her growing up years until I am much older.

My parents very rarely talk about their painful past. Besides living in poverty during the Second Sino-Japanese War (1937-45), when Japan invaded China, my parents grew up in that era. The world suffered from the devastation of WWII and the Great Depression worldwide (1929-41). My parents grew up with a lifetime of hardship. **[Ch. 13:10], [Ch. 13:11]**

Although I do not hear any snippets of my Chinatown classmates' family stories, I can imagine that they, too, have had a life of struggles. My classmates' Chinese immigrant parents are likely uneducated and do not speak or write English.

Our parents cannot help us with our homework, read bedtime stories, and have little time to interact with us. My parents never inquire what we are learning in school, probably because we only eat once a week together on their day off, and they come home late at 10. My parents' world is always working, keeping a roof over the family's head. Therefore, they rely on America's education system.

Although my parents do not know how to engage in conversation or ask questions about what we are learning, it never bothers me. My Daddy attended our PTA meetings with our teachers when we attended elementary school.

My parents see our report cards, and my Daddy signs off on them. A tremendous difference exists between immigrants from the lower socio-economic uneducated class and immigrants from the educated middle and upper socio-economic class.

Both of my parents are heroes to me. Their perseverance, sacrifices, courage, and giving and caring toward their family are much more than they ever received. My parents know they are not perfect, but they certainly do their best in what they can. I respect them, and I thank them both for being my parents.

Comparing the two ethnic communities upon reflection, I observe that Caucasian Americans are more outspoken and participatory, and a few are quite articulate in the classroom. In contrast, my Chinese classmates are primarily quiet, shy, and giggly in the classroom.

It seems reasonable to say that the noticeable behavioral difference is cultural upbringing, exposure, socialization influences, differing ways of communicating, behavior, disposition, etc. The Chinese classmates I socialize with are fluent in English and Chinese. I've observed Chinese classmates speak English as a second language, converse in Cantonese amongst their friends during recess, and are quiet in the classroom.

Living in the three Euro-American communities before Chinatown, Los Angeles, there are oral activities like reading groups, word contests, individual oral reports, and storytelling in front of the entire class. In Chinatown, there's not one oral activity as a part of our education.

Sometimes, only a handful of students read aloud in front of the class at our seats at Castelar. All students participate in a self-paced reading program called SRA (Science Research Associates). We have reading assignments and respond to questions. We must complete the entire set before moving to the next color level.

Math is more advanced in Chinatown because they learned fractions while I was doing division problems in Sun Valley. All three Euro-American communities are more advanced in English grammar than in Chinatown. The English grammar in the fifth grade at Chinatown was behind one year of Sun Valley's pace.

Upon self-reflection, I suffered an identity crisis in the first grade in Long Beach when I cried in the mirror because I was mistreated and shunned by my peers who didn't play with me, my shattered porcelain Chinese soup spoon on the floor. The boys taunted me to show I was different and unworthy. At one point, I desired to be Caucasian, even though I knew I was Chinese. Because I experienced ostracization, conflict, and dislike, I want to be accepted and feel I belong.

Subjectively, I knew I was Chinese, but the negative external messages created conflict and exclusion. I had fallen into an identity crisis due to the natural need to feel included and in harmony with others, to the extent of wanting to give up my ethnicity to be something I'm not.

Living in Torrance and Sun Valley, my classmates never talked about my ethnicity, making me feel different. My identity crisis subsides. Although I do not develop close friendships, I have neighborhood friends to play with while living in Torrance.

As each year progressed, I felt comfortable being indepen-dent and not feeling lonely. Instead, I engaged in outdoor activities and school projects that I enjoyed.

Living in Chinatown, Los Angeles, allowed me to integrate with Chinese children my age and learn some Chinese cultural ways. My Chinese classmates have reached out to create friendships, allowing me to feel included. I have Chinese friends in and out of school, going to each other's homes, playing at Alpine Playground, going downtown to the LA Public Library, walking to the carnival, and local stores and shops.

I feel a sense of community and the convenience of venturing to multiple places. Most of my classmates and the adults living in Chinatown are Cantonese speakers, with a small percentage of Mexicans and Italians residing in the community. Chinatown is fundamentally recognizable today. However, the demographics have changed to a diverse community over the past 45 years since I've moved. There's an increase in Vietnamese who both live and work in Chinatown. The 2010 U.S. census counted 20,913 residents consisting of Latino, 36.7%; Asian, 34.6%; blacks, 13.8%; whites, 12.4%; and others, 2.3%. Renters consist of 91% of residents in Chinatown.

Yesteryears, I recognize the Old Chinatown Central Plaza with its East Gate entrance, *Cathay Bank, Phoenix Bakery, Wonder Bakery, Columbus Pharmacy,* the many restaurants, gift, herbal, and grocery shops. The *French Hospital* has changed to an out-patient facility called the *Pacific Alliance Medical Center.* Sites that still exist are *Castelar Elementary School,* a remodeled Alpine Playground, some new homes, and apartments built.

Over the past four decades, many changes have occurred—demolishing long-time establishments such as *Little Joe's and Velvet Turtle* restaurants in 2014 and 2015. The construction of a couple of shopping plazas adds to the Chinatown community. Several new banks and *Thanh's Pharmacy* now serve this area.

The *Chinese American Museum* and over 20 art galleries have found a home in Chinatown. I served as a volunteer docent at the Chinese American Museum for a year. Recently, in late 2018, a statue of Bruce Lee was added to the community.

Our teacher assigns us an art activity to draw and paint whatever we like on a large sheet of construction paper to celebrate the upcoming Chinese New Year. I bring a greeting card with a dragon and a phoenix to help me draw these two mythical figures on my large sheet of construction paper. Finally, I finished my water-color painting, and I'm quite pleased with my artwork. **[Ch. 13:12]**

Mrs. Sherry pins my art on the hallway bulletin board outside our classroom. She also pins more student paintings on other hallway bulletin boards. Weeks later, my watercolor painting displays at the LA Children's Museum. Unfortunately, no one takes us there to see it, nor do I ever get my picture back.

We experiment with a new art form, pointillism, that involves creating a picture using dots from a paintbrush. I used the cover of a senior woman's storybook sitting, plucking her geese's feathers, and dropping them into a basket next to her as my pointillism image. We also learn how to paper-mâché our clown and a four-foot dragon for the class.

After we paper-mâché our clown, we cut colorful tissue paper and glue it on the paper mâché clown that becomes a piñata. We don't get to insert candy in the piñata, typically included in a purchased or homemade piñata.

Hitting a candy-stuffed piñata with a stick is a game at Latino fiestas. Kids and adults are typically blindfolded and twirled around before trying to beat the piñata that moves up and down on a rope someone is pulling and releasing. Much laughter, clapping, and cheering occurs, especially when the blindfolded person is swinging, missing, and sometimes hitting the piñata. Finally, someone whacks the piñata hard enough to break it, so the candy flies out. Much excitement occurs when kids scramble for the sweets on the floor.

Before the academic year concluded, my name is picked out of the lottery to get the four-foot dragon. Ruby, Jacquelin, and I carry the dragon across the street to my home.

Near the end of my fifth-grade year, I don't know what possesses me to trust Jacquelin to pierce my ears. Any rational-minded person would not let a fifth-grader pierce another fifth grader's ears, right? Maybe her persuasiveness, my trust in her ability, and my gullibility together agree to the homemade ear-piercing.

I'm sitting in her kitchen, and she lightly rubs the oil with ginger on both of my ears. She doesn't do an earlobe massage for a minute or two. She dabs some ginger oil on the earlobes and rubs four times.

Then she makes a pen mark on both of my earlobes where she's going to pierce. She looks back and forth to ensure the markings are even and centered.

"Okay, are you ready?" Jacquelin asks.

"Yes," I reply.

"Stay still. Don't move, okay?"

I sit quietly, keeping very still. She slowly penetrates my skin with the sharp earring stud.

Oh, how I'm feeling the slow, gradual sharp earring stud piercing my earlobe. I feel the pain in my earlobe as my head begins vibrating. She already started the piercing, and I have to go through with it. I can't tell her to stop because she's halfway through my earlobe. I'm sticking it out. No pun intended. I remain calm, allowing the process, although my head feels warm, still vibrating.

"Okay, it went through," Jacquelin says as she slides the metal backing behind my ear to secure the earring stud.

"Okay," I respond, lifting my eyebrows with each deep breath.

"Let's do the other one," she says.

Bracing myself for the second piercing, I take a deep breath. I can't back out. I want it done and over. "Okay, are you ready? Don't move," instructs Jacquelin.

Again, I feel the sharp earring stud penetrate my earlobe as she slowly and steadily pushes the sharp earring stud. I feel the warmth of my head as it vibrates inside. I remain calm, allowing the process, knowing that I have to go through it, and it'll be...

"Done!" Jacquelin says.

"Good," I say with much relief. "Glad it's over. Thanks, Jacquelin."

Whew, done. I have pierced ears. In our day, the ear-piercing stapler did not exist. Today, people get their ears pierced quickly, easily, and virtually without pain. I must have been nuts! No, insane to go through that painfully slow process! Never again! Well, I have to say that I've come a long way from running around the medical office for my first shot to now. Nevertheless, I was out of my mind. I plead insanity.

The summer after fifth grade, I return to visit Burbank Elementary School when my parents check on their four-unit pink apartment rental in Long Beach. It's been almost four years since we moved. Coming back to the playground where I spent after-school jump roping feels strange.

I ask some kids, "Where's Coach?"

They point to the building and say, "She's doing arts and crafts in the first room."

"Okay, thanks," I say with a smile.

I walk toward the building and climb a short flight of stairs. As I enter the arts and crafts room, I see Coach's back and students standing beside her. I walk up to her and tap her on the shoulder. She turns around, gesturing with wide-open eyes and a cheerio-shaped mouth cocking her neck back with surprise. She opens both of her arms wide and gives me a big hug.

"Oh, my goodness. You've grown so much!"

"How are you, Coach?"

"I'm doing fine. What are you doing here?"

"My parents are in town, so I came with them."

"You know, no one has beaten your 4,000 in double-dutch." **[Ch.13:13]**

I smiled, and we chatted a bit more before she continued back to working on the arts and crafts with the kids. We hugged, and I bid her goodbye. It feels good to see her again. It brings back memories of yesteryears as a first and second grader.

During the summer, my friend, Ruby, invites me to the Chinatown Baptist Church to participate in the week-long vacation bible school (VBS). Completing the week, I receive Jesus Christ in my heart and memorize a bible passage, reciting it to my VBS teacher.

We also have an art project that includes a sponge glued to a 2 x 4-inch thin wooden handle with silkscreen calligraphy that reads, "Cleanse me of my sins."

Leland signs me up for UCLA's Uni-Camp in the mountains that summer. Leland is among many volunteered Asian American counselors from UCLA, USC, and CSULA. Our small tent group takes a tour of the campsite. At the pool, we see a group of girls swimming in a freestyle race. Wow, they are so fast. I wouldn't be surprised if they are on a swimming team. I'm impressed with how quickly and strongly the girls swim across the pool. **[Ch. 13:14]**

We're outdoors under the stars in our sleeping bags on a cot. Early one morning, I'm fishing for the first time. We didn't catch any fish. Instead, the fish hook got caught in the palm of my hand. In the afternoon, I'm upset because I have to get a tetanus shot. It's not surprising, considering my history of how I react to shots.

After we eat at the dining hall, we do our clean-up shift. I'm in the team where we swing utensils in a plastic crate to dry them using the Roman-style method.

In the evening, we sing songs around the campfire. We sing the Uni-camp song.

Uni will shine tonight, Uni will shine.
Uni will shine tonight, Uni will shine.
We're all dressed up tonight.
We're feeling fine. When the sun goes down,
And the moon goes up. Uni will shine.

Chapter 14: Mary's Sixth Grade Experience

Early Fall semester, sixth grade, there's a Uni-Camp reunion. Two fellow Uni-Campers, Shoo-Shoo and Gracie, come by my apartment to pick me up. I asked my Daddy earlier in the week if I could go to the Uni-Camp reunion. He doesn't answer me until the morning of the event.

"No," my Daddy says.

"How come?"

"I can't let you go everywhere you want," he says strictly.

I am very disappointed and sad that I can't go to the Uni-Camp reunion picnic. The doorbell rings, and I open the door.

"Hi, Mary. Are you ready?" they ask in a chorus with a smile.

"No, I can't go," I say in a very disappointed tone.

"Why?" they say in a chorus with a frown.

"I can't go."

I look down and close the door. I questioned in my head why my Daddy did not allow me to go. It doesn't cost anything. Why? His reasoning is, "I can't let you have everything or go anywhere you want all the time." There is no legitimate reason except for restrictions. Is it not to spoil me? I am not even near being spoiled. I hardly ask for anything. I don't misbehave. As I'm growing up, I come to terms with the idea that if I want something, either I get it myself, do it without, or don't ask. Don't expect anything.

The Moon Festival in Chinese culture is the 15th of the eighth month of the lunar calendar year, or between September 8th to October 7th of the solar calendar year. This marks the Autumn Equinox, where the moon is the farthest from the earth. Many Chinese families appreciate watching a full bright moon, enjoying a family gathering, visiting others, and exchanging mooncakes.

[Ch. 14:1]

Leland has a former roommate at USC named John Tse. John always gives our family a large bag of boxes of assorted mooncakes. John's parents own a bakery in San Francisco, famous for their mooncakes.

I continue singing in chorus from the fifth through the sixth grade. Mrs. Lawton, a middle-aged chorus teacher, is passionate about singing. She prepares us to sing for different events such as Christmas and Spring assemblies at Castelar.

The chorus stands on a wooden platform at a singing event in Chinatown, singing "The Happy Wander," first stanza goes: **[Ch. 14:2]**

I love to go a-wandering
Along the mountain track
And as I go, I love to sing
My knapsack on my back
Val-deri, val-dera
Val-deri, val-dera,
Ha, ha, ha, ha, ha, ha ha
Val-dera
My knapsack on my back

During our singing event, I mistakenly sing "val-deri" at the wrong time when everyone isn't singing. I'm incredibly embarrassed, cringing inside. Fortunately, it seems that nobody noticed. My voice didn't carry far enough outdoors. Whew! **[Ch. 14:3]**

The biggest and most exciting event is singing one evening with all the chorus students from the Los Angeles Unified School District's participating elementary schools. We all sing on stage at the Music Center in downtown Los Angeles at Christmas.

On two occasions, I came across two boys who were former classmates from the fifth grade during the school year. One time, Paul notices me walking upstairs with another friend about 10 feet behind him. He stumbles a few times while uncontrollably climbing the stairs, glancing back and forth at me. He looks nervous. How annoying.

And whenever Willie sees me, he backs away from me and says, "too close, too close." Again, how stupid and weird. How annoying.

Walking home from school, I see Willie following me, ducking and hiding behind Alpine playground benches. How annoying. I'm a serious kid. I don't like silliness. What's their problem?

On reflection, I didn't recognize that Willie and Paul had a crush on me when they reacted in strange ways when I was around them. Instead, I felt annoyed by their obnoxious antics.

At home one morning, I overhear my Daddy telling my Mommy at the breakfast table about an experience he had while driving to work at the Dragon Pearl restaurant in Highland Park. The highway patrol pulled him over. Once the patrol officer comes to the driver's side of the vehicle, he says,

"Sir, do you know you were speeding?"

"Oh, I don't know," speaking with a Chinese accent.

"I need to see your driver's license, sir."

"Oh, all ligh," my Dad nods while looking in his wallet and pulling it out for the officer to see.

The officer takes it, checks the license, and looks at my Dad. The officer proceeds to walk around his vehicle, kicking each tire. He returns to my Dad.

"Mr. Fong, your tires need checking. They are over-inflated," the patrol officer says.

"Oh, all ligh."

"Mr. Fong, I'm going to let you go. But I need you to check your tires, ok?"

"Oh, all ligh," my Dad gratefully nods repeatedly.

The officer hands my Dad's license back to him.

"Drive carefully, Mr. Fong. Remember to check your tires."

"All ligh. Thank you."

"Thank you."

My Daddy expressively tells the story to my Mommy in Cantonese. He was worried at first and was so happy that the officer let him go. My Daddy feels the officer is a kind man.

My Daddy repeatedly says, "Ho choy!" while slapping his legs, smiling, and shaking his head, looking so relieved that he didn't get a ticket. My Mommy listens intensely to every moment of the story.

Too, she smiles and looks relieved by saying, *"Ho choy!"* meaning, "good lucky thing!"

In hindsight, the officer, indeed, is a kind man. I'm sure he looked at my Daddy and saw a thin, small-framed man with protruding high cheekbones and sunken cheeks. The officer knows my Daddy is an immigrant who didn't speak English well and didn't have money to spare to pay for a ticket.

Later that year, I hear my Daddy arguing with Leland not to go to law school after graduating from USC. My Daddy doesn't want Leland to go to Law School because he thinks it requires too much *"kno jup,"* metaphorically "brain juice," meaning in conversational Cantonese, too much thinking, and sleepless nights. Even when Leland has a full scholarship to USC law school, my Daddy is against it. I think that Leland would make a good lawyer. He's an excellent student and makes sound arguments.

However, Leland attends USC law school and completes his first year. Afterwards, he decides not to pursue a law degree because he says he doesn't want to do so much paperwork required in the career.

In the summer, Leland works as a youth program coordinator for the Neighborhood Youth Center, also known as NYC, in Chinatown, Los Angeles. Many Chinese American students living in Chinatown and nearby vicinities also participate in the NYC program. Leland introduces me to two sisters, Pauline and Roseanne, active NYC participants. They teach me Chinese folk dancing, like the ribbon and fan dances.

I volunteer to perform the fan dance at the school assembly at Castelar in celebration of the Chinese New Year. I wear a Chinese red top, black pants, and hair in two little buns above my ears.

At the school assembly, traditional Chinese music begins. I walk swiftly in a big circle on stage with my waist and upper torso twisted to one side while holding my fan in one hand, covering my face, and the other hand extending horizontally to my side. I'm in nature, playing the role of a girl trying to catch a butterfly.

I make several attempts to catch the butterfly, and finally, I catch one, then I show it to the audience. Then the curtain drops down.

One evening, my Daddy does not arrive home at his usual time of 10 pm from the restaurant. It gets later and later toward midnight, and he has not yet returned home. Finally, we receive a phone call that our Dad was in a car accident, but he is all right.

An hour later, a knock resounds on our apartment door. Our Dad arrives home but on a stretcher. The paramedics bring my Daddy into my parents' bedroom and place him in his bed.

My Mommy, Jason, and I stand around my Daddy. He shows his tongue where he bit about a half-inch on both sides with his upper and lower teeth upon impact. My Daddy explains later that a stalled car was in the first lane on the narrow and curvy lanes of the Old Pasadena Freeway. My Daddy had slammed into the stalled car in the moonlight darkness. My Daddy, otherwise, is not physically hurt elsewhere.

According to the lunar calendar, the Dragon Boat Festival is celebrated between late May and mid-June in the springtime. Many Chinese people eat *zongzi,* similar to tamales, but rice is the outer layer wrapped in large banana leaves folded and tied with string to boil them. Typically, Chinese sausage, beef, pork, or chicken are inside each zongzi, along with Chinese mushrooms, peanuts, preserved egg yolk, and other varieties. This is a story about the Dragon Boat Festival. **[Ch. 14:4]**

Today is the last day of my sixth grade at Castelar. There's no graduation ceremony and no party. Summertime will come in a matter of hours. In the final minutes, Mrs. Austin sits in front of the class. She says she will call our names to come up to receive our last report cards. The students quietly sit at their desks. I hear my name called and walk to the front of the class to pick up my report card.

At my desk, I glance at my grades from top to bottom in two columns. I can't believe my eyes. I received all "G's." This is the best letter grade a student can receive. I close my grade report and lookup. One of my friends at another table looks at me, wondering how I did.

I use my right index finger to draw a "G" in the air and then strike two lines to indicate two columns. Mrs. Austin continues to call students names.

Sitting quietly, I peek at my grade report again. At the bottom of the grade report, Mrs. Austin has written, "Do as well in junior high as you have at Castelar, Mary." Wow, I'm not expecting a grade report like this.

Leland is working again as a *Teen Post* coordinator this summer through a government-funded youth program in Chinatown. I'm there one-day visiting, and my brother introduces me to other college workers at *Teen Post.*

One Chinese gal says, "I heard you got all A's on your report card."

"Who told you that?" I say sternly.

The gal did not expect a questioning reaction to her attempt to engage in small talk pleasantries. Report cards are personal and only shared within my inner circle. I naturally value modesty and not showing off, so I reacted in that manner to a gal who was merely trying to develop a rapport with me.

Chapter 15: More of Karl's Childhood Memories

When I'm 10, there's a boy who thinks he's great at everything. I don't like him bragging. He tells me that I'm nothing. I feel frustrated with this kid. I don't like him bragging. He tells me that I'm nothing. I feel frustrated with this kid. I blame him for my problem, push him, and he falls.

I don't push him hard, but he falls on his butt. He starts crying like a baby. It's funny. So, he tells the teacher about me. The teacher sends me to the principal. He asks why I did what I did. I can't tell him the truth. I can't, so I start lying to make up a reason. The principal sees that I am making up a story.

I'm not a good liar. I can't do it; it's hard for me. The principal feels I have some frustrations, so he gives me a break. I understand that working out my frustrations on some other kid isn't the right way. I don't like that I hurt somebody. I realize that I have the power to harm another person. I have to lie to get myself out of trouble.

I realize that negativity breeds negativity; this doesn't solve anything. I get myself in trouble. My parents don't yell at me. They can see that I am very regretful. They can see that I am suffering from what I had done and believe it somehow or in form. I never physically attack anyone else after that.

As human beings project their frustrations onto people, the only one you're hurting is yourself. At that moment, I'm hurting myself, too. I get in double trouble and feel bad about what I have done. I'll tell him off, but I allow my anger energy to come out. I'm startled at a young age that I was able to hurt someone physically.

I have a close connection to the source. Whenever I feel I've hurt someone, I get punished for it. I feel the hurt twice as much and realized that at a young age. It helps me understand that humans can be very impulsive as I grow up. People do things without thinking. After that, I think a little bit more about something before acting on it.

My parents were born and raised in Japan. They make it a point that I attend a Japanese school for ten years. I'm not crazy about attending a Japanese school because it's very strict and has routines to discipline the students. The rules and regulations are too restrictive, but I have no choice. I have to go to a Japanese school. My parents want their children to learn discipline, Japanese heritage, and the Japanese language. They want us to remember where we came from and who we are.

I like hearing all about the Japanese heroes and historical figures that the Japanese people preserve. To this day, they worship the Samurais or Emperors. Japan was divided into all different provinces a long time ago. One of my favorite rulers is Queen Himiko. She's very connected to the Gods and the spirits.

When her father passes, she becomes the ruler who unifies a big part of Japan. She brought all the provinces together, which is pretty cool. She talked to spirits and based her ruling on these spirit conversations. People adored her because she unified the people. Many of our historical figures are samurais who killed tons of people to try and rule.

We still love them, and we put them on this pedestal. However, she didn't kill anyone. Instead, she unified people. Himiko kept everything together with the vision of love, connection, compassion, and messages from beyond. I think that is very cool. She increased the trade between all these different kinds of groups.

She never married and had a family because of her connection with the Gods. She is considered a spiritual person, so having a family wasn't in the cards for her. She died of an illness. After Himiko's passing, unfortunately, men took over, and the whole shit fell again, and Japan returned to fighting.

I have always been very interested in spirituality. Regarding religion, I'm creating my own as I go because I'm not happy with this and that. However, I always knew that something more significant and magical makes everything live and gives everything life.

As a kid, I like comic books. There is always a hero, a

supervillain, and a super guy. As a little boy, if I asked the Gods, they would give me superpowers if I asked long enough. Of course, I never do achieve superpowers.

Chapter 16: Mary's Nightingale Jr. High Years

In the seventh grade, Terry and I are in the same English class. Everyone in our English class comes from another elementary school. I don't feel right in this class. I think I'm in a slower-paced group. I convince Terry to go with me to see a counselor, Mrs. Jew. We ask Mrs. Jew if we can switch to another English class.

I also voice my dismay about the Math class. Our Math teacher, Mr. Brown, taught us nothing. He only gives us math problems to do in the textbook, and we work at our desks while Mr. Brown sits in front of the class, sleeping for the entire class period until we turn in our course work.

Terry feels uncertain if she wants to go into the English class designated a gifted class during this time. We hear that Tran is in the gifted class in English. It doesn't make sense because English is a second language for Tran, and she is not fluent in English. She came from Vietnam about three years ago. **[Ch.16:1]**

I say to Terry in a private conversation, "Look, Terry, you can do it. If Tran can do it, you can do it, too. Your English is better than hers." I encourage Terry to transfer to another English class. My purpose is not to put Tran down. There is no reason to do that.

During my first semester in the seventh grade, I'm thinking, why can't all students have the same quality education and be taught the same educational material? Students are capable of learning if both teachers and students work together. I feel like I'm in a "less than" classified student class when I do not perceive myself as such. I request a transfer to the advanced English class.

Reflecting today on the sixth grade, I scored low on one section of a state standardized test. I scored a fourth-grade level in reading when I was in the sixth grade. My low score is due to my reading pace. I'm a slow reader, meaning I like to take my time, read the contents and extrapolate the meaning of the words. I process words slowly, wanting to feel and "get into" the message.

I'm a reflective and contemplative thinker. As a slow reader, I cannot finish answering all the questions after the excerpts of readings in the allotted time. Consequently, I have a lower score. However, this does not mean I'm not capable of answering the reading questions correctly. It doesn't mean I can't comprehend the material. Because my reading rate is less than average doesn't mean I'm less intelligent.

People have different propensities. For example, some people are fast eaters. They may not chew their food as much and swallow quickly. I happen to be a slow eater. I like to take my time, chew my food thoroughly, enjoy the taste of my food, and then swallow. What's the rush? Other times I am quick, such as mechanical and non-thinking activities such as repetitive motions like running, jump roping, typing, and other bodily movement.

In other subjects, my scores were better as a sixth-grader. In the Math section, I scored at the sixth-grade level. Spelling is 13th level, and I figure it means college level, and my English section is ninth-grade level. I believe that my low reading test score prevents placement in the gifted English class.

It is very atypical of me to share my test scores with people because I think it is a private matter. I don't want others to categorize or judge me, but I would like others to see me for who I am.

However, I want to make an essential point that these standardized tests are "cookie cutters" to determine which students fit in the cookie-cutter created by members of an education committee. Members of a standardized test committee most likely are not representative of the diversity of students. That is, they have a limited capacity to understand the variations of test-takers actual abilities. I question if the committee members understand the various students' socio-cultural and economic backgrounds, world-views, exposure to life situations, and limited educational influences that are not mainstream.

Committee members create standardized test questions from their socio-cultural, economic, and educational backgrounds that might likely differ from the contrary. We understand that school districts are not equal in the budget, academic quality, and extra-curricular opportunities. That is why standardized tests have a cultural bias that favors students with a similar lifestyle to "mainstream" committee members. The committee designs the tests and makes arbitrary rules and decisions on content, types of questions, and how much time students have to complete a section of an examination.

On what basis are 30 minutes given for one test, rather than 40 minutes? Is 10 minutes more for test-taking considered wrong or "less than?" Or is 30 minutes allocated because it is arbitrarily convenient because it is half an hour on a clock? Why not designate 20 minutes to take a section of the test instead? Wouldn't that be better or superior? I'm not talking about giving someone several more hours to complete the standardized test. What is reasonable and fair?

What is the point of making test-takers speed through an analysis, which might not be their normal pace in handling tasks? Remember the expression, "Haste makes waste?" There's no rhyme or reason. These standardized tests are not predictors or accurate assessments of a student's academic performance or competency.

A culturally biased test means there are questions in which a student lacks exposure to a particular life situation, information, or a "mainstream" way of conceptualizing the topic. Therefore, it is not likely the test-taker can answer the questions accurately and will use more test time. It does not necessarily mean that one student is more intelligent than the other who did not have the opportunity to be exposed to the information.

Who defines a person's intelligence and pigeonholes them into various categories, labeling them something in a narrow and simplistic method? These educators and standardized test scores are the authorities with inherent flaws in the assessment that conveniently determines students' class placement, learning, admissions, and opportunities. Today, some universities are aware of the mentioned concerns and have implemented ways to address the issues in their decision-making, provide options, and so forth.

Mrs. Jew transfers me into the advanced English class because of my expressed educational concern, and my sixth-grade report card shows I can handle the material. Mrs. Jew also moves me to a Pre-Algebra class because I complained about Mr. Brown's lack of teaching.

To the best of my ability, I would not allow someone other than myself to determine my success or failure. I would not allow someone else to impede my progress and pigeonhole me to be someone I'm not. Being my authentic self has always been important to me. I cannot tolerate fakeness within me and in others. I'm still enthusiastic about doing my best. I like learning, growing, and expanding.

A week later, a group of girls I socialize with is quiet toward me during recess. I hear through the gossip grapevine that word is out that I made a negative comment about Tran. Donna says, "We know you made a negative comment about Tran. I don't think that was right of you to say that. It was not nice.

I don't know what to say to this unexpected comment. I have to think about what I said. I don't say anything to Donna. Donna has this judgmental attitude toward me that I was so wrong about what I said about Tran. Donna is also known to be stubborn, somewhat temperamental, and has a haughty demeanor that she is the smartest. I'm naïve and don't even think about who could have spread this rumor.

Mrs. Jew places Terry and me in the gifted English class in the following weeks. I enter the Pre-Algebra class, and sitting in the front row is Tran. I have to walk by her every morning, and her body language shows that she feels hurt and ignores me. Finally, after a few days, I stop by her desk and say to her, "I'm sorry, Tran, but that is not what I meant." She turns her body away and says nothing.

Donna's judgment and some girls' silence ostracize me. Donna judges me, and rumor travels around and back to Tran. I ask, why would someone want to distort what I said, and whoever went and told Tran? What good does that do? Except to make me look bad. Never assume and judge someone based on hearsay and not having the insider's view. Otherwise, negative attitudes, thoughts, and actions are harmful based on misperceptions, inaccuracies, and assumptions to victimize others.

I'm feeling the negative vibes, and I feel misunderstood. I don't know how Tran heard. I don't ask around. I don't know why I don't suspect Terry. She is the only one I told in private. My intentions are reasonable and supportive of Terry that she can handle the advanced English class. Sometimes, Terry tends to say things without thinking about what comes out of her mouth. She can be pretty blunt sometimes, and perhaps she misconstrued my intentions toward her. What Terry had said to the girls might have been misinterpreted and judged as wrong in what I said.

Tran is not in our social group, so it doesn't make sense why those girls seem to defend Tran and become critical of me. I honestly feel misunderstood and judged. The negative energy that I feel affects me. I begin sleepwalking now and then in junior high school. Since elementary and junior high school, I have nightmares of someone chasing me.

One evening, I get out of bed, walk outside my bedroom, and open my parents' bedroom late at night. Then I realized what I had done and closed their bedroom door.

Another night, I'm walking in my sleep. My brother told me I walked to the kitchen where my Mommy was working. She calls my name, and I don't respond. I'm walking like a zombie with a glassy eye-look. Then I walk to a chair and sit down.

Jason and my Mommy come over, wondering what I'm doing. They both call my name, "Mary, Mary, are you alright?"

Abruptly, I jump up, fling my hands and arms directly in front of me, and shout some sound. Both reactively jump back, not knowing what is going on with me. They both guide me back to my bed.

I vaguely remember sleepwalking. The next day, I vaguely sense that jolted move of shooting my hands and arms abruptly with an incomprehensible sound. Jason describes the rest of this incident to me the next day and exclaims, "You scared the living daylights out of us.

During the seventh grade, I begin menstruating. **[Ch.16:2].** I'm sitting at the kitchen table early on Saturday, getting organized in my Pre-Algebra class and creating my folder. I start feeling nauseous. I get up and pour myself a cup of cold orange juice. After taking a few sips of orange juice, I'm still not feeling well. Drinking orange juice doesn't help.

Instead, I feel chills all over my body, and I'm still not feeling well. I don't vomit. It's probably due to menstruating and the fluctuation of my hormones.

I have four bicuspid teeth extracted to wear braces in the spring semester. The orthodontist recommends wearing braces for two and a half years. Three classmates are wearing braces, too. My two older brothers don't need braces. They both have straight and nicely shaped teeth.

I complete the seventh grade, and summer arrives, taking classes at Nightingale Junior High. I'm learning to play basketball and joining the Chinatown girls' basketball league at Alpine playground for summer fun.

Sharon Lee is a new friend, meeting on the same basketball team. She is two years older, attending Belmont high school that summer before tenth grade. The other team players include Susan, who plays center, Tammy, who plays right guard, and Carol, right forward. I play left guard, and Sharon plays left forward. Our team is called the Columbians, named after our sponsor, Columbus Pharmacy, the only pharmacy in Chinatown. All of us are beginning learners of basketball.

Our initial coach, Sam Louie, says to me, "You're going to start the game." I don't know what that means. I'm guessing it means I will throw the ball onto the court to my team member to start the game. I don't recall him explaining the rules of the game. I find out eventually that I'm one of five girls from our team to start the game. **[Ch.16:]**

The next day, our new coaches introduce themselves to the team players. Both of them are at least six feet tall. Scott Yee is buff with black wavy hair, sometimes wearing a short ponytail. He also uses his fingers to pull his hair behind his ears out of habit most of the time. He's a third-generation Chinese American who recently graduated from Cal State University, Los Angeles, and used to be the quarterback of Eagle Rock high school.

Wayne Mar is lanky tall with a rice bowl haircut and is analytically intellectual. He is a second-generation Chinese American who recently graduated from Yale University. He has this habit of shaking one of his knees while standing and talking with one arm positioned horizontally across his waist, holding his other elbow with his arm vertical resting his chin on his hand.

We have our first game as beginners in the summer basketball league in Chinatown. Our team extends our hands to the center of our huddle and yell, "Columbians!" The starters walk on the court wearing beige t-shirts with Columbians and our numbers, black shorts, tennis shoes, and ponytails.

We play our hearts out! We're running up and down the court, shooting, passing, rebounding, and playing defense. What a disaster, our team is wiped out, losing 24-4! How dreadful. Scott and Wayne remain cool. I don't dare look at their faces.

After the game, we walk across the street, looking exhausted with our hand towels around our necks and our heads looking down. The team enters *Snoopy's Café.* We sit at the front counter on swivel bar stools, looking tired and defeated. Our coaches treat us to a soda. We sit there quietly, sipping our drink, slowly replenishing the life back into us.

The following week, we return to practice. We practice five days a week at 4 p.m. for a couple of hours at Alpine Playground.

In our third game, and as usual, we run back and forth, up and down the court from one end of the basket to the other. The ball bounces toward me. I grab it and shoot it up quickly and score!

Carol runs up to me, grabs both of my shoulders, and only inches away from my face, shouts, "No! You shot it in the wrong basket!"

I'm stunned, standing there with my eyes wide open, eyebrows raised, and contorting my lips. Oops! On top of that, I'm at the free-throw line thirteen times, not making a single free throw. Oops! I need to practice my free throws. After that ultimate fiasco, believe it or not, our team eventually gets better through trial and error. After every game, win or lose, our coaches treat us to a soda across the street at *Snoopy's Café.*

Scott and Wayne never yelled at us, and they are cool guys. They are generous to give us a ride home when we need it. Wayne drives an old grey VW bug, and Scott drives a silver pinto. They are pretty nice to put up with 13 to 17-year-old girls.

Sharon comes to my place, and we decide to play a prank on Wayne. I tell him I can't make it to practice because I'm calling long distance from Vegas. His speech rate starts increasing. I emphasize that I'm calling long distance, and he talks faster and faster.

I can't keep up with my pretended act and start laughing. I tell him that Sharon and I are fooling around with him. There's a long pause. Wayne feels duped. We can't help chuckling on our end. After the call, Sharon and I burst out laughing more at our devious prank. Our coaches have to put up with us. **[Ch 16:3A]**

At the end of the season, both of our coaches treat us to *Farrell's* ice cream parlor. They place an order for the Zoo. Fifteen minutes later, we hear a siren blasting in the shop. We turn our heads to see two Farrell servers scurrying through the parlor, holding onto the wooden handles of a stretcher with a large metal bowl in the center. The two servers, dressed in red and white striped shirts with red aprons, lower the stretcher at our table.

Team members gaze at this incredible display of assorted ice cream flavors and colorful plastic zoo animals hanging on the bowl's metal rim. The Zoo has vanilla, strawberry, chocolate, orange sherbet, rocky road, and chocolate chip. Cute, assorted plastic animals like monkeys, elephants, rhinos, giraffes, tigers, lions, and zebras are hanging on the bowl rim. Our eyes widen, peering at the Zoo and glancing at each other with smiles.

Wow, we've never seen anything like this before. We "pig out" on the Zoo. What an amazing treat! Thanks, Coaches!

The eighth grade starts, and I'm in the classes amongst peers I know. I sense competition in the air, and I don't like the feeling. It creates stress and a lack of togetherness and support.

It takes the fun and focus of doing and experiencing life. At this realization, I denounce engaging in competition. Instead, I choose to do the best of my ability and not accomplish something for perfection or focus on winning and beating the competition to feel good about myself. With this realized orientation, I no longer put pressure on myself. Thus, giving me a sense of peace and a newfound focus that feels right.

I'm an "A" student in all my classes except math. I do fine in pre-Algebra in the seventh grade. However, I'm finding that I'm not doing very well in Algebra I. I don't understand why. I don't find Algebra I to be meaningful or purposeful. I feel, what's the point in doing these math problems? How do these algebraic formulae and solving these algebra problems relate to me and life in general?

Perhaps it's my attitude and lack of meaningful connection to Algebra. I find it boring, which probably affects how I'm not learning. I make no effort to study at home. I show up in class and wallow in confusion and my mediocre performance.

In the fall semester of my eighth-grade year, the Columbians joined with a few other team members called the Sunkist. Falcons is our new team name, and we are more competitive because of Lisa Kwong, a sharpshooter as our right guard, and Nancy Kong is tall and plays aggressively as our center.

A few of the girls on the basketball team have a crush on Scott. One of the gals also has a liking toward Wayne. I'm the youngest, a 13-year-old who has no crush on either. Besides, they are ten plus years older. I'm a little punk.

As a team, we like to play practical jokes on our coaches. Before the game starts, we huddle together and cheer, "Falcons!" Immediately afterwards, we take off our sweatshirts on the sidelines. Five Falcon starters wearing our new yellow t-shirts walk to the court's center to begin the game.

Our new yellow t-shirts across the front of our chest read, "Scotties." Scott looks at the starters and then the bench and can't believe our new t-shirts say, Scotties. Scott's face looks like, "You got to be kidding," He shakes his head with his hands over his face as he sits down.

Team members smile broadly, cracking up when we see Scott's reaction. He continues to cover his eyes and face with his hands. He says nothing and maintains his composure. Wayne sits next to Scott and pats him on the back while grinning. Our team has a good laugh! **[16:3B]**

Even though our team's name is Falcons, we continue to wear our yellow Scotties t-shirts for the rest of the season. Not once do I hear Scott comment. The look on his face says it all. He's probably thinking, "Those little devils."

At one of our practices, I become upset during a scrimmage with our coaches and team members. Wayne pats us on the butts. I'm perturbed at him. It's inappropriate for Wayne to pat us on the butt.

I don't come to the next practice. Sharon tells me over the phone that they had a team meeting. She says Scott told the team that Mary is sensitive, so we have to be careful around her. We don't want her to quit. I come to the next practice, and the coaches figured out I didn't like the patting on the butt ritual that guys do with other guys on the basketball court for support.

In the early spring semester of the eighth grade, my family moves eastward from Chinatown, LA, to Highland Park, next door to South Pasadena. It is about the same distance by bus as attending Nightingale junior high school when I lived in Chinatown. Our home in Highland Park is a beautiful two-story home with four large pillars on the front porch. It is a three-bedroom and 1 1/4 bath with two avocado trees in the backyard.

I continue to attend Nightingale enjoying a summer class playing the guitar. Last year, Leland had bought me a rosewood classical guitar. I begin learning chords, strumming, and fingerpicking on the guitar strings while singing.

Mrs. Allen teaches us the different chords and a few strumming styles; the fanciest strum is the calypso. Since Grace moved away, I haven't seen her since the fifth grade. Grace and Ruby were the girls who invited me to stroll around the playground when I first attended Castelar. It's good to see her in the guitar class.

In the afternoon after my summer classes, I'm a paid participant of the Chinatown Youth Council (CYC), funded by the government. Leland is the social worker and coordinator at Chinatown Teen Post. He plays his guitar in the weekly *Teen Post* Coffee House. Also, he coordinates the Theatre Arts workshop. Along with a group of fifteen junior high and high school students, Sharon and I meet at the *East-West Players* Playhouse on Santa Monica Boulevard. We have acting classes with this professional group of Asian American television and movie actors. In the 1970s, Asian American acting jobs are far and few.

At the *East-West Players* Playhouse, we have activities like articulation. We practice saying: red leather, yellow leather, red leather, yellow leather. We have tongue twisters like: Around the rugged rock ran the rascal ran. How many sheets can a sheet slitter slit, if a sheet slitter could slit sheets? We would increase our rate with all of these phrases while maintaining our articulation. After a while, it gets boring because of redundancy. However, it does improve our articulation.

We also rest on the floor while one acting teacher describes different scenarios to elicit various emotional states. We engage in trust exercises in each participant have to trust the group members to take care of one's well-being. For example, one person in each group lies down on the floor while the rest of the group members lift the person high above their heads and walk around the large room.

Another trust exercise involves a person standing on a chair and falling forward or backwards with a stiff body while group members catch the person. These trust exercises teach confidence and trust in the other actors when performing together on stage. Both actors learn to be aware and responsible for helping each other when necessary, such as an actor forgetting a line or being out of position on stage. Other activities are singing and practicing a variety of skits.

Summer is over; I'm in my final year at Nightingale Junior High. I continue taking classes with familiar peers. I continue to do fine in all my courses, except for Geometry. I don't study at home. I go to class, barely passing Geometry. **[Ch.16:4]**

Eating is never a priority for me. When my Mommy returns to waitressing, no one is at home to make dinner. My upbringing conditions me not to eat much, so I eat enough to rid my growling stomach but never eat until I'm full. Sometimes, when I go to bed, my stomach growls. I don't know how to cook. Sometimes, I bike down to Figueroa Street to the *Der Wienerschnitzel* to buy a corn dog and then drop by *See's Candies* on my way back.

The 1970s and 1980s offered TV shows that I enjoyed watching. Here are some of my favorites: Sonny & Cher Variety Show, The Brady Bunch, Welcome Back Kotter, Mary Tyler Moore, The Partridge Family, Happy Days, Three's Company, Barney Miller, Charlie Angels, Here's Lucy, Kung Fu, Love Boat, M*A*S*H, Mork & Mindy, Cheers, Family Ties, Love & Marriage, Taxi, Who's the Boss? Donny & Marie Variety Show. **[Ch.16:5 – Ch.16:24].**

In the third week of September, I feel so sad hearing about the death of one of my favorite musical artists, Jim Croce, and his fellow musician, Maury Muehleisen, and four others who perished in an airplane crash. Jim Croce was only 30 years old. The feeling of loss, a nonexistent life, is hard to fathom.

I spend the entire weekend listening to his two albums on a record player in the living room. His original lyrical songs and the guitar fingerpicking sounds bring Jim Croce alive. He is an absolute musical genius and storyteller who lived unpretentiously with humor and a knack for catchy words. Hearing his voice and musicality touches my sorrowful heart and brings chills now and then while listening to his music this weekend.

I miss the real down-to-earth Jim Croce, who I consider to be one of the best lyricists because of his storytelling, vividness, characterizations, and heartfelt authenticity in reflecting on life. Although I enjoy every single song he created, my favorite songs are: **[Ch.16:25 - Ch.16:27]**

One early evening, I see through the breakfast nook window a man in a suit carrying a briefcase walking up our driveway. I walk to the laundry room back door to watch him. Suddenly, he appears at the back door, trying to turn the doorknob. He sees me. I see him.

"Open the door," he says,

"Get out of here!" I yell as I wave my hand abruptly at him while giving him an ugly, fierce face.

"Open the door," he says in a commanding tone.

"Get out of here!" I shout while displaying the same aggressive, ugly gesture.

He looks at me and walks back onto the driveway, turning right onto the sidewalk. That night when my parents arrived home close to 10:00, I tell them what had happened.

Within weeks, my parents arrived home after work with a huge box and placed it in the kitchen. I look in the large box, and to my surprise, I see a puppy! Our family never talked about having a dog. I become the puppy's primary caretaker. I name her Trojan after my favorite sports team, the USC Trojans.

I'm a bit afraid of Trojan because I have never had a dog before or been around a dog. Trojan is a German Shepherd puppy with floppy ears. She barks and whines behind the laundry room door in the early morning hours.

I go downstairs and let her out into the kitchen. I sleep on the kitchen nook booth while she sleeps next to me to keep her from making noise, waking up the household. Then sometimes, I let her stay in the kitchen if I can't coax her back into the laundry room before going to school.

Trojan and I nap almost every day together. She sleeps on my bed and usually hogs it up. I nudge her with my foot, saying, "Hey, stop hogging up the bed, move over." Then she moves over a bit. In the photo, I'm with Trojan and also wearing my "Scotties" yellow t-shirt. **[Ch.16:28]**

Returning home from school, I sneak into the house quietly to see if Trojan notices me. Usually, she sleeps on the couch. As I tiptoe upstairs, she hears me and comes running up the stairs with me.

She is so happy whenever I come home, climbing the staircase with me to my room. Trojan wags her tail like crazy. I put my books on my bed, and she jumps up and down on her hind legs while I hold her front paws on my lap. We bounce up and down together with much joy.

Every weekend morning, I play hide and seek in the house with Trojan when I wake up. She goes from room to room, sniffing for me. When she discovers me, she sits there, wagging her tail, and sees me through the crack in the door where I'm hiding. Finally, I pet her, and she follows me around the house. I walk her on weekends to the nearby Arroyo Seco Park, about two long blocks from our home.

My parents bring leftover restaurant food like chow mein, fried rice, and spare rib bones. Trojan is the first German Shepherd I know that eats Chinese food. Now, that's a lucky dog! She's an excellent watchdog, too. Every day, she barks ferociously at the mailman who slips our letters through the door slot.

During my ninth-grade year, I hear that Scott, our former basketball coach, is engaged. He invites our basketball team to his wedding and enjoyable fiesta with a lively mariachi band, good company, and delicious food. I'm attending my first wedding ceremony. Scott is kind and thoughtful in inviting us to share his happiness on a momentous day in his life.

Scott becomes an elementary school teacher. Wayne goes to

USC law school and becomes a lawyer in Northern California. They are both kind, thoughtful, and cool coaches. Thanks for putting up with us, especially me! **[Ch.16:29]**

In the mid-spring semester of ninth grade, the eighth-grade girls in Mr. Jong's Algebra I class challenge the ninth-grade girls in Mr. Owen's Geometry class. The eighth-grade girls have at least two girls in the Chinatown basketball league. As for the ninth-grade girls, I'm the only one who plays in the Chinatown basketball league. So, we have a friendly competition.

I hit two big shots, this time in the right basket! The ninth-grade girls lose. However, it's not by a sizable margin. Afterwards, I enter Nightingale's annual spring track-and-field competition to run the 50-yard dash. I come in first. **[Ch.16:30]**

During the late spring semester, I'm walking in front of the school lawn, and a thought flashes in my mind that I'm going to write a book for a broad audience someday. I don't think twice about the spontaneous idea that popped into my mind. I have no clue what kind of a book. The thought flashes at the conscious level for a split second, and then it subsides in my subconscious.

In the spring semester, I audition to be a commencement speaker at our upcoming graduation in June. I am one of three speakers who have been selected. The other two speakers speak in Spanish and Chinese. I speak English. We each write our graduation speech. My graduation theme is our class motto as Conquistadores, "We came, we conquered, and we ruled."

My parents aren't able to come to my graduation because they are working, but Leland comes to graduation. After the ceremony, my homeroom teacher, Ms. Watcher asks, "Did you write your speech?"

"Yes," I nod.

"It's good," she says enthusiastically.

I smile.

Chapter 17: Karl's Virgil Jr. High Years

I'm about 12 and think that I'm "it." I'm like, "OMG. I'm growing up. I'm getting older; look at me. I'm all cool and stuff. I'm already starting to act cooler by hanging out with the guys. I have the illusion that I already know everything. Boys have that illusion at 12.

There's a girl that lives down the street. We're the same age, but we go to different schools. She goes to a private school. I only see her on the weekends. She is pretty, and she catches my eye. I have a crush on her.

She's very confident, knows what she's doing, and has her act together. I find that attractive. This creates a wall between us, challenging me to climb over to get to her. Whenever guys have a challenge, it's more exciting to get to that point where she goes, "Okay, yeah, I'll go out with you."

So, the bigger the challenge, the more exciting it gets, physically and emotionally. However, it doesn't do much for me if a girl is easy or throws herself at me. There needs to be a hunt. There needs to be a chase, which is instinctive of the human body. It's a natural reaction where all these hormones start to work, and your adrenaline starts pumping. It's a physical reaction. So, this neighborhood gal is a little bit out of my league. There's the attraction, and she is gorgeous.

I sneak up on Gary and check out how he communicates with gals. I notice that he always does some touch. He slightly touches her shoulder or her hand.

I'm thinking about what I would say and do and how to respond when talking with her. What am I going to wear? I overthink how I'm going to approach her. I over-analyze everything.

I go by her house. I blow the whole thing as soon as I stand before her. My mind goes completely blank. I look at her, completely blowing it. She looks at me like, "You're weird." She walks off.

At that moment, I feel, "Oh my god, what if I can't talk to girls?" My insecurities about talking to girls start kicking in. From this failed attempt, I start thinking of different ways to get attention. Talking to females always seems complicated because I don't know what to say. Every time I say something, it seems to be the wrong thing, or they look at me funny. I give up on trying to communicate with gals. Instead, I try to get their attention in different ways.

As I've mentioned, growing up at home is restricting. My Dad is always the boss, and everyone in the family has to do what he says. All the children have to adjust to how he sees things. We have to make sure we fit in, and we have to make sure that he is pleased in some way. I always want my parents to be proud of me. I still have this urge to please them to be recognized. We want to be seen and our parents to praise us.

I feel my Mom understands me. She sees me for who I am. I don't feel my father wants that kind of relationship with me.

When I'm 12 years old, my father got upset with me. I tend to forget my responsibilities. I forget, and that never sits well with my Dad, unfortunately. I remember him raising his voice, then raising his hand and striking me.

At that moment, we are all alone in a room. My free will is completely taken away; I'm terrified. I don't have control over the situation. My Dad takes the control out of my hands. You know, I love my Dad, and I still do. But it is scary. I realize that anybody can take away control of your life. Anybody can do something you don't want and can't do anything to stop it.

I feel ashamed that I had pushed my Dad to do something like that. I feel guilty. It is very confusing, with very conflicting emotions and thoughts. It makes me realize that life isn't as simple. I think life is just about having fun and getting to where I want.

Life isn't as easy as it looks. Relationships can be conflicting. I feel love for my Dad, but at the same time, I'm upset with him. At that moment, I hate my Dad. I hate him for it. It's an eye-opening experience to realize that everything is not just fun, shits, and giggles. Things can instantly go bad for something stupid.

The fact that I get punished so hard for not cleaning my room on time I think it's ridiculous. I'll never forget the face that my Dad made. He was shocked by what he had just done. I can still see the shock on his face. Like, oh my god, I just did that.

I don't talk to him for a week. That is my way of revolting. He never apologizes for what he did. Although he loves his family, he believes that the father figure is the leader and you need to obey. That's just how it is. It would help if you listened because he is too proud to admit that. He could say, "Hey, I might have gone too far. I'm sorry."

After that, there are times when we get along really well, and then there are moments when I don't want to deal with him. The relationship is up and down, but I never stop loving him. Over the years, I have had this kind of hate-love relationship. It's a great lesson on unconditional love, and that is a significant turning point for me to understand that people can do things you don't expect them to do and can somehow betray you. I feel like it is a betrayal. At that moment, I become much more careful with the people I hang out with and the people I surround myself with.

My Dad probably had a bad day, and unfortunately, he uses me to express that. It feels like a betrayal. Those moments can change a relationship. When it comes to raising children, at any time, parents think they are above their children, in charge of them, control their children, and decide what their children are doing in life and where they're going. Parents act like they own their children. Commands like, "You have to listen to me. I make the rules here," "You don't decide for you, I decide for you," and similar comments. In a way, we treat our children as property.

Hurtful words, like saying to your child, "You're too stupid," or a physical attack, can completely off balance a child. It can completely take children off track for the rest of their lives. That moment with my Dad is critical because it changes a few things in me.

Luckily, I'm strong enough to overcome it. There are people, however, who can't overcome it. Some people will be affected for the rest of their lives. My advice to parents is that when children come into your life, they are individuals and choose this life by themselves. You don't choose for them. They choose this life, and they selected you as a parent.

I would have liked my Dad to sit down with me, talk to me about responsibilities and explain to me what that is and the consequences at that moment when I'm twelve. I'm all about hanging out, having fun, and figuring out the world. I don't think about the consequences. A consequence, for instance, could have been, "Hey, I'm taking away your allowance," or "You're grounded, and you can't go do this favorite activity of yours for this long. I'm not mad at you, but hey, you didn't do your job or mistreated someone."

Every decision has an effect. For instance, you can't hang out with your friends for several weeks. I would have understood that because these are the consequences if I don't do this. I chose not to clean up my room; unfortunately, the consequences are on me. That means I'm responsible for them.

Instead, he doesn't give me an explanation, and he doesn't give me a choice or an insight. He takes away the respect that I have for him. That is the difference. Some people say, "Oh, talking to him doesn't work." Perhaps that parent never talked to their children from the beginning. Parents can do better, learn and practice new teaching methods, and guide their children compassionately and lovingly. The excuse that "Oh, I was raised that way" is more of a reason to change to a better method in which your children will love and respect you rather than create anger, fear, and confusion. It's basically about mutual respect also appreciating the child's opinion.

A child's view is rarely asked in any decision-making. Everything should be discussed as a family. Before my Dad decides, asking and considering everybody's view would provide an open and satisfying solution. Parents who always make the decisions expect the rest of the family to go with it.

So, showing interest in each other's opinions will make those children feel valued as individuals, and parents will give them the tools to find self-confidence and self-love. Children will feel their ideas count, contributing to the happiness of their family.

It's all about cooperation, understanding, and teamwork. It's not about being dominant over your children. Be aware of your ego.

Children need their parents to guide them, not to put restrictions on them or obligations or anything in that manner. It's about supporting and guiding your children, asking them if they can survive in this world. It's also about allowing them to have free will in what direction they want to go. Ask your children what their passions are, what they like doing, and what they want to contribute to life. Ask them what they want to be when they grow up and support them fully.

It's all about guidance and not about, "Oh, you need to be a doctor just like me," or "You need to be in my business," or "You need to be this," "Oh, don't do that, you'll never make enough money." No, it's about allowing them to make their own choices and supporting them as much as possible. That's what parenting is. It's not about controlling and disciplining your children. It's about teaching them to understand that everything has a consequence. Decisions that they make will eventually lead to their future. That's what it's about, giving that insight.

When I'm fourteen, I learn from Gary. He's able to get a female's attention. He uses the right words at the right time. I remember observing him with a group of his friends. He has a knack for talking, and everybody listens to him.

One day, he talks to this girl, and I'm learning and observing his interactions. He is so cool. He is a natural talker, and it just comes naturally to him. He isn't nervous at all. That surprises me because I always feel nervous around girls.

He has this ease in everything he says. Girls start giggling. I think, how does he do it? What does he say, and how does he say it?

I approach him afterwards and ask him, "how do you do it?"

"You have to pretend that you care about what they say at that moment," Gary says.

As I'm listening, I think I did try that. I try to be thoughtful. I try to ask questions.

"You have to talk about what they're interested in, and then they will feel good. Then you throw in a joke now and then. They'll love you," Gary explains.

Shortly after receiving Gary's sound advice, I'm at a carnival with a group of friends. I notice a girl keeps looking at me. I'm not so sure what to say to a girl. She doesn't go to the same school, so I'll be safe if anything goes wrong. So, I figure that this is the time to try out some of Gary's advice.

I walk up to her and ask her questions to engage in some talk. Every time she asks me a question, I wouldn't answer. Instead, I would keep responding with a question back.

"Why aren't you answering my questions?" she asks.

I'm speechless. It all blows up in my face. There is sudden silence between us.

"You're weird!" and walks off with her friends.

Everybody sees how she blows me off. I feel like a hundred eyes are staring at me. I stand there, and the carnival sounds fill the air. I destroyed that interaction.

After that catastrophic exchange, I walk around with my friends and review what had just happened in my mind. I feel embarrassed that she thinks I'm a weirdo. I'm so focused on asking her questions to show interest.

However, I take it to the point that she probably feels like I'm interrogating her. I come across like I'm an FBI interrogator, and she is a serial killer. I try to figure out where she will be and what she's going to do so that I can see her again. I blow that one!

After that dismal attempt, I decide not to take Gary's advice anymore. I decide to try different methods. I try getting attention, acting cool, and having friends talk to girls for me. I do get a lot of giggles. But nothing results in a serious relationship.

As far as females think, "Oh, the guys just have to walk up to me and ask." But it's tough for a guy to approach a gal. We feel very intimidated by them. I hate to say it, but when it comes to gals, they're unpredictable.

It's tough to predict the answer, and we don't see it. Every time I think, oh, I know she's going to say yes. It's going to be fine. She's been looking at me. I would get a "no," and I'm like, why are you always looking at me then? I would get upset. I don't interpret girls' signals very well.

It doesn't work that way, and again, it's because of that difference. Guys are thinking something else than a gal. There's this miscommunication in how we interpret female signals.

Finally, in the 7th grade, I have a girlfriend. It is a good learning experience in an intimate relationship with a total stranger at the beginning. We have our ups and downs and differences in our expectations. In time, we go our separate ways.

Over the years, I have learned to be true to myself. I decide to do what is best for me and see what happens. I stop trying to read women because I am not good at it.

None of my friends is good at it either. They always say, "Oh, that chick likes you. Oh, that chick likes you." Then it turns out she doesn't like me at all. So, it's hard as a young man, especially when you're still going through the hormone phase. You're still trying to figure out how women work. It's hard and scary to approach a female, and we never know what will happen.

Chapter 18: Crossing Paths at Belmont High School

No longer living in Chinatown, I travel quite a distance from Highland Park to downtown 1st Street, Los Angeles, every weekday to attend Belmont High School. It's a long one-hour two bus ride each way.

Jason is in his senior year, and I don't want to start over again, readapting like going to four elementary schools. I don't even consider going to Franklin High School, only 1.5 miles away. My home is 2.15 miles away from South Pasadena High. Belmont is 6.5 miles away, near downtown LA on Beverly Boulevard.

At least a handful of times during my three years of catching the bus across town, I fall asleep on the long public bus ride back home. Dozing on the bus with my head prop against the window, eventually, my mouth slightly opens while drooling from the side of my mouth.

"Hey, did you miss your stop?" someone calls out.

Waking up quickly, wiping the drool from my mouth and blinking while looking outside the bus window to make sense of the location. Jumping to my feet and realizing that I had passed my stop.

Walking and swaying up the aisle, clutching one bus pole after another, saying to the bus driver, "I fell asleep. I missed my stop." Ripping a transfer slip, the bus driver hands it to me. "Thank you," I reply while holding on tight to the bus rail. The bus arrives at the next stop, the doors open, and I hop off and walk across the street to catch the bus going five stops back to where I should have gotten off.

That summer at Belmont High, I enrolled in Safety and Health classes. Many new faces come from Virgil Junior High. I met Ruth Leong in the Safety class, who has a great smile.

At recess, I meet my former basketball teammate, Sharon, at the outdoor lunch bench area known as the "Flats," where students socialize. Sharon introduces me to her friends, like Sandy, Laurie, Yvonne, and Janey. They are also classmates of my brother, Jason.

The most boring course, Health! Mr. Rawlings looks 65 plus years old. He is heavyset, wears spectacles, is semi-bald with grey, fine hair, and has a grey squiggly beard covering the top portion of his chest. Five days for six weeks of summer school, Mr. Rawlings sits in front of the class, talking for the entire period with his arms typically folded upon his chest and his cane dangling from his desk.

New faces from Virgil Junior High sit in the back of the room whom I don't get a chance to meet. I know them by name—Satori and Karl. I sit near the front in the third seat of the first row.

It's a marathon and endurance test for all students in the class! We all sit quietly, listening, and don't even have to take notes! There's no participation, no writing on the board, no group interaction, and no visuals.

We only hear the voice of Mr. Rawlings that invites me to sit and unconsciously meditate. Sitting in total stillness, with no thoughts, and Mr. Rawlings' voice jibber-jabber in the background, I learn nothing. Summer is over.

In the Fall semester of the 10th grade, I don't see any classmates from Nightingale. I have Mr. Fagan for homeroom and also for English. Mr. Fagan is in his late 50s or early 60s, primarily bald, has a mustache, and typically wears a long-sleeved white shirt with a tie. I think he resembles the cartoon character Tweety bird.

He's an excellent English teacher who takes his job seriously and speaks passionately about the subject matter. During recess, he always loves to play opera music while singing in Italian. Sometimes, I sit there eating my snack, observing him at his desk.

My favorite teacher is Mr. Matsumoto, who teaches Biology. He is clean-cut, good-looking, and polite. He is professional, organized, straightforward, and easy to understand as a teacher.

My 8 am class is Algebra II. Math has always been my least favorite class since the 8th grade. I'm the only 10th grader in that class amongst 11th and 12th graders. I do not do well on my first test. Talking with Mr. Nichols after class, I decide to transfer out and retake Geometry, a subject I struggled with in the 9th grade.

Down the hallway, Mrs. Barnes' Geometry class is at the same time as my Algebra II. I check into class and sit in the middle of the second row from the classroom doors. I know one acquaintance, Mimi Wong, a friendly, intelligent, and confident gal who sits behind me.

Karl recognizes me from Mr. Rawlings' Health class in the summer. Karl sits in the last chair in the next row, left of me. Unbeknownst to me, as each day and week goes by, Karl becomes curious about me. Karl intermittently gravitates his eyes toward me when Mrs. Barnes teaches at the chalkboard explaining the morning's lesson. **[Ch.18:1]**

Karl's thoughts: *Every day in Geometry, I look forward to seeing Mary. Glimpsing at her from an angle view, she seems to be different from the other girls. She has this beautiful blue aura. Most others have a yellow or orange aura. I enjoy looking at her beautiful blue aura. I'm feeling an energetic pull toward her. I don't know why. I just like looking at her.* **[Ch.18:2], [Ch.18:3]**

As the semester progresses, amazingly, I'm doing very well in Geometry. It seems to make more sense this second time around. I particularly enjoy proofs. Using theorems, axioms, and assumptions makes logical sense to solve the proof problems.

One morning in Geometry class, the students work on math problems individually at our desks. While working on my math problems, this girl in the back of the room in the left row makes an annoying "Ow, ow, ow, ow," sound. Continue working at my desk; again, this female student keeps saying, "Ow, ow, ow, ow." I try to ignore her broken record "ow, ow, ow, ow" sounds.

I'm slightly annoyed by the incessant "ow, ow, ow" sound. Finally, I decide to see what is going on and hopefully get her to stop making this "ow, ow, ow" sound. Slowly turning my upper torso to my left while turning my head to see where this "ow, ow, ow" noise comes from.

I see Karl smiling, twisting Fanny's pinky finger while she smiles, saying, "ow, ow, ow." Calmly looking at them with no expression, slowly turning back while thinking how silly, immature, and childish. From that point, I don't have a good impression of Karl. I'm thinking, "Who do you think you are, twisting a girl's pinky?"

Both Karl and Fanny seem to enjoy their playfulness with one another.

Exiting the Geometry class, I'm walking alone down the hallway and a thought surfaces in my conscious. I have this impression that some girls like Karl. I'm not interested in someone when several girls like the same guy. Too much of a crowd, he can pick from one of them. I'm not interested in competing. Walking down the hall, I hear my inner being clearly say: Don't get involved with him.

During the Fall semester, I join the girl's junior varsity basketball team at Belmont. Sharon and I play the same positions when we played in the Chinatown basketball league. I'm a left guard, and she plays left forward.

Mrs. Weinstein is our basketball coach. In one of the games, I make a fadeaway shot and score. During the timeout, Mrs. Weinstein points and yells at me that I should have passed the ball.

I say nothing, but I made the basket.

Although our JV team won second place in our division, I sum up at the end of the season that I don't enjoy the coaching of Mrs. Weinstein. She yells and whines too much. She has this habit of wiping her eyes and face, running her hand through her hair, and displaying irritation while coaching. My previous basketball coaches, Wayne and Scott, were cool guys.

In the Spring semester of 10th grade, my class schedule changed to another Geometry teacher, Mrs. Kornblum, in the afternoon. I'm in Mr. Fagan's English class, but this time, in the accelerated course with all my other classmates from Nightingale Junior High School. Perhaps I'm placed here because of the "A" I received in Mr. Fagan's English class last semester. Sitting near the back of the classroom, more than half of the students are new to me. I recognize Karl sitting in the first seat in the first row next to the wall of windows. Byron, one of Karl's good friends, sits behind him.

Mr. Fagan assigns us into small groups to work on a project on any topic of our choice. Our small group researches the topic of Graffiti and create a slide presentation. Karla, Milagros, and Satori are my group members from Virgil Junior High.

On Saturday, Satori and I explore the neighborhood near my home on 10-speed bikes, taking photographs of Graffiti and murals for our slide presentation. In our group's graffiti slide presentation, we cover the history of Graffiti and begin our coverage with Egyptian hieroglyphics. We also integrated a couple of interviews. Milagros narrates, and we include music in our pre-recorded presentation. Mr. Fagan selects our graffiti slide presentation as one of the best, along with another group's topic on the overpopulation of dogs and cats.

Before the annual spring concert, Mr. Schwartz, the music teacher, asks me to design the spring concert program cover. He likes my calligraphy writing on my Christmas cards. I watercolor a simple design of a man playing the flute by the stream in the woods. "*Free Spirit*," is the title of the spring concert on the program cover. **[Ch.18:4]**

We complete the tenth grade, and summer arrives. After summer school, I'm a paid participant of the Theatre Arts Workshop of the Chinatown Youth Council, funded by the government supporting the Neighborhood Youth Corporation (NYC). Jesse, an actor, authored and directs his children's musical "Mr. Narcist and the Tiger." Betty, an actress associated with the East-West Players, also assists us in the musical. Jesse and Milton's help choreograph the acrobatics in the play between Mr. Tiger and Mr. Narcist. I play the role of Mr. Narcist, Peter plays the tiger, and Evelyn plays the Monkey.

As Mr. Narcist, I admire my reflection in the water, one of my favorite lines I ham up is, "Well, Mr. Tiger, if you were as beautiful as I am, I'm sure you wouldn't want to be seen near an ugly tiger, now would you? So, if you don't mind, please leave before I get angry."

The audience enjoys a good laugh on this line while Mr. Tiger gives a funny nonverbal expression. We perform our musical in Chinatown and for the Optimist Club as our final project in the theatre workshop. **[Ch.18:5]**

Chapter 19: Karl and Mary Meet in U.S. History

The first day of my 11th grade year of the Fall semester begins in Mr. Fagan's homeroom, where we receive our new class schedule and announcements. Two former JV basketball team players sit near me, Dani and Poppy.

"Mary, are you going out for the team again this year?" Poppy asks.

"No. I'm not," as I shake my head.

"Why? Why not?" asks Poppy, wrinkling her eyebrows.

"Naw, I'm considering trying out for the girl's gymnastics team. I think both sports will overlap a bit," I explain.

"That will be all right," Dani replies.

"Naw, I think I'll pass," I respond with a slight smile.

"You should. Don't be a chicken," Poppy says.

"Naw," shaking my head and looking down.

The bell rings, and we go to our first period. Walking into the US History class, only about ten students quietly sit. We wait for about five minutes before a teacher comes in and tells us to go to another classroom down the hallway to join another group of students. So, we pick up our belongings and walk down the hall.

Walking through the new classroom doorway, Karl sits directly facing me as I enter the room. I look at Karl, reactively rolling my eyes, walking clear across the opposite end of the room, sitting kitty-corner to him. I intentionally walk the farthest away from Karl, an immediate adverse reaction to my impression of him twisting Fanny's pinky last year in Geometry class.

The classroom layout consists of two halves of rows of chairs facing toward the center of the room. A 10-foot walkway runs down the middle of the two halves. Quietly sitting at my seat, waiting for our new US History teacher, Mr. Potter, to begin class.

As the Fall semester begins, Karl glances at me several times across the room during every class session. I catch him looking at me time after time, day after day, week after week. I don't think much about why he's looking at me. Often, looking up from my desk, our eyes meet for a second before he quickly looks away.

Karl's thoughts: *In class, I'm trying to get Mary's attention and telepathically trying to get her to feel what I'm feeling. I keep thinking of her in my mind and trying to influence her with my thoughts: "look at me, look at me, look at me." Suddenly, Mary glances over at me. "Oh, shit. She looked at me." I look down at my desk, nervous that she caught me looking at her again.* **[Ch.19:1]**

As the days progress, we find each other glancing at one another several times during class. One time looking up, Karl is looking at me. Quickly, he looks away. Continue working at my desk; a few seconds later, glancing his way again, I catch him looking at me. Immediately, he looks away, clearing his throat. **[Ch.19:2]**

As the weeks pass, I no longer have negative feelings toward Karl. Instead, his glances in class every day have a subliminal effect on me. Never smiling at him but catching his glimpses. I'm neutral and focused on our assignments.

I continue doing my work without thinking about him or listening to Mr. Potter speaking at the podium next to Karl's desk. Somehow, my attraction grows toward Karl as the semester progresses. Although we never interact with one another outside of U.S. History, my thoughts and interests do not develop further because we have minimal interactions. I hardly know Karl.

At home, my parents prepare food in the kitchen. Standing on one side of the kitchen, I decide to go, "weeeee," sliding across the kitchen floor in my socks. Turning around, "weeeee," sliding back across the kitchen floor. Well, that's fun!

Realizing that the atmosphere at home is too serious as far as I can remember. My parents have been typically serious and strict in their communications within the family. Understandable, there have been hard times of survival, struggle, working all the time, and my Daddy does not have good health. For decades, my Daddy has struggled with asthma, sometimes finding it hard to breathe.

Every night, my Mommy and Daddy return home around 10. My Daddy parks his car in the carport, walking up the driveway incline and into the house. He sits in his chair, breathing heavily and rapidly. He takes off his coat and unbuttons his white work shirt. Unable to speak for several minutes, he's rubbing his chest. Removing his shoes and socks, he wears his slippers next to his chair. Eventually, he slows down his rapid short breaths to a regular rate.

My Mommy puts her belongings down on the kitchen table, removes her heels, and slips on her slippers. She turns on the TV to watch the nightly news and chats with my Daddy. Wearing her red blouse, she empties her skirt pockets of waitressing tips onto the couch. Sitting back, propping her feet on the coffee table after an exhausting day on her feet as she counts her change. She complains that some customers only tip her 25, 35, or 45 cents for an entire table. After watching the 11 o'clock news, they retire for the evening just before midnight. The routine starts over again the next day for my parents, six long work days.

I see my parents once a week on their day off and briefly a few minutes before sleeping at night. My typical interactions are greeting them when they arrive home and saying, *"Jo tau, ah Ma. Jo tau, ah Ba,"* meaning, "Goodnight, Mommy. Goodnight, Daddy."

They both nod and usually say, *"Oh, neih heui fun gau. Neih ting yat heui fan hok,"* meaning, "Oh, you are going to sleep. Tomorrow you are going to school."

I'm in a dark place in my nightmare, lying down somewhere. I'm sensing sharpness and movement coming at me like rectangle shapes closing in, at the rhythm of my pounding heart. Snapping out of my nightmare--hyperventilating. Getting out of bed, and walking downstairs, slouching on the breakfast nook booth with one hand on my chest, still hyperventilating.

My parents try to calm me down. I drink some water. I eventually calm down and return to bed. This occurred in the Fall semester of my 11th-grade. Fortunately, that nightmare was the last.

My upbringing, overall, lacks a nurturing relationship and warm interactions within my family. Our family communications involve mostly doing what we are told, being quiet, and hearing parental criticisms and lectures. When my Daddy lectures, it's a long, long time. Not one hour, not two, not three, but sometimes as long as four hours!

All three of the kids sit or stand in the kitchen while being lectured. I don't know why my Daddy talks so long. We don't misbehave or do anything irresponsible. I don't think there is any legitimate complaint. None of the kids has gone through a rebellious stage. We aren't disrespectful. We don't have significant character flaws. We don't come home late hours. We don't have any addictions.

Perhaps my Daddy feels part of his role as a father is to lecture the kids. My Daddy interweaves a few stories of his past and how difficult his upbringing was and coming to America. Maybe since we are older, he wants us to know the struggles that they went through and how much easier we have it.

I believe my Daddy had a poor upbringing, was not nurtured, cared for, and lacked warmth and affection. I understand in time that my Daddy's Mom was a gambler in China. My Daddy's Dad had gone to Canada and the US for work and was absent when my Daddy was growing up. He recollects the last time he saw his Daddy when he was five years old, holding his hand while walking down the street.

With this understanding of my parents' history, I do not have an orientation of blame toward them but rather an acceptance and understanding. It only makes sense that our parents do love us. They show it by working day-in and day-out to provide a roof over our heads, shelter, food, and necessities. My Daddy explains that he made three attempts to come to America. The immigration process was incomplete or held up in the first two occurrences. He says he was fortunate to succeed through legal immigration on the third try.

My Daddy discovered in his early years in the U.S. that his Dad was shot in Bakersfield, California. He expresses that he had dreamt about his Dad stomping on the dirt road where cars drove back and forth. Eventually, my Daddy travels to Bakersfield and locates his Dad's burial site as he had envisioned in his dream. At the time, my Daddy and the family lived in San Francisco and had his Dad's casket transported to a cemetery in San Francisco. My Daddy marvels how he could decipher the visual clues in his dream on where his Dad's burial site was.

Whenever he lectures, he speaks with intensity and emotion. Every time my Daddy lectures us, he says, "I won't be able to sleep tonight because I've had to lecture you, kids. My heart is upset, just talking about all these things." He rubs his chest with his hand.

Sometimes, it's just one thing; as he says, it feels like a hotel here with the kids coming and going as they please. My Daddy blows it out of proportion. I don't think my parents understand that Jason and Leland go to school and work.

They are busy accomplishing what they need to do. They don't come home in the middle of the night and spend their time goofing around with friends. He could also be redundant and ramble and say the same thing repeatedly. He is a bit temperamental, but he isn't a mean or angry person.

My Mommy never lectures us. Perhaps she feels it is not her place and that it is my Daddy's role. She would typically tell us what to do when needed. Whenever we do something wrong, she would blame us, say it is our fault, and tell us what we should have done.

As we get older, when something goes wrong or when we get hurt, she blames us for not being more careful. She doesn't provide warm nurturance and loving care if we get hurt but is more of a reactive response. You should have known better, or you shouldn't have done this.

At times name-calling and put-downs are used that make us feel stupid. It is unnecessary verbal abuse. My parents raised me in that fashion. They do it out of habit, raised and conditioned to say phrases as motivators to avoid errors and make behavioral corrections. However, my parents don't understand that such negative talk and energy do not nurture or teach but intimidate another.

Interestingly, one of my friends once told me that she accidentally cut herself while cutting a box. Her Mom's response is similar to what my Mom would say, "Why didn't you watch what you were doing? Why don't you be more careful? Be more careful next time." There's no expression of sympathy but a tone of blame. It's your fault for not using your head, and how you should do this.

After a rare visit from our San Francisco relatives, my Daddy says, "Chinese parents don't show they love their kids. They show that they like other kids, but not their own." Quite frankly, I think, "What? That sounds strange. Are you saying that you don't love us? This doesn't make sense at all." I don't say anything, remaining baffled by what my Daddy stated. I'm not displeased or angry at my Daddy. I'm like, "huh?"

Upon reflection, perhaps my Daddy means that with your kids, it's all about disciplining and correcting your children to be model people instead of focusing on giving warmth, affection, and love that might spoil the child. I think my Daddy bases his disciplinary approach on raising kids the way he was raised. That is, affection in the family is not expressed directly in verbal and nonverbal ways. Instead, providing shelter and food is one way to show love. Showing affection toward other people's kids through smiling, complimenting, giving treats, etc., presents "face" and good relations toward others. We were also taught to give our guests the best, whatever that may be, to show hospitality.

My family does not express love and affection directly in verbal and nonverbal ways. However, I received more nurturance as a young child than my older brothers. My parents grew up in an era of the great depression, war, poverty, struggles, the immigrant experience, and being in survival mode, create an environment that lacks happiness, joy, love, affection, and other positive communications.

This is why I slid across the kitchen floor in my socks, to be silly. I decide to get out of that box of dead seriousness, the feeling of dense energy, the lack of fun, joy, happiness, love, and affection. I recognize the feeling of the negative and stressful energies that inhabit and imprison our family, and I want to break out of it.

I sense my parents' hardship. I see their struggles as I'm growing up. I never want to trade places with my parents in what they went through. So, my thoughts are not complaining or blaming. It's an awareness I no longer desire negative, dense feelings like dark clouds hovering over us ever since we lived on Gaviota Street.

For years, I have become immune to the energy field of discomfort and heaviness because that is all I know. It becomes a normal state of living at home. It's not 24/7. Sometimes things are just neutral: nothing intense and dense, yet nothing joyful and affectionate. I understand that my parents were not raised with feelings of love and affection. So how can they know and express feelings of love and affection?

On top of that, their lives have been spent working hard and experiencing stressful events. Like many other Chinese immigrants, culturally, touch is minimal in interactions, and public expression of affection is not normative. Greeting each other, yes, usually cheerfulness with friends, neighbors, and employers. Culturally, whenever Chinese people meet Chinese people's acquaintances, a ritual of asking what village or area of China they are from. They continue chatting to identify and share common areas of China.

If both parties come from the same province or village, expect an explosive excitement of happiness with smiles, clapping, and sometimes hand touching. It's a shared magical sense of, "Wow, this is a small world!" That is, in this big world of seven billion people, we have finally met each other coming from the same village or province.

Chinese people feel a magical sense of pre-destiny and affinity during this chance meeting. The conversation entails an understanding of identifying with similar roots, lived experiences, and memories. The Chinese concept, *yuánfèn,* refers to this pre-destined relationship, fate, a chance that brings people together, or a predestined affinity with a person, place, and perhaps knowing the same people.

Living in Chinatown and schooling through high school, my classmates and friends rarely touch each other. We never hug, shake hands, pat each other on the back, or show any other affectionate expressions through touch. I only recall one Chinese friend who naturally touches her classmates at times, such as their hands, putting her arms around another's shoulder in a caring way. She has three younger siblings, and she naturally caresses them growing up, so it is natural for her to express herself in this way.

Today, in the 21st century, I have adopted communications that express positivity and warmth. Understandably, the world I live in today is drastically different from my parents' era. I'm grateful to choose positivity in how I live my life today.

During the Fall semester, at 7 am, I play the piccolo in the marching band, a new and worthwhile experience. We practice on the football field weekly to prepare for the Friday night football game. When we play an instrumental pop song, "The Hustle," four rows of band members alternate doing simple steps, shifting to the right and then to the left. Spectators in the bleachers see a zig-zag effect, and they go wild with cheers. **[Ch.19:3], [Ch.19:4]**

As the marching band prepares to go down to the football field to practice, the instructor, Mr. Schwartz, rags on me, saying, "Why are you so skinny? You look so skinny," shaking his head. Mr. Schwartz has ragged on my appearance before. My eyes well up with tears. Why does he rag on how thin I am? What does it matter to him? Yes, I know I'm on the thin side, but what's it to him? I'm still growing.

He's an immature 60-year-old single man, always wearing a cap and all-black clothing with red sneakers, picking on a teenager! Mr. Schwartz is in his second year of long-term substitute teaching, filling in for the tenured teacher on medical leave. Mr. Schwartz always makes stupid comments, makes fun of his students, loses his temper at times, and is the only one who laughs at his corny jokes. The students tolerate him.

The marching band walks outside of the band room and down to the football field. I'm still tearful. Two friends are consoling me. Mr. Schwartz walks by me, muttering sarcastically, "Well, invite me to your sweet sixteen party."

He disgusts me with his verbal abuse and immature conduct. He is unconscious of his habitual undisciplined thoughts and dysfunctional remarks. He has been conditioned in his upbringing, acting out on autopilot, unaware of his frustration, anger, and lack of self-love. Perhaps he intentionally knows his remarks are belittling due to his dysfunctional issues disguised in his warp sarcasm. He disgusts me with his verbal abuse and immature conduct. He is unconscious of his habitual undisciplined thoughts and dysfunctional remarks. He has been conditioned in his upbringing, acting out on autopilot, unaware of his frustration, anger, and lack of self-love. Perhaps he intentionally knows his remarks are belittling due to his dysfunctional issues disguised in his warp sarcasm. The bottom line is that he is exerting negative energy that reverberates, affecting others. He's like a broken record, not caring to get up and fix the scratch that continues to repeat itself annoyingly. **[Ch.19:5]**

I'm not going to tolerate his abuse anymore. Once the marching band ends in the Fall semester, I quit-- never retaking Mr. Schwartz. I respect myself, no longer allowing him to victimize me.

At a school assembly, marching band members sit on the auditorium stage. A band member keeps looking at me, intentionally singing a popular song. He sings, "I don't want to know your name because you don't look the same, like before. You think you have a pretty face, but the rest of you are out of place. You looked all right before. Fox on the run, screaming...". I ignore him. He sounds like a broken record. **[Ch.19:6]**

Growing up throughout my teens, I'm a late bloomer. I don't focus on how I look. I never get to the point of feeling miserable and getting down on myself. I don't spend time comparing myself to others or feeling jealous of others. I'm fortunate that I have never felt any sense of jealousy toward others ever since I was very young. I appreciate people's qualities if they are attractive, intelligent, and talented. My philosophy is, "If I can't have it, I'm glad someone else does." I'm grateful that I'm not ego-driven and appreciate who I am.

I've always been ambitious and active in wanting to do my best. I do not prefer the competitive mode of outdoing another person to gain attention and affection, be included or accepted and feel better about myself. Instead, I desire to be true to myself while continuing to discover who I am. I like participating in various enjoyable and creative activities to expand and expand beyond my boundaries.

On my bedroom wall, I have a poster of a forest, a bridge and a waterfall with a quote, "Give the best you have and the best will come back to you." Relaxing on my bed, I'm repeating this quote and not fully agreeing with the message. I search for why these words don't resonate completely with me. Finally, I figure out why. This phrase communicates that I will receive the best in return when I give my best. However, I feel that one ought to give their best, not to get something in return, but to give your best if it is in a situation or to someone for the pure intention of giving without having any expectation of receiving the best back or anything in return. Give because you want to give from your heart with the intention of sharing, helping, or bettering a situation or person.

With the effects of being ostracized in elementary school, I was motivated to be the best to receive acceptance. It's human nature to belong, get along, be inclusive, and be one with others. However, I don't care what others think of me as I mature. I learn I can't control others' thoughts, feelings, and behaviors who judge or misconstrue my intentions. I know my heart. I stand by being true to myself, being authentic. I no longer allow others and the externals to shake who I am or make me into something I'm not.

I engage in what I'm doing. I'm not concern about others and what they think about me. If people have negative thoughts toward others, the issue is about themselves, not the person they criticize. I understand classmates have their teenage criticisms. I hear through the grapevine negative-minded people badmouthing me. I could never understand why a person would do so since I hardly interact with them.

I do have friends, more like acquaintances. Two friends I confide in during high school. A lunch buddy and later a group of lunch buddies, although we don't have classes together. For years, lunch was my main meal of the day. Breakfast doesn't exist. Dinner was inconsistent until near the end of 11th grade, when my parents retired.

I focus on enjoying activities like playing basketball, gymnastics, drama, marching band, orchestra, competing in speech tournaments, and watching college football and basketball games. I'm in various groups of classmates, depending on the activity. However, I never feel part of a close group of friends. I never think I have to be in the "in-group," whatever group. I don't know because I don't mingle much.

Throughout my life, I'm used to being an independent party. Although I would like to have a good group of friends with whom we identify and support one another. I don't seem to click with anyone. I have many nice classmates at school, but I don't feel a deep connection with them. I'm happy socializing with supportive people and sharing life experiences. I'm engaged in various activities for interests, fun, and development. I never have the desire or need to be the center of attention. Nor do I need to have to be around or cling to people. I may appear active on the external, but I'm shy, insecure, and lack social skills, especially regarding guys. So, I don't think much about guys.

Karl's thoughts: [In US History class] *Mary seems very familiar to me. I feel an instant trust with her. I feel safe like being with my friends I've known for years. I don't even know her. I just feel this connection with her. As the days and weeks pass, I have this feeling of joy; and oh my God, yes, I want to see her. At the same time, there's a feeling of being lost, like I don't know what I'm doing; and this doesn't seem to work. These are very confusing times, but pleasant times because I love the feeling of, "she's gonna be there. I'm gonna see her." I get excited about that.* **[Ch.19:7]**

In November, students receive their set of annual self-portraits. After Mr. Potter gives us our in-class assignment, he leaves the podium to walk back to his desk. I look at arl and call his name out for the first time across the room, "Karl!" He looks up at me. I mouth, "Can I have your picture?" while using both of my index fingers to draw a rectangle in the air. He nods. We both write on the back of our photos during class.

Class ends, we walk toward one another. Karl extends his palm with a wallet-sized photo. "Oh, no! I didn't give you a large picture!" I exclaimed. He shakes his head, looking disappointed.

"I'm sorry!" I say, feeling embarrassed. I hand over a half-wallet-sized photo. We exit the class through different doors. On my way to class, I read the back of his picture. **[Ch.19:8]**

After reading Karl's comments, I'm stunned. I feel frozen in time with the aftermath of feeling good. I can't believe he wrote such positive things. I don't know how many times I've read his comments. These are the kindest words I've ever received from anyone. Karl makes me feel good about myself. However, I never thought any more than that. Always denying the idea he would have any interest. Why would he be interested in me? I'm not the most attractive gal around. I'm skinny. My thoughts never went beyond this.

Karl's thoughts: *Mary brightens up my every day just because I know I'm going to see her. She makes school days a lot more fun for me. I enjoy coming to school. I look forward to seeing her again, which changes my day.* **[Ch.19:9]**

She changes my attitude at home. I walk around, and I'm all helpful to my Mom and cheery, and people would look at me like what's wrong with him. I get into this state of longing to see her, for a chance to get a glimpse from her. **[Ch.19:10]**

In US History class, Mr. Potter takes attendance and asks, "Mary, do you have a note for being absent yesterday?"

"Oh, I was here yesterday. I came in a little late and sneaked in. We got out of marching band late."

"Oh, okay," Mr. Potter responds.

Karl looks at me once I say, "sneaked in." I glance at him, Karl smiles, and I smile back. He looks down at his desk, smiling and shaking his head. We both connect on how informal and funny it is for me to use "sneaked in" when speaking to a teacher. **[Ch.19:11]**

Karl's thoughts: *I don't think Mary notices anything for a couple of weeks. I'm trying to get her attention. I'm trying to reach out and talk to her. I'm making eye contact. I'm trying to make it like, "Hello." I'm trying to make eye contact, but she misses it. She is like, yes, okay. I don't think she is doing it on purpose. I think she isn't noticing it. She isn't focused on it the way I am. How do I get her attention without marching around with a flag and playing the trombone in front of her nose?*

So, I keep looking at Mary, thinking in my mind, "Look at me. Look at me." Mentally, I'm trying to get her to look at me. I'm trying to do a Jedi mind trick on her to look at me. Eventually, she looks at me. Yes, she hears me, but no reaction on her end. So that is disappointing. I feel disappointed because I'm trying so hard and just not seeing any results. She's a hard nut to crack. I don't have the courage to walk up to her and say, "I love you. Let's go out. Let's do something. Let's hang out." I can't do it. I don't have the balls. **[Ch.19:12]**

Chapter 20: Spring Semester of Eleventh Grade

I'm living up to my promise, no longer associated with Mr. Schwartz. Instead, I happily join the orchestra at 7 am with Mrs. Goodman, the other music teacher, a pleasant, good-looking red-haired professional in her late 30s. We play a variety of classical and contemporary favorites. Karl is also in the orchestra. I didn't know he plays the drums and percussions.

Karl's thoughts *I'm waiting. Is she going to look and smile at me? That's my thing. I'm just hoping that she would look and smile or say something. There's always this sensation of hoping for her to reach out to say something that would help me to take a different step. There's a lot of longing and hoping, a lot of nervousness. She makes schoolwork more pleasant for me because I get to see her.* **[Ch.20:1]**

My US History class switches to the afternoon with Miss Matik. During the first week, Karl and his best friend, Rocky, stand outside the open door of my US History class. Karl peers inside. He's looking for someone, sees me, and leaves. Why are they peeking into our History class? Did Karl come to glance at me like he used to last semester?

After class, I have a gymnastics class. I join the girl's gymnastics team as I intended to. Low and behold, Mrs. Weinstein is our gymnastics coach! Ugh! This is why I didn't join the girl's basketball team last semester. I can't stand her yelling and whining. Now, I have her again!

Fortunately, she doesn't scream, complain or whine during my two years on the team. Perhaps because she isn't a gymnast and doesn't feel it is her place. Maybe coaches yell at players in basketball, but yelling doesn't occur in gymnastics. As a gymnastics coach, Mrs. Weinstein is supportive and helpful.

One day, while our gymnastics class tumbles on the mats, some girls scream. I'm startled, and glancing at the open door, Karl and Rocky dart away. Mrs. Weinstein runs to the door and down the hallway. Dashing through the corridor, they both return to their gymnastics practice. Why are Karl and Rocky peeking into our gymnastics class? They're fooling around, having teenage boy fun.

The school doctor checks all the gymnasts—the doctor checks for scoliosis, which is the curvature of the spine. Fortunately, I pass because the doctor only exams my upper mid-back. However, I have a curve in my lower back, which he misses. Another teammate has upper scoliosis and needs a medical note from her private doctor to stay on the team.

Going to a female gynecologist for my first pap smear, and she recommends going to an orthopedic clinic to check out my curvature. My Daddy is going with me. They take X-rays and give me another appointment to return for the diagnosis.

I ride the public bus for 90 minutes for my follow-up appointment since my parents have vacation plans in Vegas. The doctor marks up my X-rays while I'm watching. The doctor says two surgeries require the insertion of two rods in my back to fuse my vertebrates to straighten my curvature.

"Will I be able to do gymnastics next year?" I ask.

They look at me and say, "No, you won't be able to bend your back."

As a 16-year-old, I size up the diagnosis as a radical approach to handling my condition, especially when I don't have any pain or discomfort. I leave, my eyes well up with tears streaming down my cheeks, walking to the bus stop. These doctors are drastic in their medical recommendations.

I'm waiting at the bus stop, feeling upset, wiping my tears. Someone taps my shoulder. Turning my head, a desolate man gestures at my wristwatch. I say the time. He gestures his hands to his ears and mouth. Angling my wrist, he peers at it, nods, and smiles at me.

This moment with this desolate mute man, less fortunate than me, opened my awareness. Wiping my teary eyes, I no longer cry, feeling bad for myself, knowing so many less fortunate people than me. I can talk, speak, and move about with ease--it humbles me. This interaction is synchronistic, a meaningful coincidence, opening my awareness of how fortunate I truly am.

The bus arrives, hopping on board for my 90-minute ride back home. I won't return to the orthopedic doctors. I'm able to compete on the gymnastics team on the floor exercise, balance beam, and vault.

We have a school assembly for all the student body candidates running for office. I give a brief speech in front of the entire student body on the football field. I say, "Hi, my name is Mary Fong, and I'm running for student body treasurer. If I'm elected student body treasurer, I'll keep an accurate account of all the money, ensure we don't overspend and provide accurate financial reports. So, I hope you'll vote for me, Mary Fong, for student body treasurer. So, I hope all of you will keep on bumpin' with me, Mary Fong, for student body treasurer."

"Good speech!" someone yells from the balcony of the bleachers. I appreciate the shout-out. A week later, unfortunately, I don't win the treasurer position. It doesn't make or break me. Typically, running for school office is a popularity contest, not necessarily about competence. Okay, so I'm not that popular.

I have a worthwhile experience joining the forensics team and mingling with fun-spirited speech team members. We have excellent humorous interpretation speakers such as Fernando and Robert. Both qualified to compete at the state and national tournaments. We also have an excellent duo interpretation team, Ricky and Albert. Ruby competes at the State level in expository speaking on acupuncture. We have many other forensic speakers on our team that win many plaques. Our team competes at high school locations like Sylmar, Beverly Hills, and Belmont.

Grueling to compete in forensic tournaments, going through three and final rounds. Sometimes, I feel my nerves and don't eat or drink anything all day. There aren't any food facilities, food machines or water. I don't think about bringing any food, drinks, or snacks.

Competing in every final round and winning plaques in every tournament in expository speaking and storytelling requires endurance. I'm exhausted by the end of the day, competing from 9 am until the competition is over by 5:00ish--an absolute marathon test!

I also enjoy drama in high school, playing in a couple of productions. One originates from a TV show called MASH, in which I play Agnes, one of the three Bonwit dancing sisters. Tim Kelly, the playwright, autographs my program after our MASH performance. **[Ch.20:2], [Ch.20:3]**

My Daddy's lung collapsed, and he's rushed to the hospital. A doctor inserts a tube in his lung cavity to allow the air to escape, relieving the air pressure on his lung. Discharged from the hospital in a few days, my Daddy continues his recovery at home. Both my parents retired.

Smoked cigarettes, my Daddy did as a teenager. He finally quit smoking when I was 10. Smoking no longer gives him the taste and satisfaction; besides ruining his health.

My parents' morning ritual is sitting at the breakfast nook, sipping their coffee, eating a pastry, chatting, and viewing people through the front window. Sometimes, I would make a week's worth of blueberry cheesecake, carrot cake, or banana nut bread for my parents' breakfast.

Trojan eats a couple of orange slices at times. My parents laugh and smile while watching Trojan hold down the edge of the peel. She pulls off the slice and chews on it.

Afterwards, my Daddy drives to Chinatown and shops for fish, beef, chicken, pork, and vegetables. He buys two Chinese newspapers to enjoy reading, sitting on a patio chair with legs propped up in the backyard.

My Daddy uses a sharp cleaver to cut the meat into slices on a cutting board, a six-inch tree stump used in Chinese restaurants. My Mommy marinates the meat slices with soy sauce, cooking wine, sugar, sesame oil, and chopped garlic for several hours before stir-frying it, along with a vegetable dish for dinner. We eat bowls of rice every night with chopsticks. Usually, we eat as a family almost every night, depending on Jason and Leland's work or school schedules.

Since I'm still in high school, I appreciate dinner every night at home. Sometimes at the dinner table, I goof around, flexing my biceps. I get a kick out of it, my cheap thrills. My brothers shake their heads, roll their eyes, and sometimes say, "Oh, brother." I also have this habit of talking more than consuming my meal while everyone eats away.

My Mommy often reminds emphatically, *"Yak la, nei a fan dong saai a!"* meaning, "Eat your rice. It's cold!" Cringing with embarrassment, I stop and focus on eating.

Depending on how wacky I feel, I also tend to whip out little Snakey and a few of her friends before and during dinner. Sometimes, Leland and Jason bring out their Snakey for a couple of seconds when my Daddy isn't paying attention. My Daddy usually shakes his head, smiling while looking down whenever Snakey comes out to talk to him. Sometimes, my Mommy lightly slaps Snakey's face.

"Hey, why are you hitting me? What did I do? I didn't do anything. That's not nice," complains Snakey while shaking her head.

My parents smile and sometimes chuckle at how ridiculous their daughter is. I figure I'm breaking the ice and bringing in some lightheartedness, no matter how silly.

At school, Karl and I only cross paths sometimes in the orchestra. Most of the time, we don't say anything to each other. We're in different sections. Occasionally, we say, "Hi." We don't see each other the rest of the day unless we have a class together in the afternoon. We don't have the same circle of friends, and we rarely meet each other during recess and lunch.

Karl's thoughts: *Every day at school, there's this nervousness of, should I tell her, should I not tell her? I always think there would come a time to talk to her and say, 'hey, I like you. I really, really like you.' However, her vibe always put me on hold, making me more nervous.* **[Ch.20:4]**

So yeah, I have the lovey-dovey feelings of being just crazy about a person to a point where it just doesn't make sense. That's how I feel. Then when I don't see her, I always long to see her. **[Ch.20:5]**

While at Belmont High, I feel so much expectation, desire, and pressure. I'm trying to get Mary's attention. I'm trying to fit in with everybody else. I'm trying to please my parents. A lot of times, I'm trying to please a lot of people.

In that way, I sometimes feel alone. I sometimes feel lonely because although I love everybody, I still feel like nobody knows who I am. With that feeling, with that knowledge, I can't say what I see or what I feel because people think I'm crazy or they think I'm weird.

With that knowledge of knowing I'm different, there's always a sense of loneliness. There's always a sense of trying to find out, well, who am I then? If nobody else sees that, who am I? Many insecurities affect how I see myself feeling lonely in my perspective of the world. There's the pressure of performing, the pressure of succeeding, making my parents proud, and showing them that I can be at the top. These pressures are where all my insecurities come from.

I'm a member of the girl's 11th-grade service club, the Chatelaines. I'm a flower girl at the June graduation on the football field. Dressed in a flowing mint green gown with a long-sleeved flowered chiffon wrap tied at my waist, wearing high heels and short white gloves. My long hair flows with bouncing curls, wearing mint green eyeshadow with mascara and lipstick. I feel pretty.

My Daddy drives me across town to Belmont. The orchestra plays *Pomp and Circumstance* repeatedly on the football field. I'm playing my flute for twenty minutes as family and friends arrive, seated on the balcony of bleachers.

When the flower girls assemble on the football field sidelines, they signal me to join them. The flower girls team up in pairs, holding one end of the white flower arch. In pairs, we stand about ten feet apart in a line. The orchestra continues striking up the *Pomp and Circumstance* graduation song, and the high school graduates in their black caps and gown proceed to walk under each decorative flower arch. **[Ch.20:6]**

For the first time in my life, I feel truly happy. I feel pretty. I smile and giggle as each graduate walks under my flower-decorated arch. I know many graduates, particularly the ones who competed on the forensics team.

We exchange smiles, winks, hellos, and congratulations as they walk under the flower arch during a memorable, once-in-a-lifetime ceremony marking the achievement, success, and a significant milestone. I book pressed the carnation I wore as a flower girl. **[Ch.20:7]**

The flower girls lay their decorated arches down, returning to my orchestra seat. All the graduates sit, and the audience lets out a roaring cheer as the ceremony begins. Every graduate's name is announced.

Finally, the high school principal announces, "Graduates, and you may now move your tassel from your right to your left. Congratulations!" The audience claps and cheers, the orchestra strikes up the music, and the graduates walk through the floral arches into the gymnasium.

❧ ❧

The next day, walking through the hallway on the last day of the academic year, I spontaneously pop into Mrs. LeFont's classroom to see if anyone wants to exchange yearbooks for signing. I have no clue who's in this class. Students chat amongst themselves while Mrs. LeFont assigns grades to their report cards.

Shuffling quickly into the classroom, I sit at a desk while Mrs. LeFont glances at me and returns to her task. Within seconds, Karl and his classmate, Bob Shepherd, walk across the room toward me. Bob sits in the chair next to me in the next row and says emphatically,

"Mary FONG, how's it going?"

"Oh, hi, Bob. I'm doing fine," I say.

Karl sits right in front of me, sitting on the desk, beaming at me." When are you going to sign my yearbook?" Karl asks.

"Oh, okay," I say.

As we write in the yearbook, Karl says, "Oh, I need my glasses."

"Why? Can't you see through your beady little eyes?" I say jokingly.

He looks at me and smiles. "I'm going to hit you," he says. He tightens his fist and flinches a fake hit toward me. Ducking my head, hiding my face in my arms on the desk. Slowly peeking, he flinches again. Dodging, burying my face in my arms, peering a bit.

Karl gets off the top of the desk and sits at the desk behind me. "I'm going to burn your house down," he says.

"Now that wasn't nice to say," turning around toward him, saying in a meek voice.

Karl shakes his head, smiling, and continues to write in my yearbook. I turn around and finish writing in his yearbook.

All the while, Bob sits amusingly, watching and laughing.

Afterwards, Bob and I exchange yearbooks. Class is over. Soon after, I read what Karl wrote: **[Ch.20:8], [Ch.20:9]**

That weekend, I repeatedly read what Karl wrote to me. His compliments overwhelm me. He's the only guy I know that has the confidence to use the word "beautiful" in high school. As a second-generation Japanese American male teenager, I wonder where in the world did he learn to use "beautiful" and have the boldness to write this at such a young age? So atypical to express oneself from his background.

I wonder and question repeatedly, "Does Karl like me?" The more I question, the more I keep rereading his comments, and the more I freak out at the possibility that he likes me. When he underlined the word "<u>a lot</u>," he's emphasizing that he wants to get to know me better.

I'm freaking out at home during our week break before summer school. I don't know what to do or what to think. I've never had a boyfriend before. In all my 17 years of life, I have never had a guy friend, let alone I've never really talked to a guy beyond a simple one-liner. I also feel uncomfortable around guys because I sense that guys always check out the girls. This makes me feel like a sex object. I never had any male friendships where we talked.

I'm officially a certified, socially inept person. I don't even feel comfortable saying "Hi" to a guy. I don't know how to engage in small talk. However, I can sit and have a deep conversation, but I'm not good at small talk. I've lived this independent existence all my life, and now confronted with a guy I'm attracted to who has showered me with compliments.

What do I do? That's why I'm freaking—I mean, freaking stressed! Unbelievably, there's this possibility that Karl indeed likes me. However, what in the world do I do and say? All my life, I have had to navigate through life independently, doing my thing and not worrying about others and what they think. As the week wears on, I get to the point of considering that perhaps, Karl and I would get together and share our senior events. **[Ch.20:10]**

Summer school begins, and I have US Government with Miss. Matik and Forensics afterwards. On the first day of class, Miss. Matik assigns seating arrangements. She has the entire class stand up and calls out, "Miss. Miyamura, can you please sit in the first seat here." Satori walks to the first seat and sits down. Miss. Matik says, "Mr. Karl, please sit behind Miss Miyamura."

At this point, I think it's silly for her to assign us seats, so I step outside into the hallway. I hear Miss. Matik from inside the class say, "Let's see who will sit behind Mr. Karl?" I enjoy saying hello to people walking in the corridor. Miss Matik glances around and says, "Miss Fong, can you please sit behind Mr. Karl.

I feel embarrassed while walking across the room to the first row farthest from the door while Miss. Matik comments gleefully, "Oh, there's going to be much romance this summer."

I'm super embarrassed, trying to keep a poker face. Sitting right behind Karl, his head and upper torso turn backwards about a quarter way and place his right elbow on his back chair, embarrassing me even more as I look down at my desk. Miss. Matik continues to assign every other seat to a girl, boy, girl, boy.

During the first week, Miss. Matik asks several questions during the class discussion to elicit student responses. She gives a scenario, "There's a topless bar in your neighborhood. What's your opinion about this?" She looks around, and there are no volunteers.

"Miss. Fong, what do you think about having a topless bar in your neighborhood?"

I freeze, incredibly embarrassed. What in the world am I going to say? I don't know what the heck to say; good grief. I say whatever comes to my mind that sounds at least halfway decent.

"It would be fine with me," I say.

"Why would it be fine with you, Miss. Fong?"

"It's freedom of expression."

That scenario is unrealistic. I don't know the negative consequences of a topless bar near my home. If there is one, I don't think I would cross paths with the bar. It wouldn't impede my life. I can't identify with this situation.

The following week in Miss. Matik's class, we have our usual 10-minute break. Still sitting, I'm holding my fruit on top of my desk while my head and body are turned toward the back door, debating if I should stay here or go out in the hallway to eat.

Unexpectedly, I feel a hand on top of my hand that holds my fruit. I freeze. I don't know what to do or think. Karl's hand is on top of my hand. My mind is blank. I stop breathing. He keeps his hand on my hand for almost five seconds. He lifts his hand, gets up from his desk, and walks to the back of the classroom.

I still don't know what to do. I turn back, facing forward, looking down at my desk as I hear Karl's footsteps walking to the back of the classroom, exiting. I sit with no thoughts. I take a deep breath, exhaling slowly, feeling the energy in my body diminishing like letting the air out of a party balloon. "I turned him off," my thoughts registered. **[Ch.20:11]**

Karl's thoughts: *I feel shot down. I had a lot of hope, and when I didn't get a response, it was like she took that away. I don't know what to do anymore. She's not interested in me. Maybe I should give this up. A lot went through my mind in a very short time. I feel very disappointed. I feel like a fool, thinking that this might work and lead to something. I feel my heart pull out of my chest. I feel like crying. My heart is breaking. I still couldn't let it go. I held onto it, but it isn't the same anymore. I'm emotionally damaged.* **[Ch.20:12], [Ch.20:12A]**

Whenever Mary is around, my heart starts racing a bit. I get nervous and do stupid things, acting like an idiot sometimes. She has this effect on me. Mostly when I'm around her, I'm incredibly nervous, which makes me go into an idiot phase.

Our 10-minute break is over, and students return to the classroom. Quietly sitting at my desk waiting for Miss Matik to begin class, Karl reaches over to his desk's right side across the aisle and squeezes Jasmine Nagamine's left leg while sitting at her desk. She naturally cringes and giggles. Karl sits back in his seat.

Witnessing Karl for the first time squeezing a girl's leg. He's no longer interested in me. I turned him off. I'm immensely perplexed. I can't take him seriously anymore. Miss Matik reconvenes class.

After summer school ends daily, I go to Chinatown to work with elementary school children as a paid assistant of the NYC summer program. My brother, Leland, is the supervisor and coordinator of a program for elementary school kids.

Another assistant, Carl Chang, an undergraduate at UC Davis, stays with his parents in Los Angeles for the summer. Carl plays well with the kids. He's a kid at heart. There's an assortment of activities scheduled for the kids. I do storytelling with them. We go on field trips like ice skating, swimming, Griffith Park's astronomical observatory, bowling, and a car wash fundraiser. Carl jokes around and has funny antics whenever he sees a female. He's a girl watcher. He's amusing to observe.

Karl's thoughts: *Afterwards, a lot went through my mind at home, like how something happened in school. I'm lying on my bed, repeatedly going over the scenarios. I would do that. I'm a person who tries to dissect everything that happened and figure out where I went wrong. A lot of times, I don't blame Mary. I usually put it on me like I messed up and must have said or done something wrong. Because she doesn't respond, I feel very uncomfortable and again disappointed. I expect to get a look back and maybe see her blush or have some smile on her face. Instead, there's no reaction. Perhaps she's disgusted with me. Maybe she's thinking, "My God, he's touching me. I'm going to get cooties." Maybe she's scared of me. There's no positive response or a giggle--nothing.*

[Ch.20:13], [Ch.20:14]

Chapter 21: Senior Fall Semester

Our senior year at Belmont starts bright and early at 5:30 am. I briskly walk to the bus stop about five blocks away. Sometimes, the bus comes a bit early, or I'm behind schedule catching the 6:00 am bus. I'm still a block away from the street and see the bus coming from a distance down the road, sprinting like crazy to the bus stop. Usually, the bus driver sees me running like a maniac, and he's kind enough to wait some seconds.

Hopping on the bus, huffing, and puffing, profusely thanking the bus driver as I pull my change out of my pocket to drop in the fare machine clanging down like a Las Vegas slot machine. I take a deep breath, glancing for an empty seat to plop down for a 35-minute ride to downtown LA, 2nd street, to transfer to my second bus. I'm usually in my orchestra seat at 7 o'clock.

Many students from last year return to the orchestra. Karl is back on the drums and percussions with his perfect touch on the various beats and drumming styles. I don't know if Karl and I will get together during our senior year. He treats several of the girls in a teasing way and never teases me. Several girls like him. I maintain a neutral disposition toward him.

Karl's thoughts: *I can't wait for a new day to come. I can't wait to see Mary again. This kind of yearning to say 'hi,' and to see and watch her walk and move around. That's the stuff that I know I can't talk to my friends. They would say, 'You're crazy. You sound like a girl now.' I never discuss it with them fully because I know people wouldn't understand the kind of bubbly feelings that I feel. That nervousness is my biggest one around her because I don't know her. Everything I try or say doesn't seem to work out the way I want.*

She's just a hard nut to crack. So, I always become very nervous about what is going to happen. **[Ch.21:1], [Ch.21:2]**

The senior year allows me to continue the extra-curricular activities I enjoyed in my junior year. Many apply to colleges and registering to take the SAT in November. I apply to USC, UC Berkeley, and California State University, Los Angeles (CSULA). I always anticipate attending USC. Since the fifth grade, I've been a Trojan fan, and Leland is an alum. I don't know what to major in college, either journalism or elementary school teaching. I'm not going to major in Business. Not interested in dealing with money and business matters. I want to have a job that is meaningful.

I'm not going to join a sorority when I attend college. Understanding this club's sister culture, I'm expected to perform and conform to something I'm not. I'm not putting down sororities. I want to be me and to be accepted the way I am.

I understand members enjoy their sorority and sisterhood if they are a good fit for the other gals. In my day, clubs were not diverse. Potential members go through Rush week to engage in activities and socialize. In the end, sorority sisters vote for new members of the organization.

Besides orchestra, I enjoy Physiology and learning about the body's anatomy. I'm in Physiology class in October or early November, and I overhear a student saying that Shelly Ling and Karl are going to the Prom together. I'm surprised to hear that through the grapevine. My mind is blank.

Later that day, thinking about what I had heard earlier that Karl is going to the prom with someone. I'm upset, tremendously upset. Okay, he was once interested in me. He's no longer interested in me. Let him go. Let him go. And so, I do. **[Ch.21:3]**

My thoughts reflect summer school when Karl loses interest in me. I turned him off, not responding to his hand on my hand. I froze. Karl's hand on my hand was surprisingly unexpected. His move was so forward and bold, especially when we rarely talk and interact with one another. I couldn't take Karl seriously after he squeezed another girl's leg. My thoughts are confirmed when I hear he is going to the prom with someone else. I keep my thoughts and feelings within, not sharing them with anyone. I accept that he changed, or he isn't seriously interested in me anymore. **[Ch.21:4]**

In time, I switch my attention to Carl Chang, who I met this past summer in Chinatown. He's back at UC Davis. We're writing letters to each other as pen pals. We write monthly, updating on what is going on in our lives, nothing romantic, just as friends. This helps me to redirect my attention away from Karl and to recover nicely.

I'm not angry at Karl. If he isn't interested in me, then he's not interested in me. That's plain, simple, and logical. Sure, I'm disappointed.

I feel we have a shared attraction, but he changed his mind.

Fortunately, I don't get a chance to have my heart get deep with him. So, I'm able to recover and not have a seriously broken heart. It doesn't make sense to dislike or be angry at him. I continue carrying on just like I did before he wrote in my yearbook at the end of the 11th grade. I don't treat him any differently. I act as if nothing happened. I've resolved my thoughts and feelings about Karl by letting him go. I'm okay. I can move forward as if nothing occurred.

Karl's thoughts: *When I'm home thinking about Mary, I know that I'll be seeing Mary again. I feel a little lovey-dovey feeling, a little butterfly. Get that little giggle in my head, and I'm all excited. I want to go steady with Mary, but it never feels right, or I never feel the right moment or the right words on how to express it.* **[Ch.21:5]**

It's taken me a while to figure out all these feelings. There's much confusion in my mind. I feel these emotions, but then I get mixed signals from her. She's a hard nut to crack. Maybe it's not meant to be. I went back and forth, back and forth, for a very long time. **[Ch.21:6]**

I want to see if there's any hope with Mary. One last attempt. I don't know what to do anymore. I said "yes" to another person who asked, but I want to make sure 100% that there is not a slight chance that Mary would say, "yes." So, the only thing I have left that I haven't tried is reverse psychology. It's my last option. **[Ch.21:7]**

A week later, I'm at my locker. Bob Shepherd and Karl are walking along the hallway. Bob starts acting goofy and animated, pretending to be clawing with his arms and hands toward me while saying, "Hey, Mary, FONG! Whatcha doing, Mary FONG!"

"Getaway, Bob Shepherd!" as I raise my arms and hands over my head and face keeping him from touching. "Getaway!" I air-slap with my hands toward him to defend myself.

Bob always likes goofing around and laughing. Karl laughs in the background, watching. I close my locker, and we walk down the hallway together. Karl walks in the middle, between Bob and me.

"Mary doesn't want to be my girlfriend," Karl says out of no where.

I freeze. I can't believe what I heard. I'm stunned. I keep walking straight ahead as if I heard nothing. There's dead silence.

"Mary doesn't want to be my girlfriend," Karl says it louder and with emphasis.

I freeze again. I'm confused. I'm questioning in my mind, "Why is Karl saying this to me?" I keep walking straight ahead with them, not even blinking an eye.

Karl turns to look at me to see if there's a reaction on my face. I have a frozen poker face, immensely confused inside. He turns his head and looks straight ahead. Silence.

Eventually, we depart at the end of the hallway, where I turn right, and they turn left down the hall. **[Ch.21:8]**

I'm utterly confused. It makes no sense why Karl said what he said to me. He doesn't sound like he's joking. I'm baffled. I heard he's going to the prom with someone just last week. Now he's making this indirect comment about being his girlfriend. How does anyone respond to that? I couldn't. I already resolved my issue last week to let him go. I don't think much about his indirect comment anymore. I push the thought away from what just happened. I let him go a week ago. **[Ch.21:9]**

Karl's thoughts: *I'm despondent and couldn't express it. I'm carrying this heaviness for two weeks. It's an ending of something that I'm willing to let go. Have you ever had that feeling that you wanted something, but you know in your heart that it's just not going to happen? It's just never going to happen. It's a part of my heart that gets ripped out. It's like a part of my soul. I feel empty inside and lost. I've been building it up inside. It doesn't lead to anger, but it leads to a loss. It's almost like grieving. I feel like I have to start letting go. I have to protect myself because there's too much* *disappointment. I hate myself. It took two weeks for me to make peace with the situation.* **[Ch.21:10], [Ch.21:11]**

Weeks later, I'm walking to my seat in the orchestra. Karl says to me, "Where's my carrot? Where's my carrot?"

"Oh, you want a carrot?" I think Karl says this because I'm wearing my denim overalls with a carrot and the green leafy stems hanging out of my left side pocket. Love wearing my denim overalls and having a carrot with the green leafy stems dangling out. It's quirky, different and fun for me. **[Ch.21:11A]**

The next day, I come to school with a peeled carrot in cellophane wrap and extend my hand, giving it to Karl with a four-by-six-inch stationery card with a colorful smiling turtle.

"Here's your carrot," I say.

Karl looks at it and says, "no."

"Here, take it."

He takes it and says, "all right."

After our lunch hour, we have an English class together. Karl calls me "Mary."

I turn and look at him.

He nods and says, "The carrot was good."

I grin.

A month later, we receive our senior glamor photos and exchange our portraits. Karl gives me his senior photo. **[Ch.21:12]**

Karl is always complimentary, which is meaningful to me. His quiet support and what he writes make me feel good. I'm a modest person, partly because of my Chinese cultural upbringing that values modesty. However, I also think that I'm naturally born that way.

I instinctively feel that no one is better than another. We are all equal. Karl's comments never go to my head. I think Karl is observant of what I do, making me feel good that he notices me.

I feel his comments are sincere, and he is kind to all his high school classmates.

Karl's thoughts: *I'm going to do it. I'm going to do it today. I'm going up there and talk to Mary and tell her. Although I want to move forward, I feel something always holds me back. I'm an*

intuitive person, so I follow that feeling. I get disappointed a lot. **[Ch.21:13]**

I'm done with this. The problem is, the logical mind says we're done. I can't be doing this to myself. But my heart is telling me I have a connection with her. I feel drawn to her. I'm done. Cut off the emotional connection. But it's so hard when we bump into each other. Here come the feelings again. It's immensely tough to turn my heart into rock and to deny the emotions I'm feeling. The feelings keep coming. So, it's incredibly tough to shut down my heart. **[Ch.21:14]**

Karl's thoughts: *Although there are always these feelings for Mary, I eventually start hanging out with other girls because I thought, well, either she will become jealous, or maybe I can get her to notice me that way.*

Over time, I say, I just give up. I feel like I've tried so much now that I'm going to quit. My friends try to get me to consider other girls. But, I have these feelings for Mary. There's something about Mary. **[Ch.21:15]**

My last year competing on the forensics team has been eventful. I continue to receive finalist plaques throughout the year for my expository speech on the topic of mime, and for storytelling, I present, *The Sneetches* by Dr. Seuss. I'm most excited and happy today when Belmont's speech team wins the sweepstakes trophy in our last tournament of the year, beating out Beverly Hills High School!

That evening, I show Leland the two plaques I won. My Mom walks to the kitchen and stops to see what we are discussing. This is the first time I say to my Mom, "Ma, I won two plaques at the speech tournament today."

My Mom holds both plaques and says, *"Oh, liang ge muk,"* meaning "oh, two pieces of wood."

I don't say anything. I'm neutral, and I don't feel offended. I figure my Mom's response is a way to keep me modest. My Mom understands more English than she speaks. Normatively, the Chinese culture (e.g., first and second-generation) is not a compliment-giving society. They do compliment, but sparingly in comparison to Caucasian Americans.

Culturally, the Chinese emphasize improving one's competencies through hard work and listening to advice and criticism. My parents never ask me about my homework or what I'm learning in school throughout my education. My parents have minimal schooling and are limited in speaking English, and the various subject matters taught in school. Although they value education, it's foreign to them. My parents all their lives in survival mode, working to pay the mortgage, utilities, insurance, food, etc. **[Ch.21:16], [Ch.21:17]**

After school, I'm sitting on the curb in downtown LA waiting for my second bus to go home. I feel low energy, quiet, and calm. I reflect, think, and analyze myself. Mary, you're nice. Why don't you act friendly? I'm not mean. I'm questioning why I'm not more expressive, friendly, social, and smiling at others.

I analyze why I feel and think a particular way and question it. I engage in self-talk to get to the root of my thoughts and feelings to understand why I am the way I am in various situations. For example, if I'm bothered about someone or a situation, I question why I feel and think the way I do. When I ask myself a question, it requires a response. Then I keep asking a follow-up question, and I respond. This Q and A technique enables me to dig deeper and deeper within myself. This process helps me to understand and know myself better. Also, I want to resolve any negative feelings and thoughts and be in a state of healthy alignment.

Chapter 22: Senior Spring Semester

Received acceptance to all three colleges, and I'm pleased. My first choice is to attend USC. However, I have to see if my financial package will afford me to attend.

I'm matched up for career day to visit my Chinatown stomping grounds, Castelar elementary school to experience a day with a teacher and her classroom. It's a pleasant experience meeting the fifth graders. However, I feel strange because some Chinese girls are so friendly and curious when talking to me while holding my arms and hands. They are sweet. I have never experienced so much attention with kids welcoming, looking up to me, and wanting to hold my hands and arms. During my visit to Castelar, the Hiroshima band plays in the auditorium.

I'm impressed that this fantastic Japanese jazz band entertains these kids. It's a treat for me too! **[Ch.22:1]**

Back at Belmont in gymnastics class, a girl says to me with a smile, "My brother thinks you are cute."

"Oh, who is your brother?" I say with surprise.

"Aaron."

"Oh, I don't know him. I don't think I've had any classes with him."

"Well, he thinks you're cute."

"Oh," modestly grin.

Eventually, I discover who Aaron is. I see him a couple of times in the hallway with a big smile, and he says, "Hi."

Ladyes and the Knights are senior service clubs with a square dance outing. I show up since I'm the Historian. Aaron wants to be my dance partner, but I'm not interested. I try to avoid him. One of my friends says that I'm rude. But she doesn't know the backstory. I don't like to mislead anyone.

In a matter of a couple of weeks, our class is in the library. Aaron is in the library and comes by to say, "Hi." At this point, I write a note to him. Walking by where he sits, I give him the note. I walk away to the bookshelves. Coming by his seat moments later and say, "Did you read my note?"

"Yes," he nods complacently.

"Did you understand what I wrote?" I ask.

"Yes," he responds.

I returned to my seat. I explained in the note not to have an interest in me because I don't want him to waste his time. I don't want to keep Aaron's hopes up. I don't want to hurt him, but it would be best to communicate my thoughts rather than not do anything, especially since his sister conveyed a message to me. He might think I'm acquiescing, and he might approach me, which I don't want him to do. I care about another's feelings, and I do my best to communicate when I can clarify a situation. Aaron has a sweet disposition. However, there's no mutual interest.

I marvel at gals who go out on dates and have no attraction to them. How do they do that? I must be immature. For some reason, I can't do that. Those gals are kind to accept a date and be cordial going out. Wow, I'm impressed.

If a guy asks me out, he must have an interest or an attraction toward me. If I don't have an interest or attraction, I don't accept because I feel I would be misleading a guy, and it's encouraging him, which bothers me. It is hurtful if the guy has the illusion that I'm interested when it's not the case. I would feel I'm not true to myself and the guy.

Some say that going on a date is only a date, like trying on a pair of shoes. It's a time to have fun and get to know a person. However, if I'm not attracted to the person, and the other person is attracted to me, I feel a mismatch. I have a concern not to mislead someone because I don't want to hurt a person.

If I can curtail a situation where the guy has fallen for me, I find a way to resolve the complications. It's a matter of perspective and approach. I take it seriously, while other gals might see it as a date with no strings attached. I don't want to see the ball of string get knotted and tangled. That's all.

As an 11th grader, I decide not to go to the prom in my senior year. It's a big waste of money just for an evening to get all dolled up and go out with a guy I barely know. I think it's impractical, awkward, and pretentious. However, after the 11th grade, I would have reconsidered if Karl had asked me.

But that's not happening since he chose to take another gal. I don't think twice about the prom. The entire senior cabinet of officers attended the prom, except for me. They assumed I was going and wondered why I didn't go.

In lieu of the weekend of the prom, I joined a group of gals gathering for a slumber party at Mrs. Gee's home. She is the Ladyes' advisor. Never been to a slumber party, and I figured it would be fun. Eight of us enjoy the evening eating out, bowling, watching TV, chatting, and doing a late bagel run. It's past midnight, and a few girls are dozing off. A few gals wide-awake play a prank on two of the gals sleeping with their glasses. They apply tape on their glasses.

Everyone giggles. When the gals wake up, they look disoriented. Everyone chuckles.

Eventually, I doze off on the couch. Waking up, I go to the restroom. Sitting on the toilet, I see my toes bleeding, thinking the bowling shoes caused it. I touch my bleeding toes and realize those gals had painted my toenails red! "Those dirty rats," I mutter and chuckle.

Before entering the living room, I stick my red nail-polished foot out of the doorway. I'm tapping my foot up and down to get the pranksters' attention, and they burst out laughing. I jump out and say, "All right, who's the dirty rat who painted my toenails red? I'm sitting on the toilet, thinking my toes are bleeding. I'm thinking my bowling shoes cause my bleeding."

The pranksters' burst of laughter fills the living room with big smiles and claps. It's my first slumber party, and it was fun! They got me!

By the end of my second season competing on the gymnastics team, I qualify to compete in the All-City Girl's Gymnastics Finals. Five of our team members qualify. A highlight accomplishment, considering I've been learning for only two years.

I'm feeling pretty good in the final weeks of my senior year, looking forward to completing high school and starting a new chapter of life at the university. Mrs. Goodman invites her orchestra students to her home one afternoon. I still feel socially awkward talking to guys.

Karl asks me, "What are you going to major in?"

"Education," I say.

"What are you going to do with it?"

"I'm thinking of being an elementary school teacher."

"No, don't do it! Don't do it!" he says with emphasis.

"Why?" I'm surprised that Karl is so emphatic.

"My Dad is an elementary school teacher, and he says, don't do it!"

It's the last week of our senior year, and I walk to the Flats to do my senior cabinet treasury duties, selling Grad Nite tickets to Disneyland. As I'm walking, Greg calls out, "Hey, Mary. Can you sign my yearbook?"

"Sure," I say as we exchange yearbooks. I sit down and begin writing.

Thirty seconds later, someone swings their backpack toward me and says, "Hey, when are you going to sign my yearbook?" I look up, and I see Karl.

"Oh, I'll sign it right after I finish signing this one," I say. A minute later, Greg returns my yearbook, and I hand it to Karl. Then I return Greg's yearbook to him after signing it.

Karl gives me his yearbook. As we both sign each other's yearbook, he says, "Are you going to Awards Night tonight?"

"Yes," I reply, turning my body away from him. From my peripheral vision, I can see that he notices my body language. I think what kind of question is that? Of course, I'm going to Awards Night. We're both in orchestra, and we play tonight.

I continue writing nonsensical thoughtless ideas in his yearbook. I'm feeling light-hearted. My feelings toward Karl are neutral since I had resolved my relations with him almost eight months ago.

We both finished signing each other's yearbooks. Then Karl gets up and says, "I'll see you tonight at Awards Night."

"See, you," I reply. I get up and continue walking across the Flats to do my treasury shift. During my shift, I read what Karl wrote in my yearbook. **[Ch.22:2]**

Again, he writes the best compliments I have ever received from anyone. After reading his kind and generous compliments, I notice that he mentioned the time we met in U.S. History. That time must have meant something to him to write it. I see that he writes his regrets about not getting to know me better this past year. I recall him writing his intentions last year in my yearbook that he wanted to get to know me a lot better. But it never happened.

At this point, graduation is just around the corner by the end of this week. Our time has passed. I read his words, and I don't think twice about them. I've already accepted what happened this past year, and I have no judgment or negative feelings. I feel neutral. I close my yearbook.

Awards Night occurs, and the evening is over. Everyone in the orchestra returns their musical instruments to the back room and exits. I wait for Mrs. Goodman to give me a ride home.

I sit in the front row, right in the middle of the auditorium, absorbing the last moments of ever sitting in this auditorium again. I realize that this evening was my final performance in the orchestra. Sitting, embracing this quiet moment, until someone calls out to me,

"Hey, Mary."

I turn to my right and see Karl walking toward me with a guitar in his hand. I look at him and turn away, looking toward my left. He sits down on the seat, armrest next to me.

"How are you doing?" Karl says with a smile

"Oh, I'm doing fine," I reply with neutrality

"Why don't you play me a Chinese song?" Karl asks while extending his guitar toward me.

"Oh, no. That's all right. Oh, you go ahead," I say.

Karl starts strumming his guitar and begins singing a Loggins and Messina song. **[Ch.22:3]**

Karl plays the first stanza, stops, and says, "Do you know this song?"

"Oh, yes," nodding unenthusiastically, looking away from him. In my mind, I'm thinking, I don't like the part of the song, when he sings, "come on and squeeze me, come on and squeeze me." I feel a bit uncomfortable, and I'm unsure what is happening. I was feeling, "Oh, no."

Karl pauses, and I have an inkling that he is ready to ask me something.

"Hey, Karl!" someone yells from the back of the auditorium. Karl looks back at his friends from the orchestra and looks back at me. He pauses.

"Come on, Karl, let's go home!" they call him again.

Then Karl looks back at his friends, and he looks back at me. He hesitates.

"Well, I got to go now. Ah, I'll talk to you later," Karl says.

"Okay," I respond. Karl gets up and walks to the back of the auditorium, where his friends wait.

I'm left sitting here. I feel relief. I sense that Karl was just about to pop the question to ask me out to Grad Nite. I don't want him to ask me, however. Whew! I feel total relief. His friends saved him. I don't want to embarrass him. And I don't want to be in the position of saying I couldn't go with him. I already have a date to Grad Nite.

Karl joins his friends, eager to leave after the Awards Night. Stan and Karl pile into Byron's used car.

Karl's thoughts: *I'm quiet in the car. The guys are all goofing around and making fun as usual. I'm just quiet. They think that I was hanging out with Mary. They don't know my intentions, but they can see it in my face. They can see that there is something not right. They know I'm not quiet. When we hang out, I always have something to say. I'm just too quiet, and they can see that something didn't happen the way I might have planned it. They are trying to get it out of me. But I don't want to talk about it. So, I keep responding, 'yeah.'*

I'm trying hard not to cry in the car because guys don't cry.

That's just a rule, and when guys surround you, you don't cry. I'm trying to hold it together. That's why I'm not saying anything because if I start talking, the tears will come. So, I'm trying to hold it in. I'm trying to suppress the tears by being quiet for a while until I feel the energy bubbling inside of me subsides. **[Ch.22:4]**

I'm really sad. I feel like this is the last time, my last opportunity to connect with Mary. To honestly tell her how I feel and I blew it. I couldn't say it. It makes me sad. So, I had to suck it up in the car. **[Ch.22:5]**

I tell them to drop it, and I don't want to talk about it anymore. They stop asking. They start talking about other stuff, and I start talking about that stuff. The guys are talking about all kinds of other shit, so I try to focus on that. This energy becomes too overwhelming, and crying starts. So, I put my focus away from how I'm feeling. Shifting to the bullshit, they tell in the car allows me to mellow down that energy and hold it all together.

Karl arrives home. He has his moment lying on his bed.

Karl's thoughts: *When I went to bed, I had one of those staring at the ceiling moments, replaying in my mind what just happened and what could have happened. It drove me a little crazy. My sadness turned into a little bit of anger. Once I started regurgitating everything, I become angry at my friends for interrupting. Of course, they didn't know, but I get to where my energy needs to go somewhere. I need to release it somehow, or it'll eat me alive. I hit my pillow a little bit to get that energy out of me. I become angry at my friends for interrupting. I become mad at myself for not having the courage to do what I was supposed to do. I become mad at Mary because she never responded or never asked anything, or she never said much to me either. I feel frustrated. Combining sadness and frustration, I become angry. But my anger faded quickly; and then becomes sadness again.* **[Ch.22:6]**

So, I feel like I'm on a roller coaster. I go up and down and go through all these different emotions. I'm going through all these scenarios in my head. How it could have been, how it should have been, how it should not have been. I'm going through all these things, and I keep thinking and thinking. **[Ch.22:7]**

I'm disappointed in myself that I just couldn't. It never came out of my mouth. I never said what I really wanted to say. I tried to open up to Mary, but it never happened.

I'm disappointed in myself that the fear always took over. The fear of being rejected, the fear of not getting the response that I was hoping for, always took over. It controlled what was coming out of my mouth. It also controlled what I was doing most of the time when I was around her. I couldn't say it, 'hey, I care about you. I'm in love with you. I have a crush on you. I want to do this and that, this and that with you.' **[Ch.22:8]**

On the other hand, I also feel disappointed that after all my attempts, she would pick up what I was trying to say and help me in the conversation. That is, someway, she would see that I'm trying to make something clear to her and that she would open up and tell me how she feels. **[Ch.22:9]**

Eventually, I fell asleep just thinking about things. I think I exhausted myself with overthinking, crying, and being upset. **[Ch.22:10]**

Flashback at least two months prior, I asked my pen pal, Carl, if he wanted to go to Grad Nite, which he accepted. Around this time, the orchestra met for a weekend rehearsal for the school's musical, *Bye, Bye Birdie.* During our break, I stepped outside and sat on the concrete wall next to the steps. Stan, the trombone player, sat on one side. We chatted a bit, and I told him that I'm going to Grad Nite with someone. When Karl caught a ride home with Stan and Byron after Awards Night, I'm sure Stan told Karl I had a date to Grad Nite.

The next day, I'm out at the Flats signing yearbooks. I'm wearing my coral color sundress. I feel pretty good. I'm sitting at one end of the lunch table, signing a yearbook. As I write, a tiny piece of rolled-up paper flies in my direction. I ignore it and keep writing.

I overhear a conversation between Karl and Stan at the opposite end of the same lunch table I'm sitting. They must have sat down after me while I'm signing yearbooks. I hear Karl say, "Who can I ask to go to Grad Nite with?" Karl and Stan keep chatting. Other than that, I don't hear much.

I continue writing in the yearbook, and another tiny paper ball flies in my direction again. I ignore it since I'm focusing on writing. Then another tiny paper ball flies over again. This time, it goes down into my sundress. Then, I stop writing. I use my right index finger and thumb to pinch the tiny paper ball out from the top of my sundress. I slowly toss it aside and slowly look at Karl sitting kitty-corner.

Immediately, Karl looks up in the sky, pretending to be whistling and feigning that he didn't do anything. I continue writing in the yearbook.

The next day, I'm at home, and the phone rings. Roslyn is on the phone. She is thrilled. "Oh my goodness, Karl asked me to go to Grad Nite!" Everyone knows Roslyn's longest crush on Karl since junior high school.

"Oh, that's good," I calmly respond, slightly surprised.

"And we're going to the beach tomorrow," she says joyfully.

"Oh, great. Well, have a good time," I say calmly.

After hanging up the phone, I feel neutral. After all, I had resolved my feelings toward Karl early in our senior year. I continue with what I'm doing at home. I never tell anyone that Karl had serenaded me just a couple of days ago. I don't think twice about that interaction. I want to forget about what happened. I want to avoid any embarrassment between us.

Today is graduation. All the graduates gather in the boy's gymnasium dressed in their caps and gown with their hanging tassels. Many are chatting, hugging, or taking photos with one another. I'm floating around the gymnasium, saying hello to people.

Ryan shows me a piece of paper with his name on it. He wants to see if I can pronounce his name correctly. I'm one of the senior cabinet treasurers tasked with announcing the graduates' names during the ceremony. He has a long Hawaiian name that is not easy to pronounce. He pronounces it a couple of times while I repeat it after him. I chuckle as we're parting because I have never heard such an unusual name before.

Then I walk some five feet away, and as I turn in one direction, I'm in front of three guys standing next to each other, crying. I'm surprised to see all three best buddies-- Byron, Karl, and Rocky standing there crying together.

"Why are you guys crying?" I ask them.

"Because we're graduating," they say in a chorus while sobbing.

"You shouldn't be crying. You should be happy. We're graduating! We're going to college!" I say with sheer joy.

They shake their heads. Byron and Rocky fade backwards while Karl steps toward me.

He looks at me with crinkled eyebrows, gently points his index finger at me, and asks, "By the way, who are you going to Grad Nite with?"

"Oh, uhm, I'm… going with a friend. His name happens to be Carl also," I say hesitantly while feeling awkward and not expecting a question like that.

Karl nods and looks down. We quietly part ways. **[Ch.22:11]**

I'm glad to get out of that interaction. After Karl serenaded me, I pretend that it had never happened. I'm trying to save face for him. Karl technically did not ask me out. He stopped short, his friends calling him to go home after the Awards Night. **[Ch.22:12]**

It's time for the graduates to march onto the football field to *Pomp and Circumstance.* I take my turn to announce over the microphone when each graduate steps forward and hands me their slip of paper with their name. I don't have a chance to sit and enjoy the graduation ceremony. Before I know it, the ceremony closes with over 800 graduates marching off the field. **[Ch.22:13]**

Chapter 23: After Graduation

Following the ceremony, the graduates head to Grad Nite. Many yellow buses parked along the north side street of Belmont High wait for the graduates to board for Disneyland.

Meeting up with Carl, we hop onto the bus and sit down. We chat a bit. He asks to see my Belmont student ID. While conversing, he says, "Yea, when walking across the field, you looked like a stick."

I say nothing and ignore his comment like I've ignored others who have made similar uncomplimentary comments throughout my teenage years. I remain cordial toward him throughout the evening.

Grad Nite was uneventful. It's a wasted evening—nothing fun or exciting about my time there. We hardly engaged in conversation. It was a mistake to ask Carl to Grad Nite. He wasn't good company. He was in his world.

I'm home before the early morning sunrise, feeling exhausted and disappointed. No tears; I was nonchalant. It was a disaster. It's all behind me.

I wake up in the afternoon, still feeling tired and blasé. I don't tell anyone about my Grad Nite experience. Nobody asks. A hurdle that I jumped over, and now thankfully, it's all in the past.

A week or two after graduation, I join a bus full of Belmont students on a summer camping trip with the Eulexian Scholarship Club to Bryce Canyon and Zion National Park in Utah and Humboldt State University. I'm marveling over the never-seen large albino fishes in the marine biology area at Humboldt State. Bryce Canyon has spectacular landscapes. **[Ch.23:1]**

The hiking trip to Emerald Pools requires us to climb rocks. I make wisecracks as we climb some boulders along the trail. "I sure deserve a t-shirt that says, 'Go Climb a Rock!' and 'Whose idea is this?'" I'm not keen on climbing rocks. It's laborious rather than relaxing and fun. We finally arrive at Emerald Pools, and we sit on rocks, dipping our feet in the cold, refreshing, and relaxing pool.

Arriving back at our campsite we play volleyball. I couldn't help noticing Byron wearing white socks with zoris playing volleyball. Where are his tennis shoes? On the one hand, he wants to win, and on the other hand, he plays like Mr. Cool. He handles the ball in a relaxed style. The volleyball comes to him, and he puts one open palm up, and it rolls off his fingers.

I laugh hysterically in my quiet way because he looked ridiculous. He should have bumped it with two hands together or used both hands to set it, or he could have hit it with his fist. Anyway, I'm goofing around, not caring if we win or not. We lose, and with my hands up, I cheer, "Yeah, we lost! Yes, we lost!"

During the trip, I hear through the grapevine that first-time campers will go through an initiation. The last three people will be dunked into the river. That idea doesn't sit well with me as my curiosity and adrenaline begin flowing since I'm a first-time camper. Heck, if I'm going to be one of the last ones.

We're instructed to get our sleeping bags and meet at 5:00 pm outside in a designated open area. Calvin is in charge of the initiation activity. First-time campers stand around, holding our sleeping bags while the other campers stand back, spectating the event that soon ensues.

Holding his clipboard, Calvin shouts, "Layout your sleeping bag in one row and get inside your sleeping bag." Next, he takes roll call. Calvin shouts, "Everybody, remove your jeans, and we will come by and collect them."

I'm wearing overalls, so it's easy to slip them off. One by one, our jeans are collected as we each hand them over. All the first-time campers peer at a large pile of jeans about 25 feet away. The rest of the spectators enjoy the unraveling of the initiation event.

Calvin shouts further instructions, "When I blow this whistle, your job is to hop over to this pile of jeans to find your pair. Then hop back to your spot, put your jeans back on, get outside of your sleeping bag, and let me know so that I can check your name off. The last three people will be dunked into the river! Are there any questions? All right. Get ready. Get set!" Whistle blows! **[Ch.23:2],**

[Ch.23:2A]

A mad rush of fifteen teenagers hopping toward the pile of jeans. Karl, Randy, and I jump like crazy at the forefront toward the pile of jeans. I see my overall jeans. Fortunately, I have white and dark blue striped suspenders on them--easier to find. **[Ch.23:3]**

Randy topples over, blocking me from grabbing my overalls. "Randy! Get out of the way!" I grab my overalls, hop away like a mad dog from the crowd, and back to my spot. I laid down in my sleeping bag, trying to put on my overalls. I get them on. I jump out of my sleeping bag wearing my overalls. "Oh, no!" I exclaim looking at my overalls. But I still rush over to Calvin.

"Just though, we get our pants on, right?" I energetically ask Calvin.

"Yea," he says.

"Good, because I have them on backward!" I say gleefully with relief as he checks my name off on his clipboard.

I jump back into my sleeping bag and take off my overalls, and put them on correctly. I'm feeling relief, snapping on my overall suspenders over my shoulders and buttoning up. I'm observing the rest of the first-time campers still scrambling and hopping around to get their jeans.

Ultimately, no one is dunked into the river. It's only a motivator, a fear tactic. I'm thinking, "Oh, really, it's only a motivator? It's enough motivation to get Calvin dunked into the river!"

The next day, 75 campers take a hike. A group of guys, including Karl, Byron, and Randy, who has a great baritone voice, sing a Doobie Brothers' song, Black Waters, acapella style while hiking. They actually sound pretty good. **[Ch.23:4]**

During the hike, we come across a banana slug. Everyone huddles around to look at it. "Eeeuull," a few gals say while they squirm and react to its sliminess. Later that day, we are all back at our campsite to relax a bit before dinner.

We're chowing down our dinner sitting at several wooden tables and benches. I get up to get some soup. Karl happens to be at the large pot scooping soup. I'm next to him, watching, hearing him scraping the bottom with the soup ladle. I reach for the pot handle, tilting the large pot to fill his ladle with soup easily. Seeing from my peripheral vision, Karl slightly smiles at me as I peer into the pot of soup.

Some return to their tents as people finished their dinner, toss frisbees, or stroll the campgrounds. I'm a slow eater and one of the last still eating.

"Aaauuughhh!" a high pitch scream penetrates the serene campground forest of tall, pine-scented trees. Turning heads in the direction of Sissy, running hysterically out of her tent through the forest with her hands flapping about with a horrid face screaming, "There's a banana slug in my sleeping bag!" A burst of laughter overlays her screams of panic coming from a few guys at the dinner table.

Everyone wonders what is going on. Mr. Kwan, the club adviser, investigates the tent and discovers it's not a banana slug; it's an overly ripe brown spotted banana in her sleeping bag. Those chuckling guys know that Sissy reacted to the banana slug earlier on the trail. Of course, the pranksters knew that Sissy would make an excellent butt of a joke because of her predictable animated and expressive reaction. They knew that they would get a kick out of it.

One night, a small group of us—Karl, Sissy, Randy, Brandon, and a few others are hanging around the campfire. I have my guitar and play a couple of tunes. I play a Stevie Wonder song, "You Are the Sunshine of My Life," and "Ventura Highway." **[Ch.23:5], [Ch.23:6]**

After I play, Sissy says, "Your guitar sounds out of tune." I sit there and say nothing. Everyone is silent. Shortly after, I return to my tent and call it a night. I don't think twice about what she said. I let it bounce off of me.

Our bus is ready to return home for a long ride of several hundreds of miles on the last day. Karl turns on his music boom box on our bus ride home, sharing music throughout the one-week camping trip. Hearing one particular song makes me feel and experience the present moment of life. **[Ch.23:7]**

The week flies by so quickly. Before we know it, we're back home in LA. What a nice getaway trip.

Shortly after the camping trip, I hear a mix-up of someone having Karl's kitchen utensil from the camping trip. I use the mix-up of utensils to write to Karl to let him know what I had heard. I don't know why I want to connect with him. I think if I write, it could begin a dialogue between us. Karl and I never had the opportunity to talk or interact socially in high school. We weren't in the same circle of friends, and we only had some classes together in high school.

Reflecting, my subconscious had stored away all the questions, confusions, awkwardness, denials, hurt, face-saving, disconnects, and never expressed thoughts and feelings about my relations with Karl during high school. I suppressed myself to defend, rationalize, and cope with what I never realized. Karl receives a letter from me.

Karl's thoughts: *I'm feeling confused. Fear is kicking in because I don't want to return to that little train ride. Anxiety is kicking in on making the wrong decision. I've had this longing for Mary and wanting a connection with her. It didn't happen. I'm at the point of wanting to protect myself and wanting to close off. It's an end of a chapter and an end of an era.*

Then I get this letter out of nowhere. Confronted with these old feelings that I've suppressed and hidden in a drawer somewhere inside me. It's still there, but as long as I keep the drawer shut, I'm okay.

So, this letter opens up this drawer, and all these old feelings and longings come forward. Fear kicks in because I get to a point where I no longer want to hurt. My experience with Mary in the past two years has been like a rollercoaster ride. I no longer want to go down that road of disappointment. **[Ch.23:8]**

So, I have a choice either I respond to it, allow myself to go down that treacherous path of not knowing what's going to come from this, or continue to keep the drawer locked and not go into it. That's the choice that I make. It's self-protection. I'm feeling sad. I feel that I want something really bad and a feeling that I'm not going to get it. I feel I need to let go of the idea of Mary and me. **[Ch.23:9]**

I mention this to my close friends, and they respond, "Oh, cool." They don't think it is a big deal. They don't understand how big of a deal it is to me. I kept it hidden for as long as I can remember. I don't think I ever fully mentioned to anyone how I genuinely feel about Mary. I have come to the point where I'm feeling comfortable enough in my life. I have gotten to the point that the past is the past. It's time to move forward, start a future, and go in the direction of being who I am, and what I long for is well received. **[Ch.23:10]**

`I'm still figuring out the logistics of how I'm going to attend USC. I don't have a driver's license yet. I don't have a car. I'm not crazy about traveling on the bus for two hours one-way to take classes at USC. I'm one thousand dollars short for tuition. I don't want to take out a student loan because I have learned from watching Leland trying to pay back his USC student loan for many years. It's also out of the question to ask my parents because I know they don't have the finances to assist me.

That summer of 1977, I'm a paid participant in NYC in Chinatown. I also have a job working at a husband-and-wife team operating their insurance agency. They are dysfunctional. They argue at times. It's an unpleasant work environment. Cigarette smell permeates their three-room office due to their smoking habit. The wife has a raspy, hoarse voice, probably due to her smoking habit.

I file thick manila folders of insurance clients after both husband and wife toss them on the carpet, where I squat down to pick them up. I don't know why they can't place the files on a table or a chair that's more accessible to pick up. It's my first real job. I'm saving money to pay for college.

They fired me within a month because they claimed I did not put a stamp on an envelope returned to their office. It isn't a loss for me. It takes me an hour to take a bus to get to work. Chalk it up to experience.

Meanwhile, Karl never writes back. I quietly accept it, and my thoughts of him fade away. Finally, in late August, I switch from USC to CSULA because I could take the public bus within a half-an-hour to East LA. I would have plenty of money to pay for tuition, and other expenses, save money in the bank and be debt-free.

However, I feel very disappointed and let down not going to USC. I aspired to attend USC for years, since the fifth grade when I was a Trojan sports fan, and Leland had graduated from there. I'm no longer excited about going to college.

Chapter 24: Karl's College Days at USC

A new chapter, a new beginning for me—it's college life at the University of Southern California. I've registered for my Fall semester classes. I look forward to joining a fraternity.

But first, I have to survive Rush week, an initiation process, before getting accepted into a fraternity. I'm expecting them to have us do gross stuff, but it isn't like that. Instead, they have us do the dare-or-share events like seducing girls, stealing things, asking girls out on dates, etc. It's part of a big game; It's not anything violent or anything mean. Everybody knows, even the sorority girls know it's safe and fun activities to break the ice.

There's one event where we try and get dates with as many girls as possible in one hour. I actually win that one, and I am proud of that. The guys go on their dates. However, some are canceled later on. We have to get as many girls to accept the invitation. It's a lot of fun, but the girls know it's part of a game. They would play around and play hard-to-get. For me, I think it's a lot of fun.

Some guys feel embarrassed, and some feel very shy. I see it as a game. I don't see it as anything serious. I get five dates in one hour and go on two dates. They know it's a game on the other three dates, so they don't feel hurt at all.

It gives me a boost that it's easy to ask somebody out to get to know them after all my high school failures. It was always very hard for me in high school.

I'm going to be honest. I do some exploring because it's time for me to have fun and to discover myself and things like that. So, I do go out with women, but very few of them catch my attention. Some of them are just fun, but there isn't much depth. I'm a person, I need to feel that connection, and if I don't feel it right away, I kind of get turned off.

Many people say, "Oh, you know, you get to know each other, and things grow slowly." Well, I don't believe in growing slowly. Either I have a connection, or I don't. But I know right away. It's a 'yes,' or a 'no.' So, I know.

I haven't changed my likes for females. I'm interested in two women who are unique, special, intelligent individuals who wouldn't let anybody take them off their course, including me. I also try to get close, but they don't have time for me. I don't fit in their picture. They want to accomplish what they are here to do first.

Later comes the relationship. So, I have some good friendships with them. We have some romantic, casual times here and there.

I have a thing for intelligent women who can think and stand up for themselves, know what they want to do, and go for it. Unfortunately, that isn't so good for me and a relationship. I have a relationship in college, but there's a lot of freedom in it. It's more like companionship. I don't know why, but I think of Mary for every girl I meet. **[Ch.24:1]** I reflect on the time we met in the US History class. **[Ch.24:2]**

I do enjoy college life of academics, partying, meeting people, and going to the beach. Whenever I have a chance, I enjoy the beach with my friends, sunning, and having fun on the boogie board. I love being on the water. Much to my parents' displeasure, they think I'm socializing and having too much fun. Overall, my undergrad required a lot of studying, and my academics go pretty smoothly. **[Ch.24:3]**

Chapter 25: Mary's College Days at CSULA & UCLA

The Fall quarter at CSULA begins in early October. During registration week, I apply to the campus library for a student assistant job, including a test demonstrating the Dewey library filing system. The Science & Technology department offers me a position to identify, categorize, and accurately file journals and magazines on the library shelves. My job involves archiving current and past issues in the journal stacks.

In my first quarter of college, I register for Introduction to Sociology, a Biology course called Man and His Environment, and Chinese Mandarin. My first college exam is in Sociology. There's a mix of majors and grade levels of students taking the course.

I'm blown away when a female student completes the first exam within 10 to 15 minutes. I'm barely getting started. I chug along, reading every word carefully in the questions and each multiple-choice. I like to take my time and typically use maximum time during test-taking. In the following session, we receive our test results. I'm pleased about receiving an "A-" on my first college test. It's nice to start on a positive note.

In my first quarter at CSULA, I spend some time in the Student Union listening to music or eating my lunch while watching my favorite soap opera, *All My Children*, in a packed TV room. I study in the Student Union in my first quarter, waiting to hitch a ride with my oldest brother, Leland. He's taken many psychology classes and is only one course away from getting a degree in psychology before switching to science courses to attend the Chiropractic and Acupuncture schools.

One afternoon, the *Hiroshima* band plays instrumental jazz music reverberating throughout the four-level Student Union. It's a treat to see them perform again. **[Ch.25:1]**

In the Fall quarter of 1977, I'm a Chinese dancer in the Chinatown Folk Dance group. We perform the lotus dance at the University of California, Santa Barbara, for the Chinese New Year celebration and locally at the Lotus Festival in Silver Lake in 1978.

In the Winter quarter, I take courses called Music Appreciation, Freshman Composition, and Chinese Mandarin. One day in the Music Appreciation course, the professor tells the class that he received extra credit work from a student claiming to have written a poem.

In class, the professor reads the poem "The Impossible Dream." He reads, "To dream, the impossible dream, to fight the unbeatable foe, to bear the unbearable sorrow. To run where the brave dare not go."

I laugh hysterically. The student plagiarized a classic. The student did not know that it was a well-known creative work. It's hilarious that the naïve student thinks a professor would not notice this!

In the Winter quarter, I apply for a job at the *Los Angeles Times* newspaper in downtown LA. I'm offered a customer service job to work in the Circulation Department, answering the phone for 30 hours, six days a week.

I have a busy schedule taking classes from 8 am to noon. I have only one hour to walk across campus, catch the freeway flyer to work, buy my lunch at the *LA Times* cafeteria, wolf my lunch down in five minutes, and be in my seat by 1 pm. Fortunately, I've never been late. I've always been a very slow eater all my life, but I learn to eat very fast to get to my seat on time for work.

Over and over again, I answer phones and say, "LA Times, this is Mary. How may I help you?" I serve a wide range of clientele, from irate and upset customers who didn't receive their paper, to new subscribers, to subscribers who are delighted to go on vacation. In 1978, my hourly pay was $4.05. It's a dollar over the minimum wage. One customer exclaims I have a voice like Angie Dickson, an actress in the TV show *Police Woman,* along with many other acting performances in TV and movies. I appreciate the compliment, but I have no clue how her voice sounds until I watch her on the *Johnny Carson Show*. I beg to differ. **[Ch.25:2]**

After three months, I take a typing test at the *LA Times* personnel office to transfer and get promoted to inputting new subscribers' information into the computer. I type 112 words per minute. Soon after, there's an opening, and I'm reassigned to the Circulation Department typing subsection. I enjoy typing. I find it relaxing. It's much better than constantly answering phones for 30 hours a week. I can work very fast in mechanical processing because the skill does not require much thinking.

However, when it comes to thinking, reading, and writing, I work slower because it requires me to understand, analyze, synthesize, and create new material. I like to take my time. What's the rush? As I work, I like to feel and get into the new subject matter.

After my freshman year, I take a Public Speaking course that fulfills a general education (GE) requirement. I have a few high school classmates in the same class. I feel more pressure to meet certain expectations since my high school classmates know I competed on the speech team. I prefer having colleagues who don't know me, so I don't feel I have to perform at an expected level.

When the public speaking instructor talks about the communication process model, I find it intriguing about the essential components. I'm hooked at that point and think about being a communication major. After I give my informative speech on mime, an expository I used in the high school competition, my instructor tells me that I should join the forensics team at CSULA.

I find it tiring and stressful to compete. I recall the weekend speech competitions from 8 a.m. until 5 p.m., not eating and drinking all day, and not even having breakfast! I don't know how I survived.

In my second year of college, I take a Creative Dramatics course for fun. I've always had a love for acting. It is a creative, expressive outlet for me. My professor is directing a children's musical, *Rhumba Tiya,* a Rumpelstiltskin with a Polynesian flair. I audition. The director tries different combinations of actors to cast. I'm up for the leading female role or a sister part. The director casts a drama major in the leading female role. I'm cast in two roles, playing the sister and a fire demon. Backstage, I also play the lullaby song on the flute while the lead female sings on stage.

I'm a bit disappointed not getting the lead female role. I realize that casting is not only based on the actor's talent but also the appearance. The director considers if these actors fit the image and how they match up with other actors.

It's an overall fun experience interacting with zany theatre majors who are open and receptive to me. The only drawback to putting a production together is rehearsals last until 10 pm.

I like seeing each cast member's large black and white photos prop up on the theatre lobby wall. I enjoy the artistry of acting, requiring me to play another character in the most natural, convincing, and believable way. Actors need to understand the psyche and background of the characters to get into the role to fulfill that persona. **[Ch.25:3]**

One day I'm at rehearsals with Jack, a Japanese American drama major who plays the lead role of Rumplestiltskin in *Rhumba Tiya.* Dan and I play the two fire demons, learning our choreography with Jack. As practice winds down, Jack chats with me.

"So, where are your parents from?" asks Jack.

"They were born and raised in Mainland China."

"Oh, whereabouts in China?"

"They come from the Canton area."

"Oh, what dialect do they speak?"

"They speak Cantonese."

"Oh, they speak Cantonese. They must be peasants," he states.

There's silence.

"I don't appreciate you putting my parents down. Who do you think you are?" I say annoyingly.

"I'm just kidding," he smiles.

"Well, I don't think that's funny," I say with displeasure.

"I'm just kidding."

I ignore him. Our choreographer gives us final comments before we conclude our rehearsal.

In the 100-seat *Playbox Theatre* at CSULA, the matinee fills with elementary school children eager to see *Rhumba Tiya.* The first scene begins with our fire demon choreography. **[Ch.25:4]**

Drumming fills the air in a completely dark *Playbox Theatre.* Wearing our fire demon masks, grass skirts and holding long black sticks, we burst onto the stage. The spotlight flashes on us while we yell at the height of our leap toward the audience. All the kids scream.

The drums continue their rhythmic beat while we continue our choreography, dancing on our bare feet. We are unaware of the children's frightened reaction.

After our choreography, I'm backstage, changing my costume to the sister role. I hear from the other fire demon that some kids are petrified, crying outside the *Playbox Theatre* with their teacher.

Early in my undergraduate years, my Mom shows me how to cook. My Mom washes and cuts vegetables with her paring knife.

I'm watching her rapid movements.

My eyes can't keep up with her quick, slicing motions. I ask, "how do you do that?"

My Mom stops. She turns her head at a 45-degree angle toward me, holding her paring knife and vegetable, and instructs me, *"Yung neih a ngan, mo yung neih a hao,"* meaning, "Use your eyes, not your mouth."

"Oh, okay," while complacently nodding and looking at her hands.

My Mom proceeds with her rapid peeling and washing of the vegetables.

My eyes trail her quickness. "How do you do that?"

She stops. I say, "Oh, I see. I should use my eyes and my nose," pointing at my nose. I smile and grin. She doesn't appreciate my tad of humor. "Oh, I should use my eyes and not my mouth."

She continues preparing the vegetables. The Chinese culture emphasizes learning through demonstration, observation, doing, thinking, and figuring it out rather than speaking step-by-step explanations.

Afterwards, I cook my first Chinese meal. I cook a tofu and beef dish with brown bean sauce, topped with chopped green onions. I also stir-fried broccoli with chopped garlic and oil. My Mom takes a bite from both plates. Her eyes slightly widen, indicating that my cooking is acceptable. She continues to eat and finishes her lunch.

"Hao sik," she says, meaning taste good. Amazingly, the dishes taste like my Mom's cooking!

Sometimes, I wander into Leland's bedroom at home because he has tall bookshelves after bookshelves of metaphysical books. Not dull books, but fascinating books that he bought at the *Bodhi Tree Bookstore* in L.A. I tag along with him now and then to *Bodhi Tree.* He has cool books like *Zazen* meditation, Astrology, *Feng Shui, I Ching,* palmistry, physiognomy or Chinese face reading, acupuncture, acupressure, Buddhism, Taoism, etc. Leland has studied under a Taoist Master in California.

Leland introduces me to the *I Ching,* also known as the Book of Changes or the Book of Wisdom, a Chinese divination text. It is considered the oldest Chinese Classics since the Western Zhou period, around 1000 to 750 BC.

"Hey, Mary, you want to ask a question and see what kind of an answer you'll get?" Leland asks.

"What? Any question?"

"Yeah, ask any question."

"Okay, how about, 'Should I become an actress?"

Leland instructs me how to toss three coins six times while he marks a yin or a yang line to create a symbol that looks like six levels or layers of a straight line or a broken line representing a hexagram. A commentary in the hexagram responds to the inquiry.

Unfortunately, I don't remember the hexagram that reflects my six-coin tosses. Still, I recall I received a legitimate response related to my doubtful questioning of the yin and yang lines in the hexagram.

"What if this line is yin, and that changes to yang?" I ask.

"Okay, you want to change these lines?" Let's see what it says now.

The *I Ching* response came back, stating, "Do not question what you have been advised.

Leland laughs at the amazement of the *I Ching* response. I'm a bit surprised at the coherent and relevant *I Ching* response to my questioning of it. I continue exploring the *I Ching* and understanding some ancient wisdom and practical commentary that has helped me sharpen my observation, awareness, and adaptation to various life situations.

Energy is the basis of the *I Ching's* divination process (I is pronounced like Yee or Eee). The Physics field has established that everything is energy —you, me, words, inanimate objects, animals, plants, the universe, and so on. Energy cannot be created or destroyed. Energy only can transform. **[Ch.25:5]**

When the questioner asks an inquiry, there's an energy behind the question that contains information. The energy of the question and the questioner's intention emits into the energy field. A toss of three coins can land as all heads, all tails, or a mixed combination that reflects the energy field related to the question. The coins mirror the energy field, assessing the information within the energy field related to the inquiry.

One of my friends expresses her concern about using the *I Ching* because her religious background did not approve of divination. Because of her insufficient understanding of energy, the divination process, and the rich practical wisdom, I tell her that the *I Ching* does not contain and never advises to do anything dangerous. I say the *I Ching* never tells anyone to jump off a cliff or do anything harmful. The *I Ching* assesses and reflects the current energy in the situation and offers guidance and advice in the hexagram commentary to improve the situation and condition of a person, if necessary.

One day, I repeatedly call Trojan to come upstairs to hang out in my bedroom. She refuses and stays at the bottom of the stairs. Usually eager to come, but this time, she doesn't.

A few minutes later, Trojan viciously barks, and the back door of the laundry room slams. Racing to my bedroom window, directly above the back door, I see a woman exiting our backdoor porch and onto our driveway.

Running to the bathroom, peering through the front window, I see a middle-aged, heavy-set Caucasian woman pretending to look for a dog on our lawn. She's bending over and extending her hand, appearing to call for a lost dog. Then she immediately hops into her dark green VW bug and speeds off. Focusing on her license plate, I jot it down.

No wonder Trojan refused to come upstairs. She could sense a stranger outside. She's such an excellent guard dog. Fortunately,

Trojan's instincts kept her downstairs, or else that woman would have proceeded to enter and rummaged around the house. However, that intruder would not have gotten very far. Trojan would have come after her so viciously. Trojan takes her responsibilities seriously.

I told Jason about the intruder. He has a friend who has access to information to look up the license plate of this woman. We obtained her address, and on the following day, we investigate. We see her dark green VW parked on the street. She lives a few minutes from our home--nothing more we can do.

In the spring quarter of 1979, I transfer to UCLA. I go to UCLA to explore another campus within my financial means while taking GE courses. I'm still working on the weekends at the *LA Times.* I take the bus from my parent's home at 6:00 am to be on the job by 7:00 am and get off work at 3:00 pm.

I live in a student-run off-campus housing during the weekdays, and everyone has kitchen and bathroom duties. The bathrooms are coed and typically less than clean. I live in a small triple roommate room. Both of my roommates are nice. However, one roommate sleeps at 1 or 2 in the morning or does her laundry.

My bed rests by the door, and both roommates shuffle in and out, frequently slamming the door and shaking the wall. Guys living next door also habitually slam their door, reverberating the shared wall. The environment is disruptive and unhealthy. It's not quiet—too much activity affecting my sleep and a sense of peace. At the UCLA library, I would nap every weeknight before cracking open my books.

I'm taking Political Science, Linguistics, Introduction to Communication, and Children's Literature. I attend large lecture halls with 300 to 500 students. Two of the four instructors are PhD candidates lecturing with a microphone. I don't find value in large lecture halls. They are no interaction between the professor and students and between students. It is one-way communication and a straight lecture. A brave student may shout out a question for the professor to respond which concludes the class session.

However, discussion sections meet weekly with a teaching assistant who is either a master's or doctorate student with little teaching experience. I find these discussion sections unproductive and not conducive to a learning experience.

These mass auditorium-sized lecture classes are one-way communication that does not allow students to articulate their ideas, ask questions, and become acquainted with colleagues. Students are not able to develop their identity and develop as a learner. Every class session, I sit next to a stranger. I feel like a nobody, a sheep amongst a herd, mechanically processed.

Most of my courses at CSULA consist of 30 students or less. Just a couple of classes have 100 students that are non-interactive. A significant difference in student learning occurs in smaller classes, which allows for personal, educational interactions between the professor and students. Students can develop their speaking and interactive communication while developing their identity and getting to know their classmates.

Although I'm a UCLA student, I'm still able to join my CSULA cast members in competing at the San Diego Children's Festival in the spring quarter. One evening we went disco dancing. I'm 19 years old, and they require their customers to be at least 21.

We enter as a group, so I slip in without being carded.

I enjoy theatre and have a secret desire to go into acting. However, I'm not fully committed to majoring in drama because I feel uncertain about my profession's livelihood.

Later that spring quarter, I'm fulfilling my student duties at the off-campus housing by working in the kitchen and cutting carrots with two other students. I'm cutting a carrot, and my cleaver rolls off the carrot and slices my index finger! Red blood gushes out. I'm in shock, feeling no pain.

The chef is startled. He immediately wraps my finger with a cloth, applying pressure while directing me to elevate my finger above my heart. The office manager is notified and drives me to a local doctor. I have three stitches, a tetanus shot, and a good gauze-wrapped bandaged index finger. Isn't this *déjà vu* on the same left finger gushing red blood when the hamster bit me almost 15 years ago?

The academic year closes soon, in June. I move home for the summer, working 30 hours weekly at the *LA Times.* During the summer, I'm figuring out if I'm returning to UCLA for the Fall quarter or transferring to USC, where I have a Fall semester admission. UCLA doesn't have what I want to study.

USC does have a major in Communications, particularly human communication. I don't have a car, and it's too far to travel on the bus for almost two hours one way if I decide to attend USC. I'm still stuck in nearly the same predicament as when I graduated from high school, except now I have enough tuition money.

I ask USC to defer my admission acceptance to the spring semester of 1980, and they do. Fortunately, in December 1979, my parents give me $1500 toward my first car like they did with my two older brothers. I saved enough money to buy a new blue 1980 Toyota Corolla for $4,000. I'm quite pleased and ready to attend USC. I'm still on a State Scholarship. I've saved my money over the past two years while working part-time. I'm able to pay the out-of-pocket $1,000 tuition. My ducks are lined up to attend USC finally.

Chapter 26: Mary Transfers to USC

Spring semester 1980, I'm attending USC, which takes me a half-an-hour to travel eight miles on the freeway and in my class seat. I'm majoring in Speech Communication.

I'm taking Intercultural Communication, Argumentation, Communication Theory, and Children's Theatre. I'm typically the only Asian American student in my courses in a sea of Caucasian Americans, generally from the middle to upper socio-economic class.

I don't have the chance to develop significant friendships during my undergraduate years. I don't identify with any of my classmates, and neither do they identify with me. I'm quiet. I would say that I'm the oddball in the classroom. I don't focus my thoughts on being the oddball, but I know I'm different from my homogeneous class of students.

Virtually through 10 years, I didn't quite fit in with a group of friends or even have a single pal at the elementary schools I attended. My classmates range from taunters to strangers to classmates to acquaintances. I didn't have a true friend I could look forward to seeing, and she would look forward to seeing me at school. I grew up adapting to being independent. Moving to Chinatown, LA is when I developed friendships.

Thus far, in my college experience, I haven't clicked with anyone to the point of developing a good friendship. I have good relationships with co-workers at the CSULA's library and the *LA Times,* but I never develop friendships with my classmates and co-workers outside work. Yes, we may have gone out a couple of times, but nothing more. I don't join clubs because I'm busy taking classes, studying, and working part-time. It would have been nice to have the opportunity and time to mingle and click with a social group.

Near the end of the spring semester, I go to USC's Doheny library in the reserve book section to read for my Children's Theatre course. The take-home final requires that I read the reserve books and respond to the essay questions.

As I look up my reserve book in the card catalog, a Belmont high school classmate, Young Park, walks by and notices me.

"Hey, Mary," he greets me with a smile.

"Oh, hi, Young," looking up from the card catalog.

"Are you coming here?" he asks.

"Yeah, I just transferred here."

"Oh, great."

"How do you like it here?"

"Yeah, I like it," says Young smiling.

Then, he leans toward me and points to some long tables in the back of the library. He says in a tone of voice like he knows something about the past, "There's Karl. He's sitting right over there."

"So, what! Who cares!" I respond annoyingly.

"Gosh, Mary," he says surprisingly.

I look down and continue my search in the card catalog.

"Okay, see you later," he says as he leaves.

"Bye."

Young Park returns to his library table, where Karl and his friends study. "Guess who I saw?" Young asks, smilingly at Karl. His heart skips a beat.

"Who?" Karl asks hesitantly.

"She just transferred here," Young smiles. Karl pauses and knows who exactly it is, just by the tone of Young's voice and smile. Karl's heart flutters and intuitively says, "Mary, Mary Fong?"

"Yeah, I just chatted with her," Young says with a smile.

"Oh, yeah, good," Karl says while nodding.

Karl's thoughts: *I feel relieved and happy that I didn't see Mary. I've gotten to a point; I don't know what to do or how to act around her. I have her carefully hidden away.*

I didn't know Karl attends USC. I never asked him in high school. I don't think twice about Karl. Meanwhile, I'm at the front desk, checking out my reserve book. I sit down and read for a couple of hours before leaving home.

The following week, I'm back on campus for my classes. I return to the Doheny Library to check out the reserve book to finish reading and begin responding to the essay questions on the take-home final.

Karl's thoughts: *I notice someone with long shiny hair sitting at the library table working. I take a glimpse of her, and I'm in a panic. Oh crap, Mary's here. What do I do? Panic, and then the fear overwhelms me. Should I go? Should I not? Should I pretend like I'm not here?*

Then comes a feeling kind of, fuck it, just fuck it. Just go with the flow and see what happens. I don't expect to feel so much again after seeing her. I feel that she is like my poison. I see her—Boom! Here come all these emotions flooding straight into my face.

When I see her, I had to come over and say, "hi," not start anything. I just want to feel if we still have that connection. It's more like out of curiosity. I get to a point where I'm desperately in love with her, which never worked out.

Then I see her again and want to see how much is left of that emotion. I'm just curious. I want to know if I'm over her. I want to know if I'm good. I want to see if it is done. When I talk to her, I have nothing planned. I don't know what I'm going to say. I'm just going to say hi and see what happens.

Sitting near the back of the library, I hear someone call out, "Hey, Mary."

Looking up from my reading, I see Karl.

"Oh, hi, Karl," I say as he walks toward me, sitting one chair away from me.

"Are you coming here now?"

"Yeah, I just transferred here."

"Oh, good. What are you reading?"

"I'm reading a book on reserve for my Children's Theatre course. It's a take-home final I'm working on."

"Oh," Karl nods.

"How's your sister, Sheila?" I ask.

"She's fine. She works at Vons."

"She works where?"

"Vons."

"Where?"

"Vons."

"Oh, Vons supermarket."

"I don't know, Mary. I think you've been studying too hard," Karl says in a kidding way while shaking his head and smiling.

I look at him and say nothing. There's a pause.

"Well, I better get going," he says.

My disposition is neutral towards Karl. I have no interest in him. I don't want to be yo-yo around like in high school. I don't want to experience the on-and-off-again feelings of him showing interest in me, and then no interest, then interest, then no interest.

I continue reading the reserve book while working on my take-home final. I stay another hour to finish before going back home.

Karl's thoughts: *I realize now that I have the longing stored away, it's easier for me to talk to Mary. In a way, it gives me a sensation of, yeah, we're good, we're good. It's all right, in a way, closure. It is a way of being okay with suppressed emotions I have had for a very long time. It is proof to me that, hey, I'm okay.*

However, the thing is, as soon as I see her, these feelings come back up. They aren't as intense as they were before. Did I still have feelings for her? Absolutely, but let's just say that they have changed. My feelings for her have changed. I guess I matured. I'm also seeing somebody else. I don't believe that seeing somebody has to do with the change inside of me. It has to do with me moving on. I stepped away from her, moving in a new direction. I've grown up. I have matured. I'm goofy, but I have matured internally.

When I'm interested in someone, and if someone's not, I've learned to let go. I have had that after Mary. I had that with another girl. Okay, no biggy, move on to the next. I've learned not to hold onto that anymore, accept things as they come, and not see them as desperation or failure. To view it as, okay, there must be something else that's better coming my way.

I flipped that around in my head, and so it works. It's self-protection, but it doesn't mean I don't care about Mary. It doesn't mean that I don't love her. I always have, and I always will. It's love that I can't explain. It's an attraction that doesn't make any sense whatsoever. However, it's there, and it's real to me. She might not feel that.

Yeah, it's almost like a test, testing myself. I tested myself to see how deep my feelings go. They are not as intense as they used to be. I have changed. She has changed. She has changed a lot. Her energy is more open and inviting to me than before. That's just what it feels like to me. I always go off of what I feel. Although we didn't talk a lot, I don't go off of what my mind says. It feels like she is more accessible or comfortable to talk to than before. I stepped away from Mary.

After seeing Mary, I'm thinking of her off and on. It isn't constant, like all day long thinking about her. However, she does pop into my head. It's like something reminds me of her sometimes. I go into a classroom, and I think of her. Sometimes I hum a song from a movie that makes me think of her. Seeing her opens the door again. I had buried my thoughts and feelings about her for the past few years. **[Ch.26:1]**

Karl's thoughts: *I have to move on. I have to try to block out the thought about her for my protection because my mind starts wandering off again. I don't want to get stuck again in something that isn't going to happen. I want to continue focusing on where I need to put it. Mary is a distraction. Unfortunately, she always has been. It is a nice distraction, but I don't want the thoughts and memories to come back to disrupt what I'm building because I see my future. I'm building up to something new and separate from my past. Many people will embrace their past and carry it into their future. For me, after high school it's a new beginning.* **[Ch.26:2]**

We are done with that, and I'm starting a new chapter where I can be a new me. I'm going in a different direction, and where I'm planning a future instead. I consider my path, in some way, a nice survival.

It's like surviving the parents, surviving the pressures of school, surviving the pressure of Mary, going through puberty, and going through all these changes. It feels more like survival, not in a bad way, but surviving the changes. Then once I leave that path, I know it is a new beginning. I want to continue to focus on that new beginning.

She does linger in my thoughts. They are good, positive thoughts. Just the feeling of seeing her back in high school, the excitement that I got when we would meet, even if it was only passing by each other--those were intense moments for me. They were very intense moments, and those were happy memories for me. The disappointment, the crying, and the feelings of failure in that aspect were far away. So, positive feelings and emotions arose now and then. **[Ch.26:2A]**

It's been about a week since I thought about her off and on. Then I put my focus back on moving forward from that. **[Ch.26:3]**

After typing my notes from the reserve reading room, I submit my final essays by the deadline. I go to the Theatre Department during finals week to pick up my essay papers. Dr. Fuller talks to a student in his office. So, I quietly walk by his office to the table where the stack of graded papers lay. I pick up my papers and slowly walk by looking at my results.

Dr. Fuller sees me and calls out, "Hi, Mary."

"Oh, hi, Dr. Fuller," as I backtrack my footsteps to peer at him in his office.

"You wrote excellent final essays."

"Oh, thanks," I smile.

"You should be a drama major."

"Oh, me? I don't think so. I'm afraid that I'll grow hungry," I say with a smile. "Have a good summer."

"You too."

The reality, in the early 1980s, far too few available acting roles exist for Asian Americans. I like the artistry it takes to be another character. As much as I enjoy acting and have tossed the idea around and even took a series of photoshoots, finally, I'm not pursuing an acting career. I heard a quiet voice within me not too long ago, saying, "You will lose yourself."

The academic year ends, and summer arrives. I'm taking two courses: Introduction Broadcast Production and a film course at CSULA. I'm working additional hours at the *Los Angeles Times* Circulation Department.

Arrive at work, I hear from a co-worker that Robert's mother had died that morning of a heart attack. I feel much sympathy for him. I don't know what to say. I sit at my office pod for 45 minutes, feeling inspired to write a poem to give to him called "Carry On."

Two Heart Nuts to Crack!

Waking up this morning, I realize
I have a friend who is quite so nice.
To hear of his special love
who has spread her wings to fly like a white dove,
is a new beginning for thee.

I sit here in the morning hours,
wondering what kind of flowers
that I can express to a dear friend.
To find the words, to find the way
to express and share these days.

It's been said that these days are a reflection
of your family's and friend's affection.
We gather our thoughts,
to remember that the most she sought,
was for one, to embrace her love in your heart,
to carry on forward these days.

She's here, she's everywhere, no matter where you are.
She's a part of you as much as you are with her.
Neither of you has lost
but gained the deepest special love
no one else can ever create.
Carry on...

These words, these rhymes, are only real within you.
Though I can't possibly feel the same way,
I can only express my sentiment
and empathy in this little way.
Carry on...
© Mary Fong, 1980

Later that summer, I go to USC marching band camp for tryouts in San Diego. I have a dilemma. Marching band practice is at 4 pm, when I have a Nonverbal Communication class to take simultaneously. Finally, I decide not to join the marching band in the Fall semester because I need to take this Communication course to graduate by June 1981.

In the Fall semester, I take a news writing course. The news writing course requires me to do a weekly news story for the *Daily Trojan.* I like seeing my stories appear in the campus newspaper.

One evening, I go to the movies for the first time with a friend's younger sister, a high school senior. We each purchase our movie tickets at the box office. I pay for my adult ticket first.

She steps up and bends her knees looking up at the box office counter, speaking in a soft girly sweet voice with her long black hair draping on both sides of her face while wearing her sweatshirt and jeans.

"One child ticket, please," she says while slipping some bills under the window. The salesgirl rings up a child's ticket. She turns away with a smile after picking up her child price ticket, while I say nothing after witnessing an acting performance.

A few months later, I receive a call from her older sister that her younger sister had died in a car accident. I'm shocked, blown away. It was not too long ago when we went to the movies together.

She was a passenger while a high school male friend was driving. She was not wearing her seat belt, ejected from the car. The driver survived. She is the first person I know who died so young. She no longer exists. It's an eerie feeling, and I'm at a loss for thoughts and words. I keep reflecting on the last time we were together, seeing a movie. I've never read or talked to anyone about death.

Arriving in the morning to attend the first funeral of someone I once knew. Feeling sad while signing the guestbook. Entering the chapel, straight ahead, I see her resting in the casket. Many people quietly sit in a silent room as I approach her.

I open up a small plastic container to remove the casket flower. Feeling my nerves, I reach over her body with slightly shaky hands pinning the flower to her casket. I sit down.

After the visitation time, she is laid to rest. Her father thanks everyone for coming, and everyone receives a piece of candy to symbolize leaving a sweet taste in your mouth, not a sour-tasting residue from this funeral.

December 8, 1980, a mentally ill fan assassinates a famous musician, John Lennon. I'm shocked. I buy his last album, *Double Fantasy,* which is co-created with his wife, Yoko Ono. Their sales skyrocket after Lennon's death. At the 1981 Grammy, their *Double Fantasy* receives the best album of the year. John Lennon is another musical genius who died too early at 40. The songs I particularly like are: "Starting Over," "Watching the Wheels," and "Woman." **[Ch.26:4 - Ch.26:6]**

Early spring semester of 1981, my Daddy has difficulty breathing. He's admitted to the hospital to have another tube inserted in his lung cavity to release the air that creates pressure on his lungs, collapsing them. In a few days, the French Hospital in Chinatown releases him to recover at home.

It's my last semester before graduating from USC. There's no memorable event in the spring. However, I do recall the last exam of my undergraduate career. It's a final in my Psychology of Communication course. I'm the only one left taking the exam, sitting in the back, taking my sweet time, answering carefully. Finished, I exit the room.

I'm wearing my denim overalls that day. Walking down the Von Kleisman Center steps, doing a cartwheel in Alumni Park crosses my mind. I refrain, keeping my cool, feeling liberated while walking casually through Alumni Park, across campus to my car. I completed my undergraduate degree in four years, attending three universities and taking summer courses. I had to. My state scholarship funded me for only four years. I did it. Mission accomplished.

Graduation is in two days. My parents never had the opportunity to attend any of my graduations because they had to work. My parents are in retirement now. During this time of graduation, my Dad is recovering.

My black cap and gown with the golden tassel sit on my dresser. I'm ambivalent about going to my graduation today. No one in the family knows it's graduation day. In the last hour, I wear a dress and grab my cap and gown on the spur of the moment.

I drive to USC, barely getting in line to be seated. I sit way in the back row, looking around at all the rows of graduates sitting in

Alumni Park. The speakers are on a platform near the steps of the Doheny Library. The graduates don't walk across any stage. Instead, when the USC President announces that we are now graduates, we all move our golden tassels on our black caps from right to left. The ceremony is over. Afterwards, all the graduates meet up with their friends and family.

I get up and walk down the sidewalk on campus towards my car. On the way, I happen to come across a classmate, Irma Martinez. She is the only classmate whom I remember her name.

She is the only Latina I know from my Communication classes. **[Ch.26:7]**

"Hi, Mary. Congratulations!" Irma says with a smile while waving.

"Oh, hi, Irma, congratulations to you too!" I surprisingly say as I smile and wave back.

"We did it!" she says with laughter.

"Yes, we did it!" Laughing with her.

"Where's your family?" she asks.

"Oh, my family, they didn't come. My Dad is not feeling well."

"Oh, I'm sorry to hear that."

"Oh, that's all right. They're at home."

"Here, I can take a picture of you," Irma offers.

"Oh, okay." I say.

"Here, you want to stand over here?"

"Okay."

"Smile," she says as she pauses and snaps her camera.

"Thank you, Irma."

"I'm happy to, and I'll send it to you. What's your address?"

I write down my address before we say our goodbyes. In a week, I receive the only photo of my graduation in May of 1981. Thanks, Irma. I would love to see you again.

It's a rare occasion for our family to plan a trip to San Francisco. All the kids are grown, going about daily activities, while living at home. We coordinate a one-day family reunion in San Francisco the summer after my graduation. It's my first airplane flight traveling from LAX to San Francisco with both of my brothers.

We meet up with our parents, who travel earlier to see relatives and friends. It's only the second time I've seen my first cousins and my Dad's brother. We first go to the cemetery to pay our respects, where my grandfather's casket has been relocated from Bakersfield to San Francisco. Then we have lunch with our relatives at a restaurant.

Afterwards, we sit in the living room at our relative's home in the heart of San Francisco while they converse. When evening comes, we fly back. I appreciate all the amazingly beautiful city lights through the window.

Returning to reality, I'm still deciding where to go for my master's degree in Communication. I also work the entire summer at the *LA Times* for 30 hours, six days a week. I don't do anything special that summer. However, my Dad and I attend my Mom's Citizenship Ceremony at the Music Center in downtown Los Angeles. It's the only day witnessing my Mom experiencing a meaningful and celebratory event where she is the focus of attention. It is a pleasant occasion. Afterwards, we have lunch to celebrate.

On a summer day, I hear a high pitch, loud cry from Trojan in the backyard. I race downstairs to see what's going on with Trojan. She immediately comes to me. I pet her and wonder what's wrong. I don't see any physical signs of where she hurts.

Within a week, growing lumps protrude on her body. I take her to the veterinarian, who diagnoses her with leukemia. I bring her back home. Her bumps continue to protrude—finally, her skin breaks and oozes. I put vitamin liquid on her bumps.

As I'm driving to work at 6:30 am, I cry that Trojan is dying. Tears stream from my eyes down my cheeks as I wipe them away. Trojan is my first dog, napping on my bed almost every day since the 9th grade. She always looked up to me. I know our time together is minimal.

No longer will I have that happy girl greet me when I return home every day, always walking up the flight of stairs to my bedroom. Enjoying our joyful jumping ritual with her paws on my legs while I'm sitting. Even on days when I'm tired and hungry from a long day and the day I hear about a friend's younger sister who died just months ago, I always show how happy I am to see my pal, Trojan. No more hide and seek in the house and walking her to the park.

My Mom says to put her down, and I have to. Her oozing bumps worsen. No hope. It's time. I take her to the Vet and hand over Trojan on the leash. Minutes later, the assistant returns Trojan's collar and leash. I leave the office without my pal.

Returning home, I open the back door of the house. It's quiet--No more running paws and clanging sounds of her metal license and I.D. tag on her collar. I climb the tall flight of stairs to my bedroom alone—no Trojan running upstairs beside me while patting her head and back. I miss the happy energy that Trojan always shared with me. I sit on my bed, allowing the tears to flow. I take a deep breath, wiping my tears. My pal is no longer with me.

I stretch out on my bed with my head on my pillow, looking at the ceiling and the windows. Tears continue to stream intermittently from the corner of my eyes and down the side of my face. Now and then, I cup my eyes with my hands and wipe the sides of my face, blinking to clear my vision. I can feel and see my diaphragm slowly breathing up and down. Eventually, I close my eyes to find comfort in a nap without my best pal next to me ever again.

Chapter 27: Mary's Master's Program at CSU, Long Beach

It's a fresh start in the Master's program at California State University, Long Beach, in the Fall semester of 1981 in Communication Studies. A new beginning, feeling liberated as I drive 30 miles from my parent's home in Los Angeles to campus. Seminars typically have 10-15 graduate students engaging in interactive discussions, rather than professors or graduate teaching assistants usually conducting straight lectures at the undergraduate level. I'm taking Research Methods, Nonverbal Communication, and an undergraduate course in Storytelling.

In late October, I'm the maiden of honor for a long-time friend of nine years, Sharon, whom I've known since we played Chinatown community basketball together. Sharon marries another high school classmate, Mark, playing the flute and piccolo in the orchestra and marching band.

Near the end of the wedding banquet, some people sit chatting at one of the large round tables. Walking over to that table, I sit in an empty chair next to Sharon's high school classmate, Terrance.

"Hi, aren't you Jillian's brother, Terrance?"

"Yes, I am."

"Do you remember Jason Fong? He's one of your classmates from Belmont?"

"Oh, yes."

"He's my older brother."

"Oh, is he. Who are you?"

"I'm Mary. How's your sister Jillian doing?"

"Oh, she's doing fine. She just graduated from Cal. She's going to Washington State now."

"Oh, she is. What is she doing there?"

"She's in the veterinary program."

"Oh, she is. Great."

"She's coming back this Christmas. I can give her your number."

"Oh, okay."

Sometime in December, Jillian comes home to LA and calls me up. We chat for a while, and she asks if I would like to join her and her brother, Terrance, at Cabrillo Beach and the pool tides. I invite a high school friend of mine, Janet, to join us at about 11:00 a.m.

The four of us spend a day together exploring the beach area. The siblings ate before we met, but Janet and I didn't even have breakfast. No one mentioned having lunch during our time out.

We return home by 5:30. The two siblings neglect to ask us if we want to grab a bite to eat. I'm exhausted, cold, hungry, and furious.

Terrance calls the following week to chat. He picks me up to shoot baskets at a local court.

Returning home, my Mom asks, *"Go-a nam yen, hay bing go, a?"* meaning, "That guy, who is he?"

"Keui mang hai, Terrance." Keui zhidào Jason. Keui hai Jason, hok hau péngyauh," meaning, "His name is Terrance. He knows Jason. He is a friend of Jason at school."

"Keui hai xìng, me ä?" meaning, "What is his last name?" my Mom inquires.

"Keui xìng, Sako," meaning, "His last name is Sako," I respond.

"Sako?" my Mom questions.

"Keui hai yät boon," meaning, "He's Japanese.

"Keui hai yät boon?" my Mom asks, meaning, "He is Japanese?"

"Yeah."

The following week, Terrance asks if I'm interested in going to the LA auto show at the convention center. We come across a car with a small 76 orange rubber ball stuck on the car's antenna. He's a graduate of UC Berkeley in Psychology. He tries to apply a Rorschach test that examines a person's emotional functioning and personality characteristics based on one's perceptions of various inkblot images. **[Ch.27:1]**

"What comes to your mind when you see this 76-orange rubber ball on this antenna?" He asks.

"This reminds me of the sun, where the earth orbits around it," I say.

"Wow," he laughs. "I didn't expect a response like that."

The week after, we get together and reshoot baskets. Returning home, my Mom asks, *"Nei tong go ä Yat boon heui gaai?"* meaning, "Did you go somewhere with that Japanese?"

"Yeah, ngaw dei heui dä bö," I say, meaning, "Yes, we went to play ball."

Shouting in the air, my Mom complains about going out with a Japanese guy. With intense eyes, she's speaking with agitation. She shoves the chair about in the kitchen. I don't know why my Mom is irate. She's yelling in the kitchen about the Japanese and Chinese war.

My Mom speaks with emotional intensity about being very young. She, her family, and all the villagers hid in their homes with everything shut and locked up. She recalls the Japanese soldiers' footsteps coming through the village. Everyone is in tremendous fear. For an entire week, my Mom gives me the silent treatment.

Iris Chang wrote a New York best-selling non-fiction book, The *Rape of Nanking*. She interviewed many Chinese survivors of the second Sino-Japanese War in 1937-45 during WWII to provide testimony in her non-fiction book. **[Ch.27:2]**

Leland talks to me a couple of days later. He says, "Mary, if you have a choice between a Chinese guy and a Japanese guy, marry the Chinese guy."

I look at him, surprised that he tells me this. I didn't think he would advise me in this way. Leland says, "There was a Japanese-Chinese war where the Japanese invaded China." I'm unaware of this war since it is not taught in school.

My parents talk directly to Leland, who plays an intermediary role in communicating an indirect message from my parents to me speaking directly. My Dad never says anything to me. My Mom shouts in the room, but she never talks to me directly about her disapproval of Terrance.

In Chinese culture, when there are significant conflicts and disagreements, one way to help resolve the situation is an intermediary participates. It can be a relative or friend who is the "go-between" in relaying messages and sometimes offers advice indirectly to help in the communication and resolution between the two conflicting parties. Avoiding direct face-to-face confrontation saves face and maintains in-group harmony among families and friends.

Terrance and I chat over the phone after Leland spoke to me. I tell Terrance what has transpired.

"My parents don't want me to see you anymore."

"Why?"

"My Mom has memories of the Japanese-Chinese war when she was a little girl in China."

"Oh." Terrance pauses and says, "What do you want to do?"

"Well, what do you want to do?"

"I want to see you still," says Terrance.

"The only way I can see you is secretive."

"I feel cheated."

"I want to respect my parents about how they feel. At the same time, I want to respect myself. The only way to do this is to see you secretively."

"All right," agrees Terrance.

Terrance lives with his parents in a small two-bedroom rental home throughout his upbringing. Both of his parents were born and raised in Japan.

His Dad works as a chef, and his Mom works as a dry cleaner. Both of his parents speak broken English. His Dad is very reserved, like my Dad. I don't chat much with Terrance's Dad beyond our greetings.

One weekend, Terrance's Mom shows us how to make sushi in her kitchen. She demonstrates how to prepare the Japanese sticky rice with rice vinegar placed on the seaweed sheet with our fingers. I cut the carrots, imitation crabmeat, cucumbers, and eggs into strips and put the sticky rice on the seaweed. His Mom tightly and slowly rolls all of this with a bamboo sheet. She demonstrates how to make clean cuts on the sushi roll by wetting the sharp knife and cleaning it after each cut.

Eating each sushi piece with chopsticks involves dipping it into soy sauce with hot green wasabi. The wasabi is guaranteed to clear up sinuses if the sushi is not carefully placed in the right position in the mouth to chew.

My survival eating tip is don't put the wasabi on the roof of the mouth, or else a blast of hot energy explodes through the sinus cavity, jetting to the forehead.

Another time, I question why his Mom doesn't eat with his Dad and the family. Instead, she eats after them, and in the kitchen alone. I ask Terrance, why is that so? He says that is how they've always done it. I question this, feeling that she is not equal to them. Perhaps she carries over the traditional rural Japanese style from when she grew up in Japan, witnessing these distinct roles in her own family. Perhaps in cities in contemporary Japan, the Japanese do not have this pattern of eating.

I wrote a poem, and include it in my final paper for a course on Language, Meaning, and Communication. My poem is titled, "I."

I can see the big bright sun,
high up in the sky,
shimmering its light upon
the crest of each wave
that roars and crashes
on the shore where
I sat all day.

Here I sit in solitude
reflecting far back on life's vicissitudes.
Oh, my memories carry me back
to the fun, sad, happy,
and unforgettable times.

I try to trace the patterns
and meaning of my life,
as I look back on the essence of time.
I take the good along with the bad

and thank Him for walking
me through this special path.

Hear the silence, this peaceful silence.
Wings of seagulls flapping,
the cool wind gently breezy.
The waves crashing upon
the sandy warm shore.

I sit and hear my breathing
and my heart beating...
Listening...
to what...
I...
have to...
say.

I also work weekends at the *LA Times* from 7 am to 3 pm. This weekend job provides enough income for gas, car insurance, and food. At work, an American Tribal Indian co-worker name Barney asks me,

"Have you ever had an out-of-body experience?"

"Out-of-body-experience? What is that?" I ask.

"It's really neat. Your spirit leaves your body and travels," he says.

"Oh, really? No, I never had that experience," I respond.

"You should try it sometime. It's really cool," he says.

"Oh, okay," I say.

Within a week from that brief conversation, I'm taking a nap. During my sleep, I feel this intense electrical sensation, a feeling that my spirit is separating from my body. My head vibrates like electricity. I feel a sensation like ZZZZZzzzzzzZZZZZZ. It's slow, and I feel a strong, energetic electrical vibration.

Once my consciousness leaves my body, I see myself lying down with three silhouette figures walking toward my body. I become concerned that I don't know these three silhouette figures approaching me.

I can't move my body, having body paralysis, as I watch the

three figures getting closer to my body. I want to move, but I can't.

My consciousness returns to my body, feeling the same slow, intense ZZZZzzzzZZZZZZ electrical vibration throughout me. When I wake, I feel a weird feeling. I believe I went through an out-of-body experience. Cool! **[Ch.27:3] [Ch.27:3A]**

On the weekends, Terrance and I typically see each other secretively after I get off work from the *LA Times,* and once a week, I would ride with him to USC for his classes. I always give my Mom the excuse that I'm studying at the library all day. Other times, we swim at CSULA or meet up at his home. I'm an avid swimmer, my favorite summer sport while enjoying the sunshine, getting tanned, and working out—all for free.

I visit Terrance on a hot summer's day at his parents' home.

Sitting in a warm living room with a portable fan, everyone fans themselves and watches TV. Later that evening, I talk to Leland, and we suggest that Terrance and his sister ought to think about installing a portable window air conditioner.

Terrance gives excuses; instead, his family bears the summer heat, day in, day out, night in, and night out. Again, I question why he and his sister don't pool some money together, which I know they can, and install the air conditioning unit together.

In the summer of 1982, I tell my Mom that I'm going on a trip to San Francisco with Cindy, a long-time friend. However, I don't say I'm also going with Terrance.

We attend one of his friend's weddings and meet up with his Berkeley friends. I also ask Terrance to drop me off at the cemetery in San Francisco to pay my respects to my grandfather, who I had never met. Gradually the sun sets, and the San Francisco fog rolls in. Feeling creepy walking through the cemetery with weeds here and there and erected tombstones. I see no one at this late hour. I ignore the uninviting spooky vibe of the graveyard and focus on paying my respects.

I climb the hill and find my grandfather's burial site based on my memory of when I came for the family reunion three years ago. I put fresh flowers at his site, stay for a few minutes, and leave. All three of us end up enjoying a week-long trip to San Francisco.

Back in LA, one weekend, we decide to spend time at

Barnsdall Park. While in the car, Terrance makes a comment that upsets me. His explanation regards caring for himself, not for me. I'm frustrated by his comment and the fact that I'm putting out this effort to see him secretively. He doesn't have to put out any effort on his behalf.

My eyes well up with tears out of frustration. Is it worth it for me to continue to see him? I don't talk to him; instead, I feel miserable as we walk along the park pathway. I ignore him. He tries talking to me, and I say nothing for over an hour. He's concerned, confused, and tries to apologize. Finally, we return to his home. I drive away.

In May, I'm offered a graduate teaching associate position in the Communication Studies master's program at CSULB. I tell my parents about the good news.

Later that week, my Dad says in Cantonese, "Now that you'll be teaching at the college level, don't bring out your hand puppets in class as you do at the dinner table."

I'm a bit surprised that my Dad would instruct me about my hand puppets. He is serious. I respond, "Maybe someday, I will bring out Snakey and Turtlewe in class," I say humorously with a smile. The thought never occurred to me, but now that my Dad reminds me, I might consider incorporating my hand puppet pals into the curriculum. **[Ch.27:3B]**

I teach small group discussion and public speaking courses. We receive the textbook and the day and time of our assigned classes. We are on our own to figure things out and collaborate with others.

I'm the atypical instructor who looks very young, female, and Asian American in the early 1980s, so my demeanor is serious in a Small Group Communication course with all Caucasian American students. On the first day of class, I'm not nervous at all.

I remain calm and focus on what I need to do to do well. I don't have any particular role models or mentor.

Reflecting, my entire college education consists of 98% Caucasian male professors. I had one Chinese female instructor for Mandarin, one Chinese male instructor for Cantonese and a Hawaiian male professor during undergraduate; and one Egyptian male professor in the MA. program. Less than 2% were female Caucasian instructors or professors in my six years of higher education.

When my first paycheck comes, my family goes to lunch at a Chinese restaurant. When the bill arrives, I grab it with the full intention of paying it with my first paycheck. My Dad is surprised, not expecting me to pay. I tell him I look forward to treating them out for a meal with my first paycheck as a teacher.

Overall, undergraduate students treat me respectfully. I only have one student in my public speaking course who gets out of hand. He gives a demonstration speech on how to pick up on girls. During his presentation, he makes obscene gestures toward his female helper, who giggles.

I sit in the back row, observing and evaluating him. My mouth drops open during his obscene gestures. I give him a "D" on his speech due to inappropriateness and offending his audience. When he receives his grade, he yells across the room, "I'm a 4.0 student. I'm going to have you fired!" He exits the classroom.

He meets me during my office hours that week. The department chair is there during the meeting. The student says, "If you're not going to change my grade, then I'll have to drop the course."

Not going to happen. He was inappropriate and did not adapt his message to his audience. Besides, I'd be crazy to change his grade. Thank goodness he drops the course!

In the spring, a high school friend invites former classmates to celebrate at her home for one of her kids. It's been five years since graduation that I haven't seen these high school classmates. During the gathering, two of the gals come up to chat.

"Hey, what's the big secret?" Gladys Lee says to me in an interrogative way.

"Yeah, what's the big secret?" Gretchen Ng chimes in with a demanding voice while taking a step toward me, moving one of her shoulders forward.

"What big secret?" I ask innocently, having no clue what they are talking about.

"You know, the big secret, who are you seeing," Gladys says.

"Oh, I'm seeing Terrence. Remember you were at CSULA studying in the dining area, and we came up to say hello?"

"Oh, yeah. Oh, so what are you doing now?" Gladys simmers down in her tone of voice.

"I'm in the Master's program in Communication Studies at Long Beach State," I reply.

"Oh, you are. Are you a GTA?" Gretchen inquires.

"Yes," I say.

"Oh, you are. What class are you teaching?" Gretchen asks.

"I'm teaching a Small Group Communication course," I say.

"Oh, my brother goes to Long Beach State. I'll have to tell him to take your course," Gretchen says.

"Are you going to church?" Gladys asks.

"No, not right now."

"Oh, you're a backslider," Gretchen proclaims.

The chat is short-lived. I don't know the deal about the two Chinese American former classmates who are Christians. I find them both accusatory in their demeanor, and I have no idea why they approached me in that way since it has already been five years since we graduated from high school, and we seldom socialized during high school.

Another beautiful singer and musician I admire died, Karen Carpenter, on February 4, 1983. I'm sadly surprised she died so young at 32. I also find out that she did her undergraduate studies in Music at Long Beach State. I don't realize that she had an eating disorder, anorexia nervosa. It hits me harder when someone dies young. **[Ch.27:4]**

She is an incredible drummer with a voice like no other, singing with ease, smoothness, and emotions. I love the songs of the Carpenters like: **[Ch.27:5 - Ch.27:7]**

In our first year of secret rendezvous, Terrance and I go on a rare date in the evening. He's responsible for planning this occasion. He arranges for us to see the 6 p.m. movie showing and then to dinner after 8 pm.

In my eyes, he blows it. I'm displeased with his planning and arranging of the time of the events. This is the only time he has to plan a rare evening together. I'm hungry at 6 pm., but he arranged that we see the 6 pm. movie showing. It's after 8 pm. I'm starving!

I don't understand why he didn't choose to eat first, then go to the movies at 8 pm.? At dinner, I ask what he thought of the film. He doesn't have an opinion.

The next time we speak, I express that I'm very disappointed in his ability to plan a rare occasion to go out together. I also reveal that he seems to have this habit whenever I ask his opinion or thoughts about some topic. He would always respond that his mother thinks this, his dad thinks this, or his best friend thinks this.

I'm frustrated with him and say, "What does Terrance think? I don't want to know what your Mom, Dad, or best friend thinks. What does Terrance think?"

In the early months of 1983, Terrance receives an acceptance letter to optometry school in Santa Barbara. That summer, he spends his months preparing to move. We never do anything together besides me coming over to see him now and then. I ask him if he wants to swim several times, but he is focused on preparing to go up to Santa Barbara.

I don't understand why he doesn't go swimming just once with me this summer. He says he has to plan what to take with him and how to fit everything into his car. He has two months to figure this out. He's not working. He has all day and night to figure it out. He lets this task consume him for the entire summer. He stresses about his move. I feel that his decision-making is questionable, and it doesn't matter to him if we do anything together before he leaves. He finally figures out how to pack his vehicle and takes off to his professional program in August.

Chapter 28: Mary's Second Year in the Master's Program

Late September, a stray German Shepherd hops the next-door neighbor's fence and impregnates Kimberly, the yellow Labrador. Kimberly is in heat. The stray dog loiters on our driveway and yard for days. We don't know what to do with him. I try scatting and chasing him away with a rolled-up newspaper, but he runs away and jumps over the brick wall next door with ease.

A minute later, he comes around to our driveway and sits. I try shooing him away for a couple of days, and he refuses to leave. He hasn't eaten or drank for days, staying for almost two weeks.

One day, my neighbor yells, "Get out of here! Go! Get out of here!" I look outside my bedroom window and see our neighbor trying to shoo the German Shepherd away. The dog lays in their backyard. The neighbor goes inside his house and comes out swinging a cleaver knife at the dog, yelling angrily. The German Shepherd is fearless and doesn't move. He gets closer, swinging the cleaver knife again at the dog.

The dog yelps loudly, leaping over the chain-link fence to our backyard. I dash downstairs, standing on our driveway, looking toward the yard. The stray dog, sitting under our avocado tree, I call him over. He slowly walks over to me. I see a clean knife slice on the side of his snout. Our family needs to talk about what to do with the German Shepherd, who refuses to leave Kimberly.

"What should we do about the dog?" I ask.

"Just leave him out there," my Dad says.

"We can't leave him sitting around. Either we keep him or not."

The next day, my Dad says the German Shepherd barked at a guy walking on our property. My Dad says that we should keep him. **[Ch.28:1]**

Later that day, I'm in the backyard and decide to give the German Shepherd commands to see if he would listen. I say, "sit." He looks at me. I try pushing his butt down while saying, "sit." Standing there, I say, "You've come at a time that's not good for me. I'm in my last semester of the Master's program. I'm super busy." The dog sits and looks at me.

Finally, we decide to keep the dog that adopted us. My two older brothers and I chip in, paying for a $400 wrought-iron fence installed across the driveway to keep the dog in an enclosed area.

I name him Troy. My parents smile with delight when I tell them the dog's name. The Chinese word *Choi* means luck. I hear that in the Chinese culture if a dog comes to your home, that means good luck, and on top of that, his name, Troy, sounds similar to *Choi,* meaning good luck.

In October, my Dad experiences another episode of a collapsed lung. My Dad's surgeon, Dr. Charles Ching, is humble, gentle, and competent, with good bedside manners.

My Dad has open lung surgery and for two months on a respirator. The family goes to the hospital every day for several hours, returning home in the evening. We don't eat dinner. For two months, I dart to CSULB to teach my morning classes and dash back to LA to drive my Mom to the hospital. I attend two evening graduate seminar courses the other two days until after 9:30 pm. Constantly on the go, I skip meals and drink milk and orange juice on an empty stomach.

In early December, I ask Leland if he had ever had dark stools. I also ask him if he had ever heard rushing air in his ears. Whenever I bend forward, I hear rushing air in my ears. He says he hasn't experienced any of those symptoms.

During finals week in December, I come down with a cold, vomiting a cluster of blood into the bathroom sink. My Mom is alarmed. We decide that I will go to the Student Health Center on Monday after teaching in the morning.

Terrance has finished his first term in graduate school and is back in LA visiting his parents for the winter break. Leland and Terrance escort me to my 8 a.m. class I teach and then to the Student Health Center. I take a blood test, and we wait for the results.

Within half an hour, the medical practitioner says to me, "You need to see your doctor immediately. Your hemoglobin level is 7 when it should be at least 12."

Afterwards, Leland drives me to see Dr. See. She understands my hemoglobin test results and says, "You must go to the hospital now. You might have a bleeding ulcer. We will have to take tests." I'm admitted to the Chinatown *French Hospital.*

After changing into a gown, nurses wheel me on a stretcher to the lab room. Tears flow from my eyes of the sudden health concern and all the immediate attention. Arriving at the lab, I'm standing behind an x-ray screen, drinking a chalky substance. The practitioners observe my upper and lower gastrointestinal tract on the x-ray screen, also known as my GI. Moments later, wheeled to my room to rest.

Minutes later, Dr. See enters my room and sits next to me. "I have good news and bad news. The good news is that you don't have to go for surgery. You will need a blood transfusion. The bad news is we will have to stick a tube down your nose and throat to give you medication."

"Oh, all right. I won't be awake, right?"

"You will be awake. A nurse will come in here and assist you. I will see you tomorrow morning," Dr. See says as she gets up from sitting on my bed.

"Okay. Thank you, Dr. See."

Soon after, a nurse enters the room and unwraps the long tube. She gives me a cup of ice to hold. I'm sitting upright on the bed, watching her. I can't believe I'm about to undergo this procedure, fully awake. I sit there, allowing and accepting this procedure within moments.

"I want you to put some ice in your mouth and crunch on it. When I say swallow, I'm going to push the tube. Okay?"

"Okay." I spill some ice chips in my mouth and start chomping.

"Are you ready? Swallow." I feel her push the tube into my nose and down my airway. I feel the discomfort and continue to focus on her instructions.

"Take some more ice and chomp."

I pour some more ice chips into my mouth and chomp again. I continue to focus on what needs to be done and not allow my emotions to overwhelm me.

"Ready? Swallow." I swallow as she pushes more of the tube down my nose and throat.

"One more time. Take some ice."

I tilt more ice chips in my mouth and chomp away.

"Ready? Swallow."

I swallow as she shoves the last portion of the tube that reaches my stomach. I feel relieved it's over, although my nose and throat feel discomfort. I sit there, watching her make the final adjustments on the tube.

"I'll be right back with your medication."

I sit there breathing in and out while looking into the space in my hospital room. Much has happened so quickly. I sit there, emotionless, not feeling fear or pain. I only feel discomfort with the tube in my nose and throat.

The nurse returns shortly and administers the medicine into my tubing. She also applies an IV. An hour later, Leland and my Mom come to visit me while I'm resting. I don't want to open my eyes because I can't talk with the tube in my nose and throat. I also feel a bit overwhelmed and want to remain relaxed and not get emotional. I do not want any tears to flow because my nose will start getting runny, making it more difficult for me to breathe and clear my nose.

Some hours later, a phlebotomist administers a blood transfusion that drips throughout the night. Periodically during the night, the phlebotomist checks me and says to let him know if I feel any chills.

The following day, Dr. See visits me. "How are you feeling this morning?" she asks.

I'm fine.

"Your hemoglobin level is 13. This is good. The nurse will administer medication to you again. Afterwards, she will remove your tube," she explains.

I nod with a smile.

"You will be checked out later this afternoon. I will be back then," said Dr. See.

I nod again and grin.

A nurse comes in and smiles, "Oh, your father is also in this hospital—both father and daughter here at the same time."

"Okay, I will see you later this afternoon," Dr. See says.

After the doctor leaves, the nurse administers my medication into my tube. Afterwards, she removes the tube from my throat and nose. What an incredible relief! Soon after, the nurse takes both my breakfast and lunch orders.

Dr. Ching, my father's surgeon, comes by my room to see one of his patients with whom I'm sharing the room. Dr. Ching walks in, looking at his patient on the other side of the room. He doesn't notice me.

"Hi, Dr. Ching," I greet him.

"What are you doing here?" he stops and asks with surprise.

"I have a bleeding ulcer. I had a blood transfusion last night."

"Oh, how are you feeling?"

"I'm doing better."

"When did you come in?"

"Yesterday. I went to the Student Health Center, where they took a blood test and discovered my hemoglobin level was 7. Then, my doctor had me admitted here."

"Glad you are doing better," Dr. Ching says as he proceeds to check on his patient.

As he's leaving, Dr. Ching asks, "What are you majoring in?"

"I'm in the Master's program in Communication at Long Beach State," I reply.

"Oh, you are. My wife was a communication instructor at a community college in Hawaii."

"Oh, really."

"Yea, I met her in Hawaii."

"Oh, you did. Is she still teaching?"

"Not anymore."

"Oh, you two decided to have babies," I kiddingly smile.

He smiles, "It's nice seeing you."

I'm relaxing and vegging on TV game shows while eating breakfast and lunch before being discharged from the hospital in my remaining hours. This experience teaches me not to drink orange juice and milk on an empty stomach for a prolonged period. Doing this creates too much acid in the stomach. Milk has protein in which the brain sends a message to release a particular acid to help break down the milk protein. Also, do not skip meals.

Reflecting, I don't think the doctor needed to order the procedure to stick a tube down my nose and throat. I could have taken that anti-acid medication orally as I did for weeks after being released from the hospital. That medication only serves to neutralize the acid in my stomach and coat it. I had to pay a pretty penny for the nurse to do an unnecessary and uncomfortable procedure. It's not like I was unconscious and needed force-feeding. I didn't eat that night and had an IV given to me, so why couldn't I swallow the medication? I find this very questionable. My bill for a one-night stay, testing, blood transfusion, tube procedure, and doctor visits cost me $4,000 out-of-pocket.

Later that week, I finished my student course grades. During the Christmas break, I visit Terrance at his home. I ask him why he didn't come to see me in the hospital.

He says, "I was afraid that your Mom was there." I suppose you could have waited to see her go and then come in and see me."

During my visit with him at his home, he says to me, "You look older." I look at him and say nothing. I'm thinking, well, I've been through a lot this past semester teaching two different classes, taking two-night seminars, my Dad being in the hospital for a few months, driving back and forth from Long Beach to LA, and being at the hospital almost every day, and skipping meals. On top of that, I've taken two days of comprehensive exams, another day to do my oral defense for my Master's degree, and wound up in the hospital needing a blood transfusion.

I'm thinking, what do you expect? Why make that thought-less comment when it isn't supportive but makes me feel like crap? Honestly, his insensitive comment does not make me feel less than. Instead, I see it as a reflection of his disposition--thoughtless, inconsiderate, and lacking compassion.

The department chair offers me a couple of classes to teach in the Spring semester. I spent the Spring semester relaxing and recuperating from my bleeding ulcer. The doctor says that it takes three to four months to heal.

My Mom receives one of Troy and Kimberly's puppies during this time. I name the white and black spotted mixed German Shepherd and Labrador Charles. I named Charles after my Dad's surgeon, Charles Ching. My Mom likes calling Charles Charlie. I have to say that Charles is the cutest dog I've ever seen. **[Ch.28:2]**

Although I graduated in December 1983, I attended the graduation ceremony in Spring 1984. Leland and Terrance come to my graduation. We take photos and enjoy the reception on campus. My parents are not able to come; my Dad is recovering. **[Ch.28:3]**

That summer, the 1984 Olympics is in LA. I'm home, relaxing and enjoying the various sporting events on TV. Surprisingly, the traffic is not bad at all on the freeways. I also treat myself to a summer vacation and visit an old friend, Lana, for a couple of weeks in Alaska. She's married to a civil engineer. The weather is beautiful, sunny, and fresh.

One evening, Lana pouts to her husband repeatedly while watching TV. She's whining about why he doesn't try to get his mother's jewelry when she died. She whines for nearly half an hour. I remain silent.

Finally, I try to knock some sense into her by calmly saying, "Lana, why do you want something that does not belong to you?"

She doesn't respond. I turn my head back to continue watching TV. She finally simmers down. Since I've known Lana, I've observed that she tends to be materialistic. She wants more and more. She's a hard worker but seems driven to bargain and have money and possessions.

Chapter 29: Which Path to Take?

In the Fall semester of 1984, I attend California State University, Northridge, to take journalism courses. In high school, it did cross my mind about news reporting and an anchoring news career.

Connie Chung is a news anchor in Los Angeles whom I admire. I take one year of print and broadcast journalism courses writing broadcast news for the campus radio station. I join the Asian American Journalist Association attending events.

Near the end of the spring term, I have internship interviews with KNX and KFWB. I get a call back from KFWB for a second interview, and they ask if I could handle seeing blood. I decide not to go for the second interview not because I couldn't take seeing blood. At this time, I'm leaning away from pursuing broadcast journalism.

I'm at the crossroads of what direction to go. Should I continue pursuing broadcast journalism, or should I give teaching serious consideration? I have to think realistically, projecting into the future. What kind of a lifestyle do I want? I want to eventually marry, raise a family, and have a career. I have to think about which profession would work best and be married and having a family.

I like my summers off and a one-month winter break annually. This schedule lends time to the family. I think news reporting would require too much running around and emergency reporting. It's an exciting, adrenaline-rush job. I don't want to feel drained. Growing up, I have already drained my health much, not eating well, having a bleeding ulcer, and stretching myself too much.

At this crossroads, I feel and think that I haven't yet given teaching a serious try. So, I send out a stack of resumes to various colleges such as Marymount Palos Verdes, CSU campuses at Dominguez Hills (CSUDH), Los Angeles (CSULA), Northridge

(CSUN), Fullerton (CSUF), Rancho Santiago College, Irvine Valley College, and Long Beach City College.

I receive a call and class offerings to teach at, except for two. I'm a freeway flyer referring to part-time instructors that teach from campus to campus. I enjoy my summer breaks.

For the past few summers, I enjoy swimming. I want to relax for the summer and kick back. That summer, I receive a call from the *LA Times,* and someone offers me an internship to work on the Calendar section of the newspaper. At this point, I've already decided I will no longer pursue journalism but give teaching a serious try. I decline the internship. Still protecting my summer days in the sun, swimming.

I'm in the kitchen talking to Leland. My Daddy comes in from the backyard and stands near me. He says, *"Maly, ni heui gaau tong wan a nam pengyou a,"* meaning, "Mary, you should go to church to meet a boyfriend."

"Daddy, I don't go to church to look for a boyfriend. I go to church to learn about God," I calmly respond.

"Okay," my Daddy replies turning around and exiting the back door.

My Daddy believes that since I've achieved my Master's degree, it is time to find Mr. Right to marry. My parents never mentioned having a relationship with a significant other.

For days, I hoped that CSULA would call me to teach. In a matter of a few days, to my delight, I received a call from CSULA asking if I could teach a public speaking course that summer. I'm thrilled! CSULA is local, and I'm familiar with the campus since I attended as a freshman.

I arrive at the Communication Studies department at CSULA to check my mailbox for the class roster. While walking through the halls to class, I scan the students' names on the roster. I come across a familiar name, Rocky Kang. Is he the Rocky Kang from high school? I walk up a flight of stairs and enter my classroom.

I take attendance and find that Rocky Kang is the person I know from Belmont High School. I don't acknowledge that I know him when I call his name. I don't want the class to know this. We never talked or said hi in high school or had a class together.

However, we know of each other. It's been seven years since we graduated.

I've always associated Rocky Kang as Karl's best friend. Rocky comes to my desk to greet me when the first session ends. He asks if I want to grab a bite to eat for old times' sake. I agree, but I mention that I need to put more coins in the parking meter. We walk across the campus toward the parking area. As we approach the parking lot, a thought crosses my mind.

"Hey, Rocky, I feel unprepared for an interview for a full-time teaching position tomorrow morning. Do you think I can get a rain check in grabbing a bite with you another time?"

"Oh, sure. We can do it another time."

We part ways. Rocky looks forward to calling Karl. Meanwhile, Karl enjoys his new direction in his life. He's dating women, advancing in dental school, and building toward his dreams for the past seven years. Rocky calls up Karl.

"Hey, Karl, how's it going?"

"Just busy, how about you?

"I'm good. I'm taking summer classes at CSULA. I'm taking a public speaking course. Guess what?"

"What?"

"Guess whooo is my speeeech instructor?" Rocky says in a fun guessing tone.

"I... don't know," Karl says hesitantly while his heart flutters.

"Come on, take a wild guess," Rocky says enthusiastically.

"I…" Karl says hesitantly while his heart skips another beat, but he had this feeling it could be…

"You know her from Belmont," Rocky practically sings it in a fun-loving way.

"Mary Fong?"

"Yup. I knew you would get a kick out of that," Rocky says laughingly.

Karl's thoughts: *Oh, no, not her again. Not because I don't care, but because I have gone over it again, and again, and again.*

She keeps popping up now and then. There she is.

"Hey, we ought to get a group together and grab a bite to eat for old-time sake," Rocky suggests.

"Oh, yeah, okay," Karl responds.

"When is a good time for you?" Rocky asks.

"Well, it depends. Just let me know, and I'll schedule it."

"Okay, I'll let you know the date. Maybe, I can ask her at the beginning of class one of these days and see if she wants to grab a bite afterwards. If so, I'll call you and see if you can meet up with us," Rocky suggests.

"Sure, just let me know," Karl replies.

"So, what's happening with…"

Karl's thoughts: *Meanwhile, I'm panicking when I hear it's Mary. I'm jealous of Rocky that he'll be seeing Mary in class for the entire summer quarter. I don't know what to do. Should I meet up with her, don't see her. I'm feeling confused.* **[Ch.29:1]**

At the end of the second session, Rocky and I walk out of the classroom together. As we go down the stairs, Rocky mentions Karl and says he's in dental school at USC. Hearing Karl's name, I almost flip. I don't care to hear about him. Anger comes over me just hearing his name as I continue to walk quickly down the stairs.

I say nothing in regards to Karl.

As we exit from the building and walk a bit, I ask Rocky,

"Do you want to grab a bite to eat?"

"Oh, I can't."

"Oh, why?"

"I'm a bit embarrassed. I only have some change," as he jingles some coins in his pocket.

"Oh, no worries. I'll treat."

"Oh, why don't we do it another time?"

"Okay," I reply.

After the students complete their first speech presentation, I return their grades. At the beginning of the next class session, Rocky comes to my desk and asks, "Do you want to grab a bite to eat afterwards?

"I'm sorry, but I'm not feeling very well."

"Oh, that's all right. I'll tell you what, how about we grab a bite to eat at the end of the quarter?"

"Oh, okay. Sounds good."

Meanwhile, Karl begins sorting out his thoughts about Mary.

Karl's thoughts: *I try to block it out. I don't want to be disappointed again. She has made it clear several times that she wasn't interested. That's how I see it. Although I want to see her, I want to come to meet her and talk to her -- I stop myself from doing it. Because I know that once I meet her, I would have hope again, and I would have urges still to continue everything again. I'm convinced that she is going to break my heart. She is going to let me down again. It's almost like I'm hiding. I hid from her. Although it's tough to stay away, I hid. I stayed away to protect myself.* **[Ch.29:2]**

Karl's thoughts: *Now and then, when I have a moment, just slouching on a couch, sitting there taking a breather, or just chilling, I have to admit that Rocky would come into my mind about asking for us to meet.*

I try to push that desire to meet, longing to see her as far as I could. Not because I don't want to see her, but because it brings confusion into my life. I'm trying to focus on getting through these classes, getting where I want to be, moving on with my life, starting a new future, and leaving the past. **[Ch.29:3], [Ch.29:4]**

In August, I begin teaching part-time at Marymount Palos Verdes College, Irvine Valley College, and CSULB. I'm evaluating the last round of persuasive speech presenters in Public Speaking in the last class session on Thursday, August 29th, 1985. Final exams are coming the following week.

During an evening that weekend, I call my former boyfriend, Terrance, to see if he had moved back to his parent's home in LA after graduation. The phone rings.

"Hello."

"Hi, Terrance. This is Mary."

"Oh, hi."

"How are you doing?"

"I just moved back earlier this week," he responds.

"Oh, good. Do you want to go out for some ice cream?"

"No, I don't want to," he answers.

"Well, Leland and I bought you a graduation gift earlier in the year. We want to give it to you, and then we'll leave."

"Okay."

"How about we come over and drop it off, and then we'll leave?"

"Okay."

"It's 8:00 right now. How about we come over about 9?"

"Okay."

"Okay, see you soon."

Leland and I arrive at Terrance's home and knock on the screen door. He opens up the security metal screen door. "Come in, you guys. Have a seat," Terrance says while he motions us in.

We enter, and once we sit, Terrance says, "I just got a phone call from Satori, a high school classmate of my sister. She said that a classmate of theirs, Karl, died in a car accident."

I'm in shock and disbelief simultaneously experiencing this undeniable tremendous wave of energy like a powerful ocean wave coming at me and over my head. Instantly, feeling negative energy zip out of my body.

"When did this happen? Where?" I question.

"All I know is that Satori said an RTD bus hit him," Terrance responds.

I sit there, quiet and still in shock. Then Terrance's Mom and I chat a bit in her broken English while Leland and Terrance interact between themselves. Soon after, Leland and I leave. When I arrive home, I call Satori.

"Hi, Satori. This is Mary Fong."

"Oh, hi, Mary."

"I just came from Terrance's home, and he told me that Karl passed on."

"He did," Satori responds tearfully."

"Do you know what happened?"

"He died in a car accident. A bus hit him."

"Oh, my goodness."

"He was out running errands. He was supposed to come back around 6 to go to the hospital with the family to see his new nephew. The family waited for Karl. He didn't show up. They waited and waited, and finally, they felt something was wrong. They started calling local hospitals. They couldn't find any information until later. Finally, they found him at a hospital in the Valley."

"In the Valley," I comment.

"There was no ID on Karl. When the accident occurred, there were looters. That's why it took so long to locate him."

"Oh, my goodness,"

"That's all I know. I'll call you once I find out the service arrangements."

"Thanks, Satori. Take care."

"You take care, Mary."

We hang up the phone. Sitting on the red-carpeted hallway floor with my back leaning against the wall and my arms resting on my bent knees with clasped hands together—still in shock. For moments of silence, I'm looking into a vacuum of space. No thoughts.

Life feels like it's stopped. It feels like the pause button is on--a still frame. Yet, I sense every breath I'm taking--in and out, in and out, emotionless, emptiness. Moments later, the realization begins sinking in that Karl has died. It's a fact. He no longer exists. He's no longer alive. He's no longer here. He's gone.

Moments pass as I sit silently, closed eyes with no thoughts. I take a deep breath. I'll never hear from him again. I'll never see him again, ever--feeling broken. **[Ch.29:5]**

My eyes flood with tears as each drop rolls intermittently down my cheeks like raindrops streaming down a windowpane on a rainy day. I wipe my tears from my cheeks like windshield wipers, while the other tears find comfort on my t-shirt. I slowly open my eyes while breathing slowly. Sitting in silence, feeling hollow, with no thoughts, and breathing deeply and slowly for minutes.

Eventually, I tilt my wrist to see the time. My watch displays a bit past 10 p.m. I take another breath and feel my body's heaviness and low energy as I muster enough strength from my feet, knees, and thighs to prop myself up from the floor. I'm exhausted and drained, still in disbelief. It feels surreal, but at the same time, knowing that it is all true. It's real.

I brush my teeth and get ready for bed. I slip half of my body under my bedsheets and covers and then reach to turn off the light switch. I wiggle into a comfortable supine position while laying my head on my pillow, with my eyes staring towards the ceiling in the dark. It's quiet. I can see the moonlight's reflection peeking through the window sills.

Eventually, I closed my eyes. I feel a heaviness on my chest as I breathe in and out. Questions of whys--flood my mind. Why did this happen? Why did Karl leave so soon, so young? Why? I toss and turn the more I question these whys. I have a night of drifting in and out of periods of sleep and restless sleep.

Chapter 30: Why?

Tuesday evening, and I haven't heard from Satori. I call her to find out about Karl's service.

"Hi, Satori. This is Mary."

"Oh, Mary. I try to call you. Did you change your number?"

"Oh, yeah, my number changed."

"I'm glad you called."

"Yeah, I wondered why I hadn't heard from you."

"Karl's service is this Thursday at 7:30 at the Union Church in J-town."

"Oh, okay. What's the address?"

"401 East Third Street."

"Okay, thanks. Let me give you my new number."

"Okay."

"Hey, do you have Rocky's number? He's a student in my public speaking class at CSULA this summer. I want to call him to see if he wants to take the final another time."

"Sure, here's his number."

"Thanks. I'll give him a call."

Hanging up the phone, I sense that Karl wants me to know about his passing. I feel it because of the timing of how I found out about Karl's transition.

I'm reviewing the sequence of events. I called Terrance at 8 p.m. on Sunday, and we arrived at his home before 9 pm. Within that hour, Satori called Terrance to inform him about Karl. If Terrance had received Satori's call earlier in the day or even after I dropped off Terrence's graduation gift, he would not have called to inform me. Terrence is uncomfortable seeing me because he declined to go out for ice cream.

There was only a one-hour window for Satori to call Terrance, for him to inform me when I arrived at his home. Satori didn't have my new number. The next time I see Rocky is Thursday for his final exam, the evening of Karl's service.

I leave a phone message for Rocky that night. Rocky shows up for the final; it doesn't take up the entire session, only a third. Rocky and I decide to meet up at a later time.

A thought pops in my mind while walking across campus to my car. Is that why Karl and I never got together? He had to leave early.

I pick up the casket flower at the florist for Karl's service that evening. I arrive home. I wait for my ride to come at 6 pm. I wait and wait. It's already 6:30. The service starts at 7:30. I look up the directions to get to the church in Japanese town. I can't wait any longer, so I drive there myself.

Arriving at the Union Church of LA, I recognize this church where one of my high school friends was the first to marry. Upon entering the packed congregation, someone gives me a program. I sit in the back row where additional portable chairs are, viewing a sea of people in black.

Sitting in the quiet congregation hall, I can see Karl lying in his casket in the front. I look at the front cover of the evening service program and opened it. Reading the personal history of Karl, I learn a few things about him. I didn't get to know him in high school. **[Ch.30:1]**

I tilt my head down, and my eyes begin to fill with tears--feeling grief. Someone, please tell me that this is a joke, a horrible joke. My eyelids could not hold back my tears, dropping one by one onto my lap. I'm in disbelief this is happening, wiping my tears away as the service begins--the program sequence proceeds. **[Ch.30:2]**

The service concludes. A receiving line flows by Karl's casket and in front of his family, seated in the front pew. Karl's hair and forehead, wrapped with white bandages, lying there. A white transparent veil covers his open casket.

"Hi Karl," I say in my mind, glancing at him. The white transparent veil covering his casket did not allow me to pin my flower beside him. I hold onto it.

My spot in the receiving line moves closer and closer to Karl's family--much crying and immense sorrow. I only know Karl's sister, Sheila, one year older than him. Her head down, weeping with intense grief, clutching white tissues in her hands.

Feeling a heavy heart standing in front of her, I say, "Sheila." She stops crying for one moment and looks up at me with eyes filled with tears.

"Please give this to Karl for me," as I hand her the clear container with the casket flower. She takes the casket flower and nods. "Thank you. Take care," I say. She nods again while looking down, wiping her tears.

Exiting from the congregation, outside a large crowd of people, some of whom I recognize from Belmont High School. We greet each other and chat a bit since we haven't seen each other for seven years. I stay for about 20 minutes before I return home.

The next day I couldn't attend Karl's burial service. I teach at Irvine Valley College from 9 to noon.

September begins a month of reflection. Tossing and turning in my sleep, asking why Karl had to leave so soon — feeling bad for having a negative attitude towards him. I continue thinking about the "what if" scenarios.

Why couldn't Karl only get hurt and end up in the hospital? That would melt my heart. I would come and see him. I would pray for him to get better. Maybe he would recover. Why couldn't he just be hurt in the hospital? This would soften my heart and break my negativity toward him. Why couldn't this happen? **[Ch.30:3], [Ch.30:4]**

Sleeping one night, I have a dream visitation from Karl. I'm dreaming that I'm in a vast room, the size of an auditorium, standing in the back. I see caskets lined up row after row. The dim auditorium has one open coffin where Karl sits with a bright light shining on him from above.

Oh, there's Karl. What should I do? I feel creeped out. Two visitors stand next to his casket. Should I go up there to see him, or should I leave? But, if I leave, and he sees me, that wouldn't look good. What should I do?

The two visitors leave. That decides for me. I slowly walk up the aisle towards Karl. Standing beside Karl sitting in his casket, I hesitantly say, "Hi Karl," as I peer up at him.

"Oh, hi, Mary!" Karl says in a lively, upbeat manner.

"How are you doing, Karl?" I hesitantly say again.

"Oh, I'm doing fine," Karl says in a zippy way.

"Oh, that's good," I say, still feeling spooked out.

"Oh, I can move so much faster, and I can read so much faster," Karl says excitedly.

"Oh, that's good," I reply. I stand to ask, "Is it true about…"

The visitation dream fades away. Did Karl come and visit me in my dream? He seemed so happy and doing well. Although a bit eerie. It was a clear visitation dream that I can remember and retell easily. **[Ch.30:5], [Ch.30:6]**

For weeks I'm questioning why he had to die so early. Why couldn't it just be a close call, a brush with death, and survive to continue to live? My heart would have melted. I keep asking why couldn't he have survived. Night after night, day after day, I think about this.

I dreamt about Karl being in a wheelchair bouncing down the staircase for a few nights. I interpret this to mean that even if he did survive, he would have been in a wheelchair and would have deteriorated eventually and died. Finally, I conclude that it was his time. **[Ch.30:7]**

Although I could not attend Karl's burial service, I have directions to the Memorial Park area he rests. Before teaching at Marymount Palos Verdes College, I pay my respects at his burial site.

When I arrive, I'm looking about and realize that he does not have a nameplate yet. I walk around and look for a new burial site. I find one, assuming it's Karl's resting spot. I place the flowers in the holder and visit for a while.

The following week, I visit Karl's burial site before teaching. I come to the same burial site as the last time. Standing there, I notice a couple of newly buried sites that don't have nameplates. I wonder if I'm at Karl's burial site?

I hop back into my car to inquire at the front desk. The man checks the location of Karl's burial site and circles the map with specific directions.

I follow the directions and realize I have been visiting the wrong burial site. This time, I'm at the right spot where Karl rests. I add my flowers to the already freshly filled flower containers.

Sitting next to his site, I chuckle and say aloud, "Hi Karl. Oops! I guess I haven't changed that much. Goofy me, going to the wrong site."

I sit in silence, experiencing the green, peaceful landscape and sunny blue skies. "I'm teaching at Marymount Palos Verdes College on Tuesdays and Thursdays, so I'm able to come to visit you before going to work," I say.

I sit silently, absorbing the present moment. "Life is so strange, huh? Life is such a mystery, isn't it?" I say aloud.

Sitting for several minutes in quietude, I gaze at the blue skies and the peaceful greenery. **[Ch.30:8]**

"Well, it's time for me to go to work, so I'll see you next time." I get up, brush and straighten my clothing, walk down the slight incline and hop into my car.

As the weeks pass, I call Rocky to see if we could meet up and chat. I left several phone messages over three months, and he never returned them. I finally give up. I figure he isn't feeling up to meeting after the loss of his best friend, Karl.

Twice a week for two semesters, I drive to Marymount Palos Verdes College. Whenever I drive through Rancho Palos Verdes, I think of Karl. I feel guilty for having such a negative attitude toward him. In a whisper now and then, "I was too young. I didn't know better." I continue to carry regret. For an entire year, I carried the burden of his death.

Springtime comes, and I meet up with Satori. We get together to go swimming at the CSULA pool. Satori sunbathes while I swim my ten laps. I get out of the pool to sunbathe with her. We chat, and I tell her about my visitation dreams of Karl.

"How come that doesn't happen to me? You should tell his parents," she says.

"Oh, I don't know. They don't know me."

Summer soon comes, and I'm happy. After my first year of teaching part-time at several colleges, I need a summer break to recuperate. It's exhausting to drive over 100 miles daily in Southern California traffic. Now, I can enjoy my days swimming laps, sunbathing, and relaxing.

Mid-August, my Dad has difficulty breathing and is admitted to the hospital's IC unit for a couple of weeks. We visit him daily.

Satori calls to tell me that Karl's first anniversary will be at his parents' home. I'm planning to attend on August 30, 1986.

On the morning of August 30, I anticipate going to Karl's anniversary. About 9 am, the phone rings.

"Hello," I answer.

"Is this the Fong's residence?" the woman asks.

"Yes."

"I'm calling from the IC Unit of the French Hospital. Your father, Mr. Fong, his heart has stopped. Come to the hospital right away."

"Okay, we'll be there soon." I hang up the phone and tell the family.

My Mom, Leland, and I quickly pile into my car. Jason isn't home at the time. Driving on the freeway with tears filling my eyes, I'm thinking, "Karl, don't take my Daddy away. Don't take my Daddy away."

Within 20 minutes, we arrive at the IC unit. The nurse leads us to our Dad's bedside, pulling back the partition drapes. We look at our Dad. He looks unconscious. His eyes are closed, his head tilted back, and his mouth wide open with a plastic tube stuck in his mouth.

My Mom calls out to him; he doesn't respond. She pats him on the legs. No response. She begins panicking, touching his body and arms. He still doesn't respond. My Mom cries out in Cantonese, "Someone, help him! He's still warm! Why isn't anyone helping him?"

The Chinese nurse holds my Mom as she is in shock and crying. "Mrs. Fong, his heart has stopped," the nurse says.

"No, he's still warm! Someone help him!" my Mom shouts desperately.

"His heart has stopped. I'm sorry, Mrs. Fong," the nurse says comfortingly, holding my Mom's upper arms.

The nurse escorts the family outside into the hall to a seating area. The doctor shortly arrives and speaks to us.

We return home. My Mom is grieving. Leland, Jason, and I collaborate to make the funeral arrangements.

My attention shifts entirely from Karl's first-anniversary gathering to my Dad's death. I am no longer able to attend Karl's memorial anniversary that day.

Today, I feel the burden of guilt and sadness I've been carrying toward Karl has lifted from me. My energies have been redirected toward preparation for my Dad's funeral and being there for my Mom.

A week later, our family and relatives gather for an intimate wake. The next day, my Dad's burial service is at the Forest Lawn Memorial Park in the Hollywood Hills.

Our family burns incense to purify the surrounding environment. Each of us briefly prays and bow three times while holding sticks of burning incense. We gather all the burning incense sticks together and place them upright in the soil at the nameplate, slowly burning. 'Chinese money' is also burned in a large metal container, symbolizing sending support and whatever my Dad's needs are on the other side, the heavens. Afterwards, we have a Chinese banquet thanking everyone for coming to celebrate my Dad's life.

My Dad and I didn't have a particularly close relationship because my parents worked six days a week and came home right before bedtime. However, my parents were retired in the last ten years of my Dad's life, so I saw them every day. I became busy going to college and work. However, I was home for dinner every night while I lived at home.

I respect my parents very much for their perseverance, courage, work ethic, sacrifices, care, love, and doing the best they knew how. I always feel that my parents began their childhood at a negative ten and made something out of nothing, making their lives in the positive zone.

I will never forget all my Daddy has taught and done for me in love. I will always remember his smiles whenever I brought out Snakey and his friends at dinner time. My Daddy no longer resisted my silliness and lightheartedness in the brief moments we shared during his retirement. I will see my Daddy again when it is my time to return home in the heavens on that one sweet day, together again. **[Ch.30:9]**

In our family, role reversals occur in which we, the grown siblings, become our Mom's caretakers. We take care of the bills that need paying and other responsibilities. I continue part-time teaching at several colleges.

I begin dating again. A year later, I develop a relationship with someone whose Dad is Chinese, and his mother is Japanese. They live in Rancho Palos Verdes. We spend time together every weekend. The sadness of losing two people a year apart is dissipating. I continue to move forward in what life offers and what I want to create.

Sharing some of my thoughts and Karl's thoughts upon reflection. No matter what life situation we are in—struggling or not. Strongly consider prioritizing our expression of love and affection through verbal and nonverbal communication. Expressing authentic kind words of appreciation and gratitude toward others in what they say and do builds connection and support. A sincere compliment praising another lets them know what you admire, which makes that person feel acknowledged and creates positive energy. A smile, a nod, or a gentle pat on the back, arms, or hands at what they've said or done that is worthy will make a positive difference, especially for our young generation. A hug, a handshake, or even a "high five" or clapping communicates your love and appreciation. A small note, card, or video that expresses your heart toward one another is a treasured keepsake. Show encouragement and care, especially for those experiencing a disability, loss, shy people, lack confidence, or didn't do well at something.

People will feel your energy of warmth, happiness, affection, support, sincerity, and love. Building an emotional bond that permeates between people will last forever. Simultaneously, developing and maintaining a positive and genuine relationship of love and affection amongst people will forever be remembered.

These positive ways of communicating don't even cost us one penny, yet it's worth more than a trillion dollars. Love is the real wealth of who we genuinely are that helps us grow as individuals, creating consciously from the inside and impacting the outside as we communicate in multiple and varying relationships and situations. Love is the golden bridge of energy that creates warm, positive, authentic, heartfelt relationships.

Recognize, let go, and drop how we create fear and belittlement to discipline and control children and people. Let go of the negative talk of destructive criticism, imperfections, accusations, name-calling, verbal abuse, and even the physical, emotional, and psychological abuse we do unto ourselves and others. This is an old, destructive, and abusive energy approach. Learn to talk heart-to-heart with children and adults to guide, understand, and nurture them in a kind, gentle, positive, patient, constructive, and peaceful manner. Making conscious efforts and reflections on our behavior, thoughts, and feelings is a developmental process of spiritual growth.

Give children and adults a voice to express their feelings and thoughts so that you can understand their state of being. Listening and observing provide insight to connect and relate valuable knowledge and wisdom we wish to impart and learn from one another.

Parents are meant to be caretakers, and partners are intended to be team members collaborating, not as owners or bosses over another. We desire to understand one another's points of view and needs, adapt and accept uniqueness, and allow our relationships the freedom to express constructively and discover what each person has come to create in their life journey.

Explain ideas and decisions for youngsters and adults to understand, rather than barking orders to satisfy and please yourself with your expectations. Have productive two-way communication exchanges in explaining, listening, and receiving feedback to reach mutual understanding, and acceptance of differences. Amicably agree to disagree. As people, we live unique experiences, perspectives, desires, and beliefs, allowing one another to be who they truly are. Developing respect, responsibility, understanding, honesty, mindfulness, unconditional love, compassion, peace, truth, forgiveness, and ethics are essential to loving communication toward self and others.

Gary Zukav has expressed that authentic power aligns our personality with our soul, living our lives and recognizing and fulfilling our divine nature in our thoughts and behavior. I say we are not here to live a life to fulfill our ego that could drive us along the path of dysfunctional and destructive behavior.

Communicating supportive expression will strengthen our well-being while demonstrating support, appreciation, and care toward others. We can learn to create and maintain healthy communications, whether rich or poor, educated or uneducated or raised in a functional or dysfunctional manner.

First, be aware of what you say, do, feel, and think. Observe and reflect on your interactions and question your intentions. Choose the higher road. It takes practice and discipline, repeatedly, and eventually, we make ourselves anew that becomes conditioned and automatic behavior and thoughts, bringing forth natural feelings of happiness, peacefulness, etc., within ourselves.

Being an expression of love will change lives, making a better world for self, families, communities, and the world. Prioritize and make the conscious effort to learn and practice loving communication methods that generate positive energy, higher vibrations, and higher frequencies within yourself and others.

Based on societal judgments, standards, and commercialized media, we have been culturally conditioned to define our worth through material things, awards, money, and appearances. Most people are conditioned to focus on the exterior aspects of themselves and others and compare who is better and less to puff their egos while diminishing their spirit and others. Many unconscious people focus on projecting an image humans judge as culturally favorable rather than being authentic. Our years of education virtually study everything external to us, neglecting an understanding and development of ourselves as people in terms of character, authenticity, heart-centered, understanding ourselves and building healthy relationships.

We are culturally conditioned to ignore our true feelings, self-worth, passions, and even what we think. Do what everyone else is doing, follow that person, be like that person, follow these rules, behave this way to fit within the norm and please others to be accepted, don't be selfish by considering yourself over others, etc. We've been conditioned to not listen to our hearts, feelings, thoughts, and uniqueness to find our way as creators and be authentic to contribute our positivity and creativity.

We lose sight of who we are when engrossed in a survival and struggle mode or fulfilling the societal-cultural demands, or the cycle of pursuing happiness and love outside of us. We lose sight of who we are when we race for society's high bar to fulfill our ego to have people judge us as praiseworthy to feel good.

Many fall into the trap of projecting a fake image to society, and we haven't done the work to know and develop our authentic selves. We compromise our integrity and our self-worth for external gain.

Most of us are not conditioned to find love and treat ourselves with self-love, self-care, self-respect, self-compassion, gratitude, and appreciation. Recognizing this, we choose healthy ways of being. When we ignore and lose ourselves, we feel an emptiness and a meaningless practice of chasing external artificial happiness that no longer fulfills us.

Walk away without needing to absorb and accept another person's negative energy. Be aware not to interpret the destructive energy personally. Instead, it's their negative energy that they need to look within to resolve. Look within, allowing self-compassion, self-love, and truth enabling this light to grow exponentially within the self.

We cannot expect life to automatically hand us love and support and blame others for not doing so. It starts with being aware of ourselves in what we do, say, think and feel. Change begins with oneself, refining and standing in one's truth and love.

No one says it is easy, but gradually, we become stronger when we value positive qualities and prioritize and implement them in our lives.

Treat yourself with compassion and love, and treat and bless others with compassion and love, too. Setting reasonable boundaries is a step toward self-respect. To have self-love, a person has self-respect.

One of my mottos is: Don't take crap from anyone, and don't give crap to anyone. Nice and simple. The change begins with each person who will change the world for the better. Be a blessing to another through your positive, meaningful, and heartfelt expressions in words and actions. Once we discover the joy within our being and practice appreciation and gratitude for many aspects of our lives, we realize our lives' pure love and happiness are freely available for ourselves and others. **[Ch.30:10]**

Have you discovered your internal cheerleading squad supporting, caring, and loving who you are, day in and day out? Are you ready to nurture, appreciate, respect, express gratitude and thankfulness for who you are, what you can creatively be, and share with others? Listen to the expression of your pure heart and eternal soul, and be your true beautiful self. **[Ch.30:11]**

Chapter 31: Beginning to Connect the Dots

Coincidence is defined as a "situation in which events happen at the same time in a way that is not planned or expected," according to the Merriam-Webster online dictionary. Another definition of coincidence is "an occasion when two or more similar things happen at the same time, especially in a way that is unlikely and surprising," as stated in the Cambridge English Online Dictionary.

A Swiss psychiatrist, Carl Jung, wrote in 1952 that coincidences are meaningful events that can't be explained by cause and effect, but another force, outside of causality could explain them. Jung calls this phenomenon of synchronicity an "acausal connecting principle": a meaningful coincidence rather than mere random, meaningless, and nonpurposeful. **[Ch.31:1 - Ch.31:2A]**

I remember telling Leland, "I don't know why I get into these weird situations. These situations feel awkward, complicated and strange—between Karl and I in high school, seeing Terrence secretively, Karl's best friend, Rocky who happened to be in my public speaking class the summer that Karl passed on. Also, my Dad passes on the same day, a year after Karl."

"That is pretty weird," says Leland.

"I don't know what's going on, but something is going on. I don't know how I get into these weird situations."

As the weeks go by, I can't help from reflecting and thinking about certain synchronicities during the 10-year period I knew Karl. What are the odds of my Dad dying precisely one year after Karl's death on August 30, 1985?

What are the odds of unexpectedly being called to teach the public speaking course at CSULA, and having Rocky Kang, a former high school classmate who happens to be Karl's best friend, enrolled in my public speaking class during the summer that Karl dies? Highly unlikely, I would say.

What are the odds of Karl and I having the same US History class and becoming attracted to one another? None of our US History classmates was in my other courses at Belmont High school for three years. I sensed that Karl and I were plucked out of our usual classmates. If Karl and I were never in the US History class together, and everything else remained the same during the three years in high school, I would have never noticed Karl and had an attraction toward him.

What are the odds of Satori calling Terrance within that one-hour window, after I call Terrence at eight o'clock and that I'll visit him in an hour at nine o'clock to only drop off his graduation gift and leave? Terrence would not have voluntarily called to inform me about Karl's death after visiting him or earlier in the day. Satori did not have my new phone number to notify me. My senses tell me that there's a significant timing of events that occurred so that I would find out about Karl's death to attend his memorial service rather than miss the event.

Are these four events related to Karl and me only random and meaningless coincidences and not connected somehow? If someone states "yes," one says that my Dad's and Karl's death are purely accidental and meaningless. If death is pointless and nonpurposeful, would someone say that life is meaningless and serves no purpose?

For me, my Dad and Karl's death have purpose and meaning. I metaphorically felt a tidal wave of energy coming at me and over my head and then negative energy zipping out of my body once I heard of his passing. My Dad's death enabled me to relinquish the burden, guilt, and regret I felt for one year towards Karl by shifting my energetic focus to my Dad.

Some would say death is meaningless, but one's life is meaningful and purposeful. Phenomena in life do not have meaning or purpose per se. Only when a person, attributes meaning and purpose; is it so. Those who know Karl are meaningfully impacted in varying degrees, depending on their awareness and relationship to him.

I also wonder about Karl's burial site in Rancho Palos Verdes, where I taught at Marymount Palos Verdes College in my first year of serious teaching. I was reminded of Karl repeatedly. His parents' home is about 29 miles from Karl's burial site. I wonder why they didn't choose a closer and more convenient memorial location.

How is it that I experienced visitation dreams from Karl? The first visitation dream of Karl was telling me that he is alive and doing fine. Also, I have repeated visitation dreams of Karl communicating that he would have deteriorated and not survive even if he survived. My interpretation of Karl's transition is not a random accident. I believe that it was his time to transition for a purpose.

How about the flash of thought I recall since the late Spring semester of my 9th-grade year that I would write a book someday for a broad audience but had no clue what the topic would be? How about the thought I had in the 10th grade, after Geometry class, walking to my next class, and a thought popped into my mind: *Don't get involved with him.* When I considered pursuing acting as an undergraduate, another thought popped into my mind: *You will lose yourself.* Walking across campus to my car to go to Karl's memorial service, a thought occurs: *Is that why we never got together. He had to leave early.*

All four of these thoughts popped naturally into my mind. These are not thoughts that came about during and after thinking about a relevant topic. They were thoughts that, presto, flashed across my mind with no effort on my part. Where are these spontaneous thoughts or messages originating? Are they meant to guide me in my journey in life?

Reflecting on high school, I'm able to identify this unspeakable energetic struggle between Karl and me after his 1985 transition. I observe and feel the energy of attraction coming together, then being separated, then coming together, then being separated, and so on. During the ten years of knowing Karl, I feel this constant energy flow coming close, then separating—eight occurrences. Why did we remain acquaintances or classmates and not have the opportunity to develop our relationship further as friends or in a romantic relationship?

I observe these synchronicities and factors forming a pattern, a thread that connects Karl and me. I don't think and feel that these events are separate, disconnected, random, meaningless, and purposeless. The timing and substance of these events are cooperating and collaborating for some reason, for some purpose.

After connecting these occurrences, one could think his death is coincidental, random, and meaningless, or one would think it was his time, his destiny serving a meaningful purpose. I feel too many of these significant 'coincidental' occurrences are connected somehow to be truly meaningful synchronicities.

What mysterious purpose do these related synchronistic events cooperate and collaborate to serve? What do these unusual events mean? I genuinely feel that something is happening here, but I don't know what's happening here.

It's not my imagination. I can't seem to put my finger on it. Could it be that I have known Karl from a past life? Could the U.S. History course title signify that Karl and I have had "US History" before? Why did he die so young, so soon? Why am I so affected by his passing when we barely knew each other as friends? My relationship with Karl is a total mystery. I can feel the energy telling me that something is going on here, and I'm curious about unraveling this mystery. **[Ch.31:3 - Ch.31:5]**

This mystery compares to a pond of water that ripples concentrically from each pebble of questions I have tossed into the water, creating ripples and cloudy water. Watch each ripple the pebble formed. Each group of concentric ripples eventually meet one another--interacting, exchanging, and creating energetic synergetic ripples that merge into one. The ripples eventually subside, and the cloudy water gently settles into a clear reflection in the pond. In my consciousness and being, the ripples of questions, emotions, and confusion subside to an internal state of clarity.

Until this time, I wait patiently, opening my awareness and my senses to all that is. Opening my awareness will require me to leave my suitcase of beliefs, attitudes, biases, and culturally conditioned ways of learning, understanding, and knowledge outside my front door. I will discover the real answers to my life's big questions during my mystery tour. In that case, I'm committed to leaving my heavy suitcase of preconceived, culturally conditioned ideas and human ways of thinking outside my door.

Leaving the heavy luggage will help minimize these influences that will not hamper, burden, and keep me locked in a culturally conditioned and limited small box of existence. This allows me to fearlessly learn from my experiences and the current research and discover answers to my big life questions that will expand my understanding, learning and knowing that resonates with the truth within me.

Therefore, allowing clarity within me to understand each pebble of question I have tossed. A clear, peaceful reflection of myself and the surroundings I see in the pond will enable me to decipher the mirror of meaning and truth behind the mystery of these synchronistic events and the big questions of my life journey. **[Ch.31:6]**

Epilogue

In early February 2016, I attended a two-day mediumship workshop taught by a credible, authentic, competent medium/channeler/spirit translator, Jaime Butler. After each seminar, Jaime did a public channeling session in the evening. The online Merriam-Webster Dictionary defines a channeler as "a person who conveys thoughts or energy from a source believed to be outside the person's body or conscious mind specifically: one who speaks for nonphysical beings or spirits."

It was my first public channeling/mediumship experience in which Jaime was in a full trance. Since I paid 40 dollars, I want to get my money's worth. I assertively asked a question, although I didn't know what to ask. I inquired if Karl is present. Jaime energetically connected with Karl for almost three minutes.

Did I truly speak to the consciousness or spirit of Karl? Wow, it's been 36 years since I last saw and briefly chatted with him at the USC Doheny Library. Was this truly happening? Was this for real? That's why I attended the public channeling to investigate, participate, and experience the integrity of this mediumship phenomenon. I had no expectations.

Karl's thoughts were translated in this memoir by Emanuelle McIntosh, an authentic, credible, competent medium/ channeler/ spirit translator. Thus far, I have over 40 hours of recorded channeling sessions communicating with Karl through the translation of Emanuelle for almost 18 months.

My reacquaintance and connection with Karl through the channeling sessions unexpectedly reignited our friendship's flame, giving me the punch I was looking for to move forward in writing my memoir. That's synchronicity again, a meaningful coincidence appearing at the right time and place. Honestly, Karl and I have a much better relationship now than in the years we knew each other in high school. Every channeling/mediumship session is like talking on the phone with an old acquaintance chatting about our high school days, and getting to know each other better.

This event is the most incredible phenomenon I have experienced in my life! Reconnecting with Karl from the nonphysical dimension and realizing he is alive and well is phenomenal. It's a mind-blowing experience, and yet it makes sense!

Before Karl and I reconnected, I studied the spiritual literature and research for four years, which helped me prepare to teach three new spiritual communication courses at CSUSB. This familiarity with the spiritual literature and research enabled me to understand and be open to what was happening rather than reject or be in disbelief. Take a deep breath and pinch me.

As a professor for 30 years, I've conducted intercultural communication research studies, publishing my findings in journals and books. Also, I have taught in the university classroom with leading-edge research and approaches in my specializations of human interaction in cultural, intercultural, spiritual, and instructional communication contexts.

I have gone beyond textbooks, books, and documentaries on spirituality by participating in and attending conventions, seminars, and hands-on workshops to learn and have first-hand observation and questioning of phenomena, particularly mediumship or channeling. From both my professional and personal experiences, I appreciate having Emanuelle McIntosh as my medium/ channeler/ spirit translator since December 2016. She is gifted and quite good in translating spirits' energy and communications, primarily through her clairsentient ability. I trust the work she does that's credible and authentic because I have received validation.

We understand that the Physics field has already established that everything is energy, which cannot be created or destroyed. Energy can only transform. Humans receive energy wavelengths through our senses; our mind translates it as a solid or abstract entity. Credible and authentic mediums/channelers/spirit translators have the developed sensitivity to perceive and translate energy than people without this developed ability. Her task is to translate the energy of Karl's consciousness or spirit that contains information in wavelengths of frequencies.

Understand that translation is not 100%. People hear, see, smell, and feel but are never perfect in receiving, sending, and interpreting an event or communication between people. We typically don't have this expectation of perfection, even in communicating on the same physical dimension. Interactants negotiate to help clarify the intention and meanings of their conversational messages. People have their field of experience containing beliefs, attitudes, values, customs, knowledge, experiences, etc. Their conditioned cultural way of communicating and living influences how they perceive and interpret information within a particular context.

Authentic, credible mediums /channelers /spirit translators receive and translate energy with a higher frequency from the nonphysical dimension through their senses. They receive images, sounds, and blocks of information telepathically and intuitively translate the energy containing information that involves interpretation.

Furthermore, the accuracy of the translation consists of a combination and contingency of both the medium/channeler/spirit translator's ability to interpret the energy based on one's field of experience and also the consciousness/spirit's ability to communicate the idea in a variety of ways through sound, images, symbols, blocks of information, and so forth. Mediumship is not simply reiterating words and sentences.

Therefore, it's reasonably fair not to have a high standard or expectation that mediums/ channelers/spirit translators always need to be accurate and detailed in their translations to be credible and competent. It's important to understand that the inquirer's quality of the question increases the translated response quality. If inquirers ask vague, general, or imprecise questions, the spirit and spirit translator's response will most likely reflect the type of question asked.

It doesn't make sense, nor is it rational for people to have high or perfect expectations for mediums who cross from physical to nonphysical dimensions to translate spirit energies. And yet, people don't have the same high or absolute standard when communicating with people on the same physical dimension.

Negotiation of meaning and communication between the questioner and spirit translator facilitates refining the interpretation or translation of the messages. I also acknowledge some people represent themselves as mediums/channelers/ spirit translators who have unrefined abilities to fraudulent manipulations. Consumers have to do their homework to ask for referrals of credible recommended spirit translators/ mediums/channelers from someone who has repeatedly had a quality translation. Some mediums/ channelers/spirit translators may post YouTube videos for viewers to witness and evaluate their credibility. Some consumers prefer spirit translators who are certified. Also, read reviews on them.

Perhaps, there are questions such as, "How do I know it is Karl?" and "How do I know Emanuelle is not making up information and doing an internet search?" These are legitimate and fair questions that I, too, have asked and was able to validate.

I only told Emanuelle Karl's first and last name and nothing more. She did not know any details of my past relations with Karl.

Rather than senseless or illogical translations, she made sense of my questions and discussed past situations that I experienced with Karl. There was an accurate translation of the same information I only knew about in the situation, for example, where I sat in Geometry class. Emanuelle described or naturally performed the gestures of shyness, nodding, looking up in the air, and whistling to communicate innocence. These are examples of behaviors I can identify as Karl when I knew him in high school.

She also stated that he died in a car accident. She sensed that Karl had an attraction toward me. I asked Karl, "What department store is near the home you grew up in?" Emanuelle translated, "K-Mart." Emanuelle is familiar with Walmart; but has never heard of K-Mart because there is no American K-Mart chain store in Belgium, where she resides. She stated that she kept getting the message "K-Mart," so she said it.

Sometimes, she is accurate with names; other times, she cannot interpret the names. The five specific examples mentioned are not published or on the internet, and I did not divulge any information. Emanuelle also stated that she did not do an internet search on Karl, nor is it a practice.

Her job is to translate the energy, similar to a person translating from one language to another. A credible translator does not invent information or do an internet search.

Competent, authentic, and credible spirit translators have one or multiple mediumship abilities. Emanuelle is most skilled as a clairsentient, meaning that she interprets the energy through her feelings and sense the emotions and feelings of people, animals, spirits, and the environment. Sometimes, she translates images and telepathic messages.

Clairaudient is the ability to hear messages or voice that is inaudible to others. Some mediums are clairvoyant, able to see the spirit, images, situations, the future, etc. Some mediums are evidentiary, meaning they can translate energy to give specifics and details. Some spirit translators do conscious channeling, while some mediums can trance channel, and some channelers do both styles.

Researchers have conducted separate experiments involving authentic Mediums/Channelers/Spirit translators: Gary Schwartz (PhD Harvard) at the University of Arizona, Julie Beischel, PhD (University of Arizona) at Windbridge Research Center, Dean Radin, PhD (University of Illinois, Urbana) Chief Scientist and Helane Wahbeh, Director of Research at the Institute of Noetic Sciences, and faculty at the Division of Perceptual Studies at the University of Virginia have conducted separate experiments involving authentic mediums/channelers.**[Epilogue:1 - Epilogue:5]**

The mediums who participated in the experimental studies showed a statistical significance of having the ability to communicate accurate information that goes beyond the probability of chance. The police, FBI, and military utilize mediums to help solve criminal cases and increase national security intelligence. **[Epilogue:6 - Epilogue:10]**

This memoir has come to an end. However, more of Karl and Mary's life journeys continue. For Karl, his journey continues on the other side, a nonphysical dimension of life, back home in a higher energetic vibrational dimension we call Heaven. In contrast, my journey continues on the earth's physical plane.

Karl has left an indelible impression on me in the short time I knew him in high school and the summer of his transition. I continue to pursue answers to the questions I set forth at the beginning of this memoir through my spiritual studies and interviews with Karl through the mediumship/spirit translator. I do feel Karl's presence every day.

We're just beginning to embark on a magical mystery tour of *A Magnificent Mess!* Trilogy from this illusionary ending of the memoir, *Two Heart Nuts to Crack!,* to the next adventure of our evolving life journey, continually transforming as immortal spirits in the second memoir, *A Beautiful Blueprint.* Indeed, we are all eternal spirits, having a temporary human experience on earth. **[Epilogue:11]**

About the Author

Mary Fong, PhD (University of Washington), is a writer and research emeritus professor in the Communication Studies department at the California State University, San Bernardino. Her teaching and research specializations are Cultural, Intercultural, Spirituality, Language and Social Interaction, Instructional, and Ethnography of Communication. Mary's second memoir, *A Beautiful Blueprint* (2023), third edition is available both in print and e-book. She is the coauthor and coeditor of a textbook, *Communicating Ethnic and Cultural Identity.* She particularly enjoys teaching Intercultural, Communicating Compassion and Love, Dying and Afterlife Communication, and Personal Growth. In the near future, she will make these university courses available to the public to help expand their knowledge and awareness in their journey of life. She is also a board member of www.ReincarnationResearch.com, in which Walter Semkiw, MD is the late founder, director, and researcher. My author page with hyperlinks is at: https://maryfong.academic.csusb.edu/.

Instructions: Accessing Memoir Hyperlinks

Two Heart Nuts to Crack! the first memoir of *A Magnificent Mess!* Trilogy is in print for readers who prefer to read from a book. This first memoir allows the reader to access hyperlinks to informative videos and songs. How? Reading this book, you will encounter **[labels]** representing hyperlinks. Before you begin reading:

ONE. Have your iPad, laptop, or cell phone with you and go to this website: **https://maryfong.academic.csusb.edu/.**

TWO. Click on *Two Heart Nuts to Crack!,* and a list of hyperlinks will appear. Copy all the hyperlinks in this memoir to a word document so you have your own copy stored on your computer. Occasionally, I will revise the broken links; and you can return to my website for an update.

THREE. Easily click on each hyperlink on the webpage when a **[label]** appears in the book.

NOTE: By 12/1/25 or earlier, I will transfer my academic faculty webpage of hyperlinks to a new author webpage when I officially retire from CSUSB. Please go to my Amazon author book page for my future author webpage of my memoirs' hyperlinks. Thank you!

Made in the USA
Las Vegas, NV
29 August 2023

76826280R00159